BORDERLINE PATIENTS:
PSYCHOANALYTIC PERSPECTIVES

The Kris Study Group of the
New York Psychoanalytic Institute

Monograph VII

Borderline Patients:
Psychoanalytic Perspectives

By

Sander M. Abend, M.D., Michael S. Porder, M.D.
and Martin S. Willick, M.D.

INTERNATIONAL UNIVERSITIES PRESS, INC.

Madison   Connecticut

Library of Congress Cataloging in Publication Data

Abend, Sander M., 1932-
   Borderline patients.

   (Monograph/Kris Study Group of the New York
Psychoanalytic Institute; 7)
   Bibliography: p.
   Includes index.
   1. Borderline personality disorders. I. Porder,
Michael S., 1933-   . II. Willick, Martin S.,
1933-   . III. Title. IV. Series: Monograph
(New York Psychoanalytic Institute. Kris Study
Group); 7. [DNLM: 1. Personality disorders.
2. Psychoanalytic therapy. W1 M0558N v. 7/
WM 460.5.P3 A142b]
BF173.A2N4313 no. 7 150.19'5s [616.85'82] 83-12750

[RC569.5.B67]
ISBN 0-8236-0576-0

Third Printing, 1986

Manufactured in the United States of America

CONTENTS

FOREWORD

The Kris Study Group of the New York Psychoanalytic Institute, under the chairmanship of Dr. Charles Brenner, discussed and reviewed the concept of borderline states over the four-year period from 1973 to 1977. In addition to our monthly two-hour meetings, we met on two occasions for a full day of discussions. During one of these extended meetings, Dr. Otto Kernberg was a guest participant, and he graciously went over his views with us, utilizing for that purpose clinical material of his own as well as reviewing cases of ours.

The membership* of the Kris Study Group included advanced candidates, recent graduates, and experienced members of our Institute. Some of the participants did not remain for the entire four years, whereas others joined our group after it had already begun its deliberations. Ten members were present throughout the four-year period.

The material we present in this monograph is based in part on the work of the Kris Study Group, but it would not be accurate to regard it simply as a summary of that group's conclusions. For one thing, the membership did not by any means reach unanimity of opinion. Indeed, the diversity of views added to the richness of the discussions. We have made liberal use of the clinical material and of the extensive deliberations which took place but have not attempted to include all points of view or incorporate each of the many thoughtful contributions offered by one or another of the participants. A preliminary summary of the group's conclusions was presented to the

---

*Participants: Sander Abend, M.D., Klaus Angel, M.D., Leon Balter, M.D., David Beres, M.D., Charles Brenner, M.D., Kenneth Calder, M.D., Gerald Epstein, M.D., Richard Glass, M.D., Herbert Gomberg, M.D., Jay Harris, M.D., Winslow Hunt, M.D., David Hurst, M.D., Daniel Justman, M.D., Robert Kaplan, M.D., Richard Kopff, M.D., Yale Kramer, M.D., Neil Lebowitz, M.D., Edward Nersessian, M.D., Teruko Neuwalder, M.D., Winfred Overholser, M.D., Michael S. Porder, M.D., Bruce Ruddick, M.D., Robert Scharf, M.D., Hilda Shanzer, M.D., Susan Sherkow, M.D., Matthew Tolchin, M.D., Herbert Waldhorn, M.D., Sherwood Waldron, Jr., M.D., Henry Weinstein, M.D., Martin Willick, M.D.

New York Psychoanalytic Society on April 25, 1978. The preparation of that report was undertaken by the three authors of this monograph with Drs. Yale Kramer, Edward Nersessian, Robert Scharf, Susan Sherkow, and Sherwood Waldron, Jr. That material also has been useful to us in formulating the ideas which we shall set forth in the following pages.

We have, moreover, felt free to go beyond the boundaries of the actual work of the Kris Study Group. We have continued to discuss its findings among ourselves, and to elaborate on them, to synthesize and selectively emphasize them according to our own point of view. In addition, we have repeated and extended the review of the pertinent literature on borderlines, including a number of important articles and books which have appeared in print since the Kris Study Group ended its work. We should like, therefore, to make it clear that the ideas expressed here are derived from the collaboration of the authors, who accept sole responsibility for them. These ideas are not necessarily shared by the other participants in the Kris Study Group on borderlines, although we believe that many of our colleagues would be in substantial agreement with our conclusions.

We would like to express our appreciation to those who met with us during the four years of deliberations. We would especially like to thank Dr. Charles Brenner, whose chairmanship of the group provided the atmosphere for the serious, critical, and vigorous examinations of the topics which arose. Dr. Brenner's encouragement and assistance were also invaluable in helping us to complete the task of reporting our conclusions. In addition, his willingness to read the drafts of our work and to provide us with helpful criticisms, advice, and suggestions has earned our heartfelt appreciation.

SANDER M. ABEND, M.D.
MICHAEL S. PORDER, M.D.
MARTIN S. WILLICK, M.D.

1

Historical Background of the Borderline Diagnosis

The term "borderline" appeared in the psychoanalytic literature for the first time in a paper entitled "Psychoanalytic Investigation of and Therapy in the Border Line Group of
Neuroses" by Adolph Stern of New York, published in the
Psychoanalytic Quarterly in 1938. In the forty-odd years that have
elapsed, the term has been used with increasing frequency by
psychoanalysts everywhere. Nevertheless, there remains a great
deal of controversy as to precisely what the term means and
how specifically it may be applied as a diagnostic construct.

Although as psychoanalysts we do not group our patients in
rigid classifications based on phenomenology alone, we recognize the importance of diagnostic assessment and criteria. Every
evaluation of a patient includes an effort to place him in a
diagnostic category, however uncertain of that placement we
may be at the beginning of treatment. Certain diagnoses generally suggest a recommendation other than classical psychoanalysis, whereas others point to analysis as the treatment of
choice. But the issue of diagnosis does not only concern choice
of treatment; it is related as well to our concepts of etiology,
dynamic conflict, character structure, ego organization, and
psychic development. Thus, placing a patient in the diagnostic
category of obsessive-compulsive neurosis carries with it some
notion of the kind of major conflicts involved and the nature
of the predominant defenses utilized, and some idea as to how
well the ego is integrated. Similarly, the diagnosis of schizophrenia, despite the heterogeneity of the manifest symptoms,

1

implies some idea of the nature of the patient's object relations, his or her propensity for regression to psychotic episodes, and the integrity of the ego functions.

As psychoanalysts have used the term "borderline," it has not always been clear whether the term refers to a specific diagnostic entity, as the terms "schizophrenia" or "obsessive-compulsive neurosis" refer to specific diagnostic entities, or whether it is used to designate a *group* of disorders or diagnostic entities. When used in the latter sense, "borderline" would correspond in nosological status to "psychosis" (encompassing schizophrenia and manic-depressive illness) and "neurosis" (including obsessive-compulsive, phobic, and hysterical patients).

If we use "borderline" in the latter sense—to designate a group of disorders that occupies an intermediate position between psychosis and neurosis—it would be necessary to determine the common features present in patients who exhibit such disorders. In order to be of both clinical and theoretical value, a list of common features would have to include not only the phenomena associated with the disturbance but considerations as to the object relations, developmental factors, ego function (including defenses), vicissitudes of the drives, and etiology. And however we use the term, we would have to consider whether the diagnosis "borderline" carries with it some judgment about analyzability. We would be interested to know whether certain variations of technique are required to obtain the best results.

As the Kris Study Group discussed these various questions, it became clear that some analysts still use the term "borderline" to refer to a schizophrenic process that is hidden or covered over. These analysts believe that careful evaluation or treatment itself will eventually reveal the underlying psychotic illness. Other analysts feel it unwarranted to introduce a new diagnostic label and believe we should refer to such patients as having severe character pathology. In their view such cases may be differentiated from other neurotic character disorders by the greater severity of the observed illness as well as by the facts that the psychoanalytic treatment of such patients proceeds with greater than usual difficulty, and that the outcome may be less satisfactory than in the more typical cases of milder neurotic character disturbances.

One of the major sources of nosological difficulty confronting both the general psychiatrist and the psychoanalyst in the past was their adherence to the view that mental illness could be divided into two major categories—neuroses and psychoses. Clinical psychiatrists treating very sick patients who did not seem clearly to be schizophrenic or manic-depressive utilized such diagnostic labels as "ambulatory schizophrenia," "pseudoneurotic schizophrenia," or "schizoid personality." Psychoanalysts treating a wide variety of patients with severe character pathology struggled to differentiate them from neurotics who were clearly analyzable. Patients with severe perversions, impulse disorders, anorexia and bulimia, addictions, self-mutilating traits, or profound infantile traits and distorted ego development often did not respond well in analysis and seemed to be considerably sicker than neurotic patients.

It therefore became increasingly apparent that the conception of mental illnesses as divided into the categories of neuroses and psychoses was no longer adequate to account for the great variety of clinical observations that have accumulated in the literature of the past forty to fifty years.

In this chapter, we provide a brief historical background to the question of the borderline diagnosis. It seems appropriate, before reviewing some of the major psychoanalytic writings on the borderline patient, to summarize Freud's views on neuroses and psychoses in order to demonstrate both his adherence to this original distinction as well as some of his doubts about it.

Freud's Views on Neuroses and Psychoses

Freud did not use the term "borderline" in his published work. Although he devoted a great many papers to explaining the similarities and differences between the various forms of neurosis and psychosis, he accepted throughout his career the view that there were two major groups of mental illness. It is true that he occasionally made exceptions to this idea. In *Three Essays*

on the Theory of Sexuality (1905) Freud called the neuroses the
"negative of the perversions," although he did not actually place
perversions in a distinct category of mental illness. He frequently used the term "narcissistic neurosis" for schizophrenia,
and yet, in "Neurosis and Psychosis" (1924), distinguished
among transference neurosis, narcissistic neurosis, and psychosis on the basis of his new structural model. "Narcissistic
neurosis" in this paper referred to the melancholias, in which
the central conflict lay between the ego and the superego. Freud
contrasted this conceptualization with that of the pathogenic
process in neurosis, where the conflict lay between the ego and
the id, and that in psychosis, where the conflict lay between the
ego and the external world. Freud himself was not very satisfied
with these "simple formulas" and probably viewed the melancholias as belonging to the group of psychoses. In any event,
his major emphasis was that the distinction between neurosis
and psychosis was to be found in the area of reality testing. In
the psychoses there was a "break with reality." Freud was to
refer to this issue repeatedly in his attempts to distinguish the
two forms of mental illness.

In one of his earliest papers, "The Neuro-Psychoses of Defence" (1894), Freud argued that the defense of conversion in
hysteria and the defense of displacement in obsessional neurosis
were to be contrasted with that used in a particular kind of
psychosis he termed "hallucinatory confusion." In hysteria and
obsessional neurosis the affect to be converted or displaced was
first separated from "the incompatible" idea [with which it was
associated;] the idea itself remained in consciousness, even
though weakened and isolated" (p. 58). In "hallucinatory confusion," on the other hand, the "ego breaks away from the
incompatible idea" so that the ego has "detached itself wholly
or in part from reality" (p. 59). In "Further Remarks on the
Neuro-Psychoses of Defence" (1896), Freud added the important finding that the defense of projection often led to the
presence of delusions.

Freud went on to describe other differences between psychoses and neuroses in the Schreber case (1911a) and in "On
Narcissism" (1914). In these papers he attempted to demon-

strate that the mechanism of repression was very different in these two major illnesses. In psychosis, he maintained, there was a detachment of libido not only from preconscious and conscious object-representations, as in the neuroses, but from unconscious object-representations as well. The detached libido returned to the ego, thereby giving rise to the symptoms of megalomania, hypochondriasis, and "end of the world" delusions.

In hypothesizing a developmental sequence for the disposition of libidinal cathexis, Freud postulated an initial stage of autoerotism, followed by a stage of narcissism, culminating in the stage of object love. The importance of this early theory of the development of object relations lay in the fact that Freud used it to explain the observation that object cathexes were apparently "given up" in schizophrenia, so that a "primitive objectless condition of narcissism" was "re-established" (1915c, p. 197). Thus, regression in psychosis was much more profound than it was in the neuroses, and led to more archaic, primitive modes of functioning. Although most of these ideas concerned changes in the disposition of libido, Freud was careful to point out in the Schreber case that, in psychosis, "a secondary or induced disturbance of the libidinal processes may result from abnormal changes in the ego" (1911a, p. 75). Thus we have an early indication of what was later to be Freud's understanding of the role of the ego in pathogenesis.

Within the category of schizophrenia, Freud (1911a) drew a further distinction between the degree of regression in paranoia and that in dementia praecox ("paraphrenia" [1911a], "paraphrenia proper" [1914]). Whereas the regression in dementia praecox was complete—to the stage of autoerotism—regression in paranoia was less severe—to the stage of narcissism (1911a, p. 77). Thus, a foundation was laid for a different conceptualization of psychopathology—one in which degrees of developmental fixation and regression could be used to account for the severity of the illness. If we recognize that the concepts of fixation and regression can be applied not only to the libidinal and aggressive drive organizations but to ego functions and object relations as well, there is room in this thesis for the suggestion that other mental illnesses might exist along a developmental continuum between severe psychoses and mild neuroses.

There is perhaps further support for this suggestion in the fact that Freud was not entirely consistent in his view that psychosis and neurosis were fundamentally different *in kind*. In particular, he expressed doubt about the validity of the distinction he had drawn on the basis of the psychotic's "turning away" from reality. He addressed this issue in his paper on "Fetishism" (1927). There he noted that the "disavowal" of "a piece of reality" by two young men—the death of their father—seemed to cast doubt on the distinction he had drawn, since "neither of them had developed a psychosis" (p. 156). But, Freud continued, these cases differed from that of the psychotic in that the disavowal existed as but "one current in their mental life" (p. 156), alongside a second current in which the death was acknowledged. This type of "splitting" was similarly found in the fetishist and served to distinguish neurosis in general and fetishism in particular from psychosis, in which the current that "fitted in with reality . . . would have in fact been absent" (p. 56). Now it is true that the symptom picture in psychosis remained sharply different from that in the neuroses: In the former, the "reality current" remained entirely absent. But it is noteworthy that the symptom pictures of neurosis (at least in certain instances) and fetishism (in all instances) could now be characterized by compromises of reality testing: "Disavowals" of reality existed side by side with "acknowledgments" of it.

Freud took this analysis a step further in his subsequent remarks on splitting in "An Outline of Psycho-Analysis" (1938a), apparently retracting his earlier claim in "Fetishism" that the reality current in psychosis "would have in fact been absent." Now the *complete* detachment of the psychotic's ego from reality seemed "to happen only rarely or perhaps never" (p. 201). The distinction between fetishism and neurosis, on the one hand, and psychosis, on the other, was apparently based on factors that were *quantitative* in nature. Splitting of the ego occurred in each of these forms of illness:

> Two psychical attitudes have been formed instead of a single one—one, the normal one, which takes account of

reality, and another which under the influence of the instincts detaches the ego from reality. The two exist alongside of each other. The issue depends on their relative strength. If the second is or becomes the stronger, the necessary precondition for a psychosis is present [p. 202].

Freud went on to compare the repression of instinctual demands typical of neurosis with the disavowal of reality characteristic of fetishism. The difference, he stated, was largely "topographical" (p. 204). But he was careful to indicate that both forms of defense could be present in the same symptom picture, whether that of fetishism (1938b, p. 275) or of neurosis (1938a, pp. 202, 203-204). Thus, toward the end of his career, at least, Freud apparently viewed neurosis—insofar as it was characterized by splitting—as manifesting a compromise of reality testing different only in degree from that seen in psychosis.

It should be noted that the term "splitting of the ego" is frequently used to describe various aspects of psychosis exclusively, despite Freud's careful description of its presence in the neuroses as well. It should further be noted that Freud's use of the term is not the same as that by Melanie Klein or, more recently, by Otto Kernberg to refer to a specific defense of borderline patients. We will return to this issue in Chapter 6.

The publication of "The Ego and the Id" (1923) and "Inhibitions, Symptoms and Anxiety" (1926) led to a shift in Freud's focus from considerations of libido theory alone to ego psychology. Patients could now be assessed within a broader framework, with attention given to all aspects of the functioning of the ego, not just to libidinal conflicts. The examination of a range of ego functions permitted greater refinement in the assessment of reality testing. Distinctions could be drawn on the basis not merely of gross withdrawals from reality but also of gross relatively circumscribed compromises of reality testing in specific ego functions.

However, in addition to concerns about the intactness of reality testing, the ego-psychological point of view was now used to assess ego functions in a much more comprehensive way. Analysts became concerned not only with recognizing the patient's symptoms and character traits but with assessing the nature of the patient's object relations, defensive organization, autonomous ego functions, and overall ego integration. Within this broader framework appeared many patients who could not be classified as either neurotic or psychotic and in relation to whom distinctions based merely on reality testing were inadequate to account for the great variation and complexity of their psychic development and their ego organization. It is to this group of patients that the term "borderline" began to be applied.

A Selective Review of Psychoanalytic Literature on Borderline Patients

It is not possible to review all of the writings devoted to patients who seemed much more disturbed than neurotics but who were not really psychotic, but some of the more important papers will be mentioned. Our purpose here is to provide a selective account illuminating certain trends in the development of psychoanalytic thinking on the borderline concept. These trends, we believe, implicate precisely the issues that our review has shown Freud himself to have been concerned with throughout his career: the nature of the distinction between neurosis and psychosis, and the usefulness of the break with reality as a diagnostic criterion. In addition, these papers demonstrate the increasing recognition of the importance of assessing the patient's object relations and general ego functioning and also take up the question of the capacity of such disturbed patients to undergo psychoanalytic treatment.

The first sentence of Stern's 1938 paper stated the problem succinctly: "It is well known that a large group of patients fit frankly neither into the psychotic nor into the psychoneurotic group, and that the border line group of patients is extremely difficult to handle effectively by any psychotherapeutic method" (p. 467). Stern stressed the high degree of narcissistic disturbance in these patients, which he attributed mainly to faulty mothering. He pointed out that the parents of borderline patients, especially the mothers, are often very disturbed themselves, their poor responsiveness to their children extending over many years. Other clinical features included hypersensitivity, negative therapeutic reactions, deeply embedded feelings of inferiority, masochism, a deep organic insecurity or anxiety, the use of projection mechanisms, difficulties in reality testing, and rigid defenses leading to psychic rigidity.

Stern devoted particular attention to the transference manifestations of these patients. They are extremely dependent and desperately cling to the analyst; they develop extremely immature attitudes and are easily wounded or feel rejected by interpretations. Thus, in Stern's view, a modification of the usual psychoanalytic technique was warranted in that these patients need more supportive measures. Although Stern did not attempt to explain the etiology of these disturbances in any detail, he ventured the opinion that ". . . the anxiety which seems to be the motor for symptom or defense formation is earlier in point of time than the castration anxiety of the transference group of neuroses . . ." (p. 487). In other words, as early as 1938, Stern had ascribed an important causative role to preoedipal factors in the development of the borderline disorder.

In 1942 Helene Deutsch's paper on the "as if" personality was published in English. The patients she described showed severe disturbances in sense of self. Their relationships to the outside world and to their own egos appear impoverished or absent Deutsch wrote" . . . the individual's whole relationship to life has something about it which is lacking in genuineness and yet outwardly runs along 'as if' it were complete" (p. 263). She went on to describe severe narcissistic and identity disturbances. The emotions of these patients are without any real warmth; expression of emotion is formal. They are passive and suggestible and take on the emotions as well as the values of the people around them. Any object serves as someone with whom to identify, and there is more mimicry than true identification. They readily attach themselves to groups in order to counteract their feelings of inner emptiness. And, like Stern, she attributed their disorders to faulty parenting.

Deutsch was of course describing patients with profound disturbances in their object relations. These patients exhibit a fail-ure of adequate identifications and a lack of integration of conflicting identifications. She noted that a similar "as if" stage often precedes the onset of outright psychosis and yet was care-ful to point out that the same symptom picture could, on other occasions, have a "more 'normal' resolution" (p. 280). Deutsch felt that these patients are "schizoid":

> Whether the emotional disturbances described in this pa-per imply a "schizophrenic disposition" or constitute ru-dimentary symptoms of schizophrenia is not clear to me. These patients represent variants in the series of abnormal distorted personalities. They do not belong among the commonly accepted forms of neurosis, and they are too well adjusted to reality to be called psychotic [p. 280].

Thus, although Deutsch cited a number of characteristics, such as "loss of object cathexis," usually associated with a schizo-phrenic process, she felt justified in distinguishing these from psychotic patients by virtue of the fact that their reality testing is preserved, falling back, in other words, on Freud's major criterion for psychosis—the absence of the capacity to remain in touch with reality.

In contrast, Robert Knight (1953) argued that the apparent absence of a break with reality is not sufficient justification for a borderline designation. Like Deutsch, he noted that the symp-toms associated with borderline illness generally precede the onset of frank psychosis. But because such patients frequently present an adaptive façade, greater attention must be paid to all aspects of the patient's ego functioning, specifically, second-ary process thinking, integration, realistic planning, adaptation to the environment, maintenance of object relations, and the defenses, not merely general orientation to reality. Such atten-tion, and the use of unstructured interviews and psychological testing (by nature, an unstructured situation), will reveal the "type and degree of psychotic pathology" (p. 108): "Borderline patients are then likely to show in bolder relief the various microscopic and macroscopic signs of schizophrenic illness" (p. 104). For Knight, then, "borderline" symptomatology merely

disguises the presence of various degrees of psychic functioning. His therapeutic recommendations were for supportive psychotherapy with educative measures.

Leo Stone's "The Widening Scope of Indications for Psychoanalysis" (1954) was an important paper in the evolution of
psychoanalytic thinking about borderlines because it addressed
itself to the issue of whether these disturbed patients could be
analyzed. Although he did not address himself specifically to
the issue of reality testing per se, he pointed out that these
patients are not clinically psychotic, presenting largely neurotic
symptoms but inducing in a clinician a conviction or strong
suspicion of grave illness. They often reveal "psychotic fragments," marked narcissistic phenomena (bodily, emotional, or
intellectual), and a massiveness or multiplicity of symptoms.
There is frequently an immediate, primitive transference reaction with terror of the analytic situation or insatiable unrealistic demands on the analyst. Stone stressed the appearance of
early archaic material, omnipotent, grandiose fantasies, severe
acting out, and a fear of primitive intensity which leads the
patient to detachment or narcissistic retreat. The patients may
attempt to control or tyrannize the therapist or to remain sub-
missive. Stone recommended a cautious psychoanalytic approach to these patients, employing parameters of technique
as necessary to maintain a positive transference. He felt that
despite the difficulties in working with such sick patients, the
results were often rewarding although the effort required great
patience.

In his paper "Psychoanalytic Considerations of the Psychotic
Character" (1970), John Frosch argued that the term "borderline" coincides with his (1959) concept of the "psychotic character." Contrasting neurosis and psychosis, on the one hand,
with neurotic character and psychotic character, on the other,
Frosch stated that:

> the psychotic character represents a specific and recogniz-
> able clinical entity, as does the neurotic character, albeit
> with all the limitations of the latter category. It is not a
> transitional phase on the way to or the way back from
> symptom psychosis, nor is it a latent or larval psychosis

which may become overt, any more than we define neurotic character as a transitional phase on the way to or
from full symptom neurosis. Like the neurotic character,
the psychotic character is a crystallization into a character
structure, reflecting predictable modes of adaptation and
responses to stress [1970, p. 25].

Frosch's statement is thus one of the earliest expressions of the
current view that borderline symptomatology refers to a stable
pathological organization. At the same time, his analysis betrays
some resemblance to that of Knight. Just as Knight had argued
that psychotic traits would emerge in varying degrees in stress-
ful, unstructured situations, so Frosch concluded that "decompensation or regressive adaptations" would occur under the
impact of certain "stresses and strains" (p. 25). But Frosch
stressed not only that such decompensations and regressions
are rapidly reversible (pp. 28, 34) but also that it is entirely
possible for the individual to "go through life without showing
such psychotic symptomatology, preserving all the while the
identifiable features of the psychotic character" (p. 25).

Frosch distinguished the psychotic character from the neurotic character on the grounds that the former's conflicts are
over disintegration of the self with concomitant dedifferentiation of self- and object-representations. The ego of the psychotic
character is vulnerable and ego boundaries tenuous. In contrast
to neurotic patients, whose defenses include repression, displacement, reaction formation, and conversion, the psychotic
character utilizes defenses of splitting, projective identification,
denial, dedifferentiation, fragmentation, and somatization. The
psychotic character also experiences frequent altered ego states
with oceanic feelings, cosmic identity, and feelings of dissolu-
tion. The capacity to test reality is preserved, but there are
significant impairments in the sense of reality (depersonalization and derealization) and of the relationship with reality.

Frosch attributed the ego defects of the psychotic character
to "real and actual severe traumata that were experienced
mainly in the late symbiotic and early separation-individuation
phases of psychic development" (p. 48). The main goals of
therapy are: "encouraging differentiation, establishing feelings

of identity, facilitating the development of mature reality testing and reality constancy" (p. 49).

Kernberg (1967,1975) took the position that borderline patients have a relatively stable form of pathological ego structure, one that places them within a group of patients whose ego organization is on a more advanced level than that of psychotics but not as well integrated as that of neurotics or patients with less severe neurotic character disorders. The main distinguishing feature among these forms of psychopathology is the degree of differentiation of self- and object-representations. In this regard, Kernberg (1967) posited two tasks for the early ego: (1) the *differentiation* of self- and object-representations, and (2) the *integration of affectively polarized* self- and object-representations. That is to say, once the early ego has accomplished the task of differentiating self- and object-representations, it faces the developmentally subsequent task of integrating those *self*-representations "built up under the influence of *libidinal* drive derivatives" with self-representations "built up under the influence of *aggressive* drive derivatives" (p. 664; italics added), and those *object* representations built up under the influence of libidinal drive derivatives with those built up under the influence of aggressive drive derivatives (p. 664). In effect, "idealized 'all good' object images have to be integrated with 'all bad' object images" (p. 665), and "all good" self-images integrated with "all bad" self-images. In psychosis, Kernberg stated, the first task is only imperfectly accomplished: ". . . there is a severe defect of the differentiation between self and object images, and regressive refusion of self and object images occurs in the form of primitive merging fantasies . . ." (p. 665).

In the borderline personality organization, on the other hand, it is the second task that has not been accomplished: There is a *"lack of synthesis of contradictory self and object images"* (p. 666). When, subsequently, this lack of integrative capacity is used defensively by the ego, we have the mechanism of "splitting," which more than any other characteristic distinguishes, in Kernberg's view, the borderline patient from the psychotic. Thus, Kernberg stated:

In an attempt to differentiate psychotic, borderline, and

neurotic patients, one might briefly say that psychotic patients have a severe lack of ego development, with mostly
undifferentiated self and object images and concomitant
lack of development of ego boundaries . . . borderline patients have a better integrated ego than psychotics, with
differentiation between self and object images to a major
extent and with the development of firm ego boundaries
in all but the areas of close interpersonal involvement; they
present, typically, the syndrome of identity diffusion . . . and
neurotic patients present a strong ego, with complete separation between self and object images and concomitant
delimitation of ego boundaries. . . . [p. 677].

Kernberg (1967) contended that the borderline personality organization can be distinguished by (1) "typical symptomatic constellations," (2) "a typical constellation of defensive operations
of the ego," (3) "a typical pathology of internalized object relationships," and (4) "characteristic genetic-dynamic features"
(p. 643). Whereas borderline patients may experience psychotic
episodes and compromises of reality testing under certain severe stresses, these "usually remit with relatively brief but well-
structured treatment approaches" (p. 642). In any case, the
borderline personality organization "is not a transitory state
fluctuating between neurosis and psychosis" (p. 642).

According to Kernberg's *descriptive* analysis (1967), patients
presenting the following symptoms may be borderline: (1)
chronic, diffuse, free-floating anxiety; (2) polysymptomatic
neurosis; (3) polymorphous perverse sexual trends; (4) "classical" prepsychotic personality structure (paranoid personality,
schizoid personality, hypomanic and cyclothymic personalities);
(5) impulse neurosis and addictions; (6) "lower-level" character
disorders (infantile personality, narcissistic personality, depres-
sive-masochistic character structure). His *structural* analysis
(1967) reveals these common characteristics: (1) nonspecific
manifestations of ego weakness (lack of anxiety tolerance, lack
of impulse control, lack of developed sublimatory channels);
(2) shifts toward primary-process thinking; (3) specific defensive operations (splitting, projective identification, primitive
idealization, denial, omnipotence, and devaluation); and (4)
pathology of internalized object relationships.

In summarizing his *genetic-dynamic* analysis, Kernberg (1967) stated that in both sexes an *"excessive development of pregenital, especially oral aggression tends to induce a premature development of oedipal strivings, and as a consequence a particular pathological condensation between pregenital and genital aims under the overriding influence of aggressive needs"* (p. 681).

Further Reflections on the Borderline Question ⚹

Although brief, our review has provided evidence for the following conclusions: that, under the pervasive influence of ego psychology, with its wide assessment of a range of ego functions, psychoanalytic thinking on the borderline concept has evolved from a view in which the borderline patient is defined in terms of the presence or absence of various neurotic or psychotic traits (in particular, the absence of an outright break with reality) to a view in which borderline symptomatology is seen as reflective of a stable pathological ego organization. We have seen how Deutsch was forced to distinguish the "as if" patient from the neurotic patient by virtue of the former's disordered object relations, and from the psychotic by virtue of the former's relatively intact reality testing. We have seen Knight's rejoinder to this position: that even where no break with reality is apparent, closer examination of the borderline patient's whole complex of ego functions will reveal compromises in reality testing of psychotic dimensions. For Knight "borderline" symptomatology is simply psychotic functioning of a lesser degree than that ordinarily seen in frank psychosis. Stone pointed to the importance of masked transference reactions, especially early in the treatment, which would make the analyst suspect more serious pathology even in the absence of a clear-cut disturbance in reality testing. Frosch examined the same evidence that Knight considered and concluded, in contrast, that the psychotic functioning of the "psychotic character" is generally rapidly reversible and, in many instances, never even apparent in the individual's lifetime. From this he deduced the presence of a crystallized character formation. Kernberg's analysis, then, represents the ultimate statement of the contemporary view of borderline functioning as reflective of a stable pathological organization. We shall, of course, be considering these questions in a much more systematic way throughout this volume.

In addition to the papers reviewed, there has been a growing interest in patients who exhibit severe ego pathology. Our understanding of patients of these kinds has increased as attention and interest have been devoted to many aspects of developmental psychology.

Although an extensive review of all of this work is clearly not practical, it is important to mention that our growing interest has been stimulated by work that may not have dealt directly with the borderline patient. We are referring here to the important studies of Margaret Mahler (1971) and her co-workers (Mahler and Furer, 1968; Mahler, Pine, and Bergman, 1975) and to Phyllis Greenacre's work on early ego disturbances and their relation to anxiety and perversions (1971).

There has also been a re-examination of the contributions of Melanie Klein (1948), and a great deal of attention has been given to the object relations theorists of the British school of psychoanalysts such as Fairbairn (1954), Winnicott (1965), and Bion (1957). Jacobson's (1964) work on developing object relations has enriched our understanding, and Boyer and Giovacchini (1967) have addressed themselves specifically to the treatment of severe characterological problems. Masterson and Rinsley (1972, 1975, 1977) have also contributed to the literature on borderline states.

There have also been two panel discussions (Rangell, 1955; Robbins, 1956) of the American Psychoanalytic Association devoted to the study of the borderline patient. A more current review by Meissner (1978) covers many of the issues discussed in this monograph. Most recently Calef and Weinshel (1979) have raised questions concerning Kernberg's contributions. In this paper, they point to the paucity of detailed psychoanalytic studies of borderline patients which might aid us in understanding the complexities and uncertainties in this difficult area of investigation.

We have obviously omitted from consideration numerous influential studies of the borderline concept published within the past forty years. Rather than be comprehensive, we have tried to provide a rough historical sketch that illuminates the concept and suggests the ways in which certain broad trends in the development of psychoanalytic thinking have resulted in the dominant view today most closely associated with Kernberg. That is to say, we have tried to account for the current status of the syndrome. But the reader should note that there are many psychoanalytic theorists who do not share the prevailing view. We shall be examining their positions in some detail in Chapter 2, and indeed throughout the volume wherever they are relevant. Perhaps more important, we should indicate that the current view is not necessarily our own view (or that of the Kris Study Group). Indeed, our entire purpose in this volume is to test the various positions of psychoanalytic thinkers on the borderline concept against clinical evidence derived from well-documented psychoanalytic treatments of borderline patients. The succeeding chapter will describe how the Kris Study Group approached this endeavor.

2.

A General Introduction to the Work of the Kris Study Group

Unresolved problems in regard to the borderline concept in general influenced the proceedings of the Kris Study Group throughout its deliberations. This was so both in the area of methodology, particularly in respect to case selection, and in the ongoing effort to clarify our preferred conceptual approach as well. Our purpose in this chapter is to detail the way the group settled some pragmatic questions, to indicate certain of the broader theories it considered, and to present in outline the ways of thinking in an overall way about borderlines which emerged gradually over the course of our work together. Thus we hope to prepare the reader for the discussions of specific features of the behavior and functioning of these patients, and of their psychoanalytic treatment, which will follow the presentation of clinical material in Chapter 3.

Choosing Case Material

The traditional approach of the Kris Study Groups of the New York Psychoanalytic Institute since their inception has been to select topics of current theoretical interest in psychoanalysis and examine them in depth, making particular use of accumulated psychoanalytic case material from the practices of the participants, who include as a rule members of varying degrees of clinical experience (from advanced candidates to senior analysts of the Institute faculty). Our group, typically, was determined to base whatever conclusions we might reach on a detailed examination of such clinical data, and we were aware that the nature of the cases chosen for review would naturally be of critical significance. Inevitably the characteristics of the population selected for inclusion would influence what we found. Our situation was particularly vexing, since there was no generally accepted definition of the borderline syndrome, either among ourselves or in the literature. Indeed, there was not even agreement that the term "borderline" describes a discrete clinical entity.

This situation posed an immediate procedural dilemma at the outset of our work. Before we had had a chance to achieve agreement on any substantive issues we had somehow to establish criteria for determining which cases were appropriate for inclusion in the study. In light of the aforementioned absence of reliable diagnostic criteria, how were we to decide which of the cases to be submitted for consideration was likely to prove pertinent and instructive?

As a practical solution we decided to compile a clinical description of borderline patients from a sample of the literature, which we hoped would at least serve as a convenient point of departure. We had already commenced to review the analytic literature on the subject of borderlines, and for our task of constructing a diagnostic guideline we chose some of the early classic papers, by Deutsch (1942), Knight (1953), and Gitelson (1958), added the major contributions of Frosch (1964) and Stone (1954), and then also included the detailed, systematic presentations of Kernberg (1966, 1967). From them, we made an effort to draw up a composite clinical picture using, as far as possible, only the *descriptive* features of the clinical material presented by these authors. Those formulations which rested heavily upon a more theoretical interpretation of the data of observation were omitted, since we soon discovered that they were likely to call forth critical discussion and disagreement within the study group. We tried therefore to restrict ourselves to less controversial, essentially phenomenological features, which we assembled into a list we entitled "Descriptive Features of Borderline Patients":

1. The pathology tends to invade the entire character structure and to be of relatively stable degree. This apparently means that such patients do not become psychotic, at least not for long, nor do they get very much better. The borderline state is not a way station in an upward or downward direction, respectively, of progressive compensation or decompensation. However, these patients certainly change transiently (regress), within their own portion of the pathological spectrum.

2. The relationship to reality is impaired, with perceptual distortions, poor judgment, and states of disturbed sense of reality. However, either the rapid reversibility of the defects or the persistent intactness of some degree of reality testing often gives an impression of *less* impairment than might otherwise be expected from the clinical phenomena.

3. Object relations may best be characterized as infantile, with egocentricity, demandingness, and exploitiveness, with or without extreme passivity, childish overidealization, and submissiveness; the latter may or may not be accompanied by resentment.

4. The life history will probably reveal the evidence of rather severe impairment: poor achievement, instability of relationships, chronic sexual maladjustment, and multiple symptoms.

5. Borderline patients present a polysymptomatic clinical picture, covering almost the entire range of neurotic symptomatology. Uniformity of symptomatology is not to be expected as one case differs very much from another.

6. Some authors emphasize that "psychotic fragments" may be found. By this they appear to mean they discover undisguised representation of "primitive" wishes and fantasies, or they observe primary process mental operations "too thinly disguised." Yet opinion is divided even among the authors who describe this clinical finding; some are most definite that formal aspects of thought, concept formation, and language will betray the encroachment of psychotic disturbance, at least episodically, but others are as firmly convinced that this is not the case.

7. Some writers give specific emphasis to the narcissistic features of these cases. Whereas some of the points of description

mentioned above could also be classified as narcissistic phe-nomena, this characteristic should also be included as a separate descriptive feature, although it would require amplification to indicate what specific qualities are considered under this heading.

8. Much has been made of the way these patients behave in the treatment situation as compared with more usual analysands. Often, there are atypical, intense, early transference reactions. Borderlines may show unusually strong affects, contradictory unintegrated attitudes toward the analyst, or both. They often have poor capacity to perceive or understand the unrealistic nature of the feelings, attitudes, and beliefs which develop in their relationship with the therapist.

9. Several writers remark on the prominence of aggressive conflicts, often characterized as "primitive," with evidence of an unusual degree of self-destructiveness.

10. The disturbances of affect may be of different kinds. Affects have been characterized as inappropriate, labile, absent, false, over-intense, poorly controlled, and so forth. Of course, any given patient may reveal a fairly consistent pattern of affective disturbance, but as a class, the borderlines seem to impress observers as frequently revealing some substantial degree of disturbance in this sphere of mental life.

11. These patients may evoke specific and characteristic countertransference reactions.

The Decision to Concentrate on Analytic Material

During the course of our work we discussed many patients who conformed to the clinical guidelines set out in our composite. Eventually we decided to concentrate our efforts on four analyzed cases which had been particularly well studied. The duration of these analyses ranged from five to ten years. All four cases had been supervised as they had been undertaken early in the respective analysts' careers. Although subject to the limitations imposed by the relative inexperience of the analysts, the cases offered a number of advantages for our purposes.

Careful notes had been kept, and supervisors' opinions were available as part of the case records. Furthermore, each case had been presented at formal clinical conferences for which summaries had been prepared. At these conferences, other analysts' opinions of the pathology, and of the treating and supervising analysts' formulations of their cases, had been put forth and were available for our review.

Some of us felt that by concentrating our attention so fully on patients who had been able to undergo the more or less classical psychoanalytic technique, we had skewed our data, limiting ourselves to a population of patients who functioned on a higher level than borderlines who could not be analyzed. We recognized the possible validity of this argument, and the reservation that this study may have limited application is reflected in its title, "Borderline Patients: Psychoanalytic Perspectives." It was our feeling, however, that what we as a group could bring to the study of borderline patients that might prove especially useful was precisely that order of understanding which derives only from the analytic situation. By way of comparison, in our own deliberations anecdotal material and cases seen in psychotherapy by our members seemed less valuable; consideration of such material invariably raised many questions which could not be answered in a satisfactory way. Indeed, we believe it was the unique detail and richness of analytic material which enabled our discussions to progress beyond broad generalizations and speculation.

We felt it was even more pertinent to our task to ask how our analyzed patients compared to the analytic patients utilized by other authors. It is surprisingly difficult to assess this question merely by reading the literature. In this connection, it was of great interest to us that Kernberg commented during the course of our meeting with him that the two patients whom we presented met his criteria for borderline personality organization.

Limitations of space make it possible to reproduce in this volume only an abbreviated summary, prepared by the respective analyst, of each of the four cases which we used in our work. The summaries, to be found in the next chapter, "Case Material," should be sufficient to familiarize the reader with the cases and to facilitate the understanding of the discussions of specific aspects of the borderline patient which are to be found in the following sections of this report.

The Struggle to Clarify the Concept

Once we had determined how we would proceed, we were engaged for many months in discussions in which we attempted to reach agreement on how to conceptualize the borderline problem. Several possible approaches were presented for consideration, espoused by one or another member, usually with support from some segment of the psychoanalytic literature. The most traditional view seemed to be derived ultimately from Freud's original formulations about psychosis and neurosis (Chapter 1). He believed these major, more or less distinct, classes of illness to be characterized by fundamentally different kinds of underlying mental phenomena, comprising different mechanisms of symptom formation, as well as by different relationships to reality. We all agreed that the gradual accumulation of clinical experience, especially with cases showing more severe pathologic features, had led to increased dissatisfaction with these categorical distinctions. Clear and ready differentiation of the two classes of disturbance had become more difficult, as the introduction of the term "borderline" was meant to indicate.

Logically enough, the earliest efforts to explain the phenomenology of borderlines had supposed that they demonstrate an admixture of both psychotic and neurotic features. Analysts who propounded this theory held that a careful examination of borderline cases would show evidence of both types of disturbance. In essence, according to them, borderlines therefore constitute a subtle, milder variant of psychosis. A close reading of Knight's (1953) paper shows that he held precisely that view. The more severely ill patients said by Hoch and Polatin (1949) to have "pseudoneurotic schizophrenia" and by Zilboorg (1941) "ambulatory schizophrenia" may be thought of as representing other examples of this interpretation of the borderline states.

Among more recent theorists, Dickes (1974) also unambiguously stated the view that borderline patients display unmistakable evidence of psychosis, albeit only in psychological equivalents of what neurologists have been accustomed to label "soft signs."

We considered this viewpoint, but it was not widely supported among our participants. Most of us doubted the validity of its theoretical basis and also felt that our clinical data did not support its assumptions. We were much more interested in exploring the idea, which has gradually emerged in recent years, that borderlines constitute a distinct class of pathological entities, of more or less stable configuration, with characteristic mental phenomena peculiar to them alone. Kernberg (1966, 1967, 1975, 1976) has become the most prominent spokesman for this way of conceptualizing the borderline states. He proposed that the diagnostic criteria for what he has suggested we call "borderline personality organization" include the presence of certain characteristic mental phenomena which are pathognomonic; among them are particular, unique defenses and distinctive forms of internalized object relationships. These are related to phase-specific developmental disturbances and prominent conflicts over aggression. Characteristic transference behavior derived from these underlying defects is another feature which distinguishes borderlines from other, neurotic analysands, according to Kernberg's hypothesis.

In our group there were, as we noted above, some analysts who from the beginning held a certain amount of doubt about the accuracy and utility of the theoretical formulations which ascribe to psychosis, neurosis, and perhaps borderlines as well unique metapsychological underpinnings. These analysts tended instead toward what might be termed a quantitative interpretation, seeing psychopathology as constituting a continuum of sorts in which different degrees of severity exist on a gradual gradient. They would then describe borderline cases as those which occupy an intermediate position on this proposed continuum, but one not so readily differentiated from the neuroses on the one side or the more gravely disturbed psychotic illnesses on the other. One of our members, Dr. David Beres, was a particularly articulate advocate of this point of view. He suggested that "borderline" is such a poor term that it be discarded altogether, since it designates merely a loosely linked group of patients with severe character pathology. It was his contention that analysts would do better to set aside generalizations about these sicker patients and concentrate instead on the specific variables encountered in the symptom picture and character structure of each such case.

It was by no means easy for our group to reach a working consensus on these fundamental conceptual matters. As noted, we were, to mention one difficulty, divided on the question of the postulated differences between neurotic and psychotic symptom formation. However, it was made clear that analysts could continue to maintain the view that psychotic and neurotic illnesses are fundamentally and qualitatively distinct from one another without necessarily subscribing to Freud's early formulations regarding the metapsychology of these kinds of disturbance. Despite this division, then, there was, as mentioned, a high degree of correspondence among us on the opinion that our clinical material does not support the thesis that borderlines constitute a mild class of psychotic patient, irrespective of the analyst's views on the nature of psychotic pathology.

Much of our effort went into a thoroughgoing study of Kernberg's formulations. We read and discussed his publications with great care and interest, since they comprise the most complete, thoughtful, and systematic presentation of a unified view of borderlines as a separate class of pathological entities to be found in the psychoanalytic literature. We studied our own case material in the light of his observations and his theories. Our consideration of his work culminated in a conference with Dr. Kernberg. We devoted an entire day[1] to this endeavor; a candid exchange of scientific opinions and ideas took place. The authors speak in this instance for the entire group in expressing appreciation for Dr. Kernberg's participation, in the course of which he gave his views of two of our study cases (II and III) and presented some clinical material of his own. He pursued with us many questions about the theory presented in his writ-

[1] Saturday, January 22, 1977, at the New York Psychoanalytic Institute, 247 East 82nd Street, New York, N.Y. 10028.

ings. Our understanding of his thinking on a number of issues was much clarified by this interchange, and we became more aware of those areas in which many of us are in general agreement with him, as well as of the points of difference. These will become evident throughout the body of this report.

As we debated and discussed the issues among ourselves, we found that, while we readily agreed that borderlines display a greater severity of illness than do other, more typical analysands, it was not easy to express this empirical judgment using concepts that had explanatory value. We struggled to test the theory that borderlines reveal common unique features. We certainly noted the evidence of regressed levels of functioning, both within and outside of the analytic situation. We found ourselves turning again and again to generalizations having to do, for example, with differences in "ego organization" in our efforts to account for their clinical appearance and behavior. This was as unsatisfactorily vague to us as it has been to others in the past, and so eventually we arrived at a determination to attempt a more specific delineation of the various ego functions of our borderline patients, and to try to understand the genesis of the disruption of these capacities as best we could on the basis of our analytic data.

As noted, our study material was drawn from office analytic practice. Although these cases were more difficult to manage analytically than the more usual ones, none required hospitalization at any stage nor were major, nonanalyzed parameters of technique regularly employed. Thus our material may rightly be regarded as coming from the less severe part of that portion of the spectrum of pathology which we designate as the borderline states. The patients were able to work, albeit with difficulty, in the analytic mode for long periods of time, five to ten years, and to profit from the experience. The formulations and conclusions which we eventually reached reflect both the selective nature of these cases and also the special comprehension of them which only prolonged, extensive analytic study of individuals can possibly provide.

In deciding to concentrate on the various ego functions of these patients as a way to better describe and understand how they differ from other analysands, we were breaking no new ground Dr. Beres, for example, systematically applied this approach to schizophrenic patients some years earlier (1956) and Kernberg's comprehensive diagnostic survey (1967) was also organized along similar lines. Many others employed such global concepts as "ego weakness" or "ego deviations" to account for the borderline clinical picture. It was our hope to gain more useful information by undertaking a more tightly focused examination of certain critical ego functions, but our attempt to achieve more specificity proved to be no easy task.

Difficulties in the Study of Ego Functions see #'s

We were soon confronted with what must be a familiar practical difficulty. It seems quite easy when constructing theoretical schemata to define gradients of ego functions which appear to offer convenient, clear distinctions and which may therefore be used in turn to establish clinical differentiations. We realize that all such definitions are to some degree artificial, essentially conventions adopted to facilitate organizing and discussing data. Whenever clinical material is examined according to such proposed guidelines, the inherent difficulty in applying them quickly becomes evident. Any one analyst, or discussant, may find it easy to assay data according to such schemata. Group discussions, by contrast, generally disclose that clinical material does not really lend itself so readily to neat subdivision, even when the group is composed of more or less like-minded members, of similar training and essentially homogeneous viewpoints, as was ours. Disagreements most often arise as to interpretations of the data, of the definitions, or of both. Even when preliminary differences have been more or less resolved, there inevitably remains room for argument over whether a given sample of clinical material *really* illustrates a given point, criterion, or distinction.

We concluded that within each aspect of ego functioning there may be said to exist a continuous range, from intact, or normal, to extremely deficient, or pathological. If this is so, graded distinctions of ego functioning may be applied only very loosely. Thus some may prove convenient to apply to actual clinical material, others less so. The best result which a group can hope to attain is a rough consensus, which was what did occur in our group. The foregoing may appear to belabor the obvious, but we assure the reader that it did not seem so to us until after many months of discussion of our material.

H | Consider, for instance, that aspect of ego functioning we call *reality testing*. It is, for one thing, no simple entity; authors such as Hartmann (1956) and Frosch (1964) have emphasized its complex and compound nature. It has been said to subsume the following: consensual validation of perceptions; logical consistency of ideas; the ability to distinguish ideas from perceptions, or fantasy from fact; differentiating self-representations from object-representations; feelings or ideas having to do with the real or unreal qualities of external and internal perceptions; social versus objective reality; the capacity to act in accordance with conscious judgments of reality; and even the special case of the way the analytic transference is experienced. Each of these have been emphasized by one or another worker, and all were considered in our deliberations. Reality testing can never adequately be described merely as either intact or defective; neither can varying degrees of intactness be demarcated, like the click-stops on certain instruments, in any way which is readily applicable to clinical material.

What seems to be common to all aspects of faulty reality testing is that *some degree* of distorting influence is exercised upon thought, judgment, or perception by wishful or fearful unconscious fantasies. From the slight misinterpretation of a social situation in a so-called "normal" individual, through the varieties of neurotic symptomatology, to the delusions and hallucinations of blatant psychosis, this explanation would seem to apply, although it does not account for the differences among these forms of disturbance. The degree of distortion and of social discordance and functional incapacity which results will vary greatly in each case. What is more, these influences can and do fluctuate in intensity in normal subjects as well as in all patients. It has been suggested that intermediate degrees of difficulty, such as our study population were presumed to display, are likely to manifest unusually severe fluctuations in reality testing, perhaps with ready reversibility. It has also been suggested that borderlines as compared with yet more seriously disturbed individuals whose relation to reality is more grossly impaired, retain some capacity to acknowledge the distorting influence of their fantasies on their interpretation of reality. They may do this either directly, that is to say consciously, or more often indirectly, as indicated by a need to rationalize the illogicalities and distortions which are present. These were possibilities which we were able to clarify through discussion and clinical presentations. They are offered here in advance, so to speak, primarily to indicate the complexity of the task of assaying reality testing. A following section of this report will concern itself more fully with this subject.

Another problem in the evaluation of ego functions is that they are not, upon close examination, always so readily separable as one might like to think. Let us take the *regulation and control of instinctual drives,* for example. We can probably agree that it is supposed to be one of the functions of the ego to modulate the expression of libidinal and aggressive drive tension in a fashion commensurate with the need for gratification, on the one hand, and the limitations imposed by reality on the other (leaving aside for the moment the role of the superego). However, is not adequate reality testing essential to the appropriate regulation of drives, and are not the control of motility, the functions of memory and judgment, and the part played by particular defenses necessary as well? The artificiality of subdividing ego functions is evident; only for convenience in discussion can it be justified.

Another example of the complexity involved in evaluating ego functions is furnished by our attempt to assess *object relations.* Surely it is unnecessary to document the complexity of this subject. Suffice it to say that we spent considerable time and effort in trying to delineate the characteristics of the object relations of our patients. The prominence of this topic in current psychoanalytic thinking made it essential for us to compare our findings with those reported in the literature. These results also will be set forth in a separate section of our report.

4

Thought processes have received special attention from some workers, who follow the usage of descriptive psychiatry in distinguishing slight evidences of formal thought disorder in borderline patients (Knight, 1953; Frosch, 1964; Dickes, 1974). Such observations are reminiscent of the neurologists' use of "soft signs" and are especially likely to be subject to disagreement (cf. Kernberg). Here too, the notion that thinking processes are either intact or not, or perhaps only "slightly impaired," seemed to us inadequate to the standards of clinical explanation which should be expected of psychoanalysts. As every analyst knows, the capacity of analytic patients for maturely logical thought varies tremendously from one session to the next, even from moment to moment within the same session. This variability seems to involve not only the capacity for logic and objectivity, to which we pay most attention in our clinical work. In some individuals at least, variability extends so far as to lead at times to idiosyncratic usages, contaminations, malapropisms, word play, and neologisms. In other words, the formal elements of thought as revealed in speech, upon which Frosch, Dickes, Knight, and others have placed great diagnostic emphasis, may be affected. We could agree that some patients are more likely than others to show a high degree of this kind of dysfunction, and also that patients we think of as sicker are likely to reveal more frequent, more blatant interferences with logical thought. But we also have noted severely ill patients who did not display this propensity for errors of the kind we are considering, and others, less disturbed in many ways, whose speech was quite likely to reflect such evidences of difficulty in logical organization of thought.

Certainly when we encounter such disruptions of thinking and its expression in speech to a marked degree, particularly during our evaluation of prospective patients, we tend to assume that greater pathology is present, and we anticipate more difficulty in analyzing them than usual. Conversely, the absence of such "signs" is assumed, perhaps not always correctly, to be a more favorable prognostic sign. However, we have come to believe that the usefulness of these distinctions as diagnostic and predictive criteria may be less than is often supposed.

In respect to the *defenses* of borderline patients, we made a #5 sustained effort to understand and synthesize what our analytic experience had taught us about our own cases, and to compare it with what had been reported elsewhere. Once again, our findings will be summarized in detail in a subsequent section of this report. Here it will suffice to indicate some broad questions we kept in mind in approaching this aspect of our study.

1. Is it possible that borderlines are not differentiable from other analyzable patients in respect to defenses? If that is indeed so, then favored defenses would be related to the specific prominent symptoms and character traits of each individual patient. Since symptomatology and character types vary within the group of patients classified as borderline, corresponding variation in defense pattern will likewise be observed.

2. Perhaps, however, we may find that the same defenses do not appear in sicker patients in forms identical to those seen in less sick ones. In other words, defenses may show a variable range as do other ego functions. Another way to formulate this possibility might be to see defense manifestations in clinical material as a result of defense mechanisms and their interaction with other ego functions, such as reality testing. Some might prefer to put it that the nature of the ego organization as a whole affects defense organization diffusely; that is to say, similar mechanisms may appear more rigid, more fluid, more pervasive, less successful, and so on, in certain sicker patients.

3. Another suggestion often encountered in the literature is that there exists a hierarchy of defenses, with some considered more "primitive" than others. Denial and projection are frequently referred to in this way, for example. Their prominence in a given patient presumably reflects some developmental difficulty, i.e., fixation, and generally produces more maladaptive behavior. Whereas these defenses are found in less sick patients as well, they are believed more likely to predominate, or at least be more in evidence, in borderlines.

4. One last possibility to be considered is that borderlines characteristically display special defenses, whose presence may be pathognomonic of the condition or at least have strong di-

agnostic significance. This is the viewpoint associated particularly with Kernberg (1966, 1967, 1975), who developed it fully in his publications.

Sometimes in our discussions such complex and subtle aspects of ego functioning as the *synthetic function* and the *autonomous function* would be mentioned. By and large, this was very much *en passant,* perhaps because the difficulty of detailing these functions from clinical material appeared too formidable. At any rate, no useful assessment of their manifestations in our patients resulted from our efforts. Limitations of time led us to concentrate on those areas which aroused the most interest and to relegate other topics to the background. As we have said, we studied *object relations, reality testing,* and the *defenses* in sufficient depth to warrant our reporting on them in detail. We will devote a separate section to our observation of the *transference* behavior of our patients. We will also address ourselves to the important issue of the technique of treatment for these cases. Finally, we will devote a section to our understanding of the etiology of these disorders. Before we turn to these selected topics, however, we will present abbreviated clinical summaries of the four analyses we studied in depth.

Toward the end of the study group's deliberations it began to assemble its findings to present them to the membership of the New York Psychoanalytic Society and other interested professionals at a scientific meeting of the Society.[2] The introduction to that program concluded with a brief compendium of the main questions which the group had addressed in the course of its work. It was thought that these would be of some help to the audience as it listened to the mass of data which might otherwise have proven more difficult to absorb. We will bring to a close this introductory material by repeating that list of questions here, in the hope that it may likewise help the reader to approach our findings with a greater sense of organization and clarity.

[2] April 25, 1978.

1. Does the term "borderline" refer to a specific diagnostic entity, or does it merely refer to a group of patients, better described by their individual diagnostic labels, who merely are more severely disturbed than other neurotics, although not as impaired as psychotic patients? If the latter usage is more accurate, what if any justification is there for separating them from less ill patients? Are there any features common to this group as a whole to which the term "borderline" may be assumed to refer?

2. Can we come to any conclusions as to the etiology of this condition? Are there specific genetic, dynamic, economic, and developmental considerations involved, i.e., are there particular kinds of conflicts involved or a particular developmental period that is of crucial importance?

3. Which ego functions are seriously impaired in this group of patients? Can we describe specific defensive operations? What is the nature of the reality testing in such patients? Can we specify the significant pathology of their object relations?

4. What is the nature of the transference established by such patients during their treatment and how can we understand its development?

5. Can patients who are diagnosed as borderline be psychoanalyzed in a traditional way, or is it necessary to introduce various modifications of technique in order to be successful? Is it possible to make an accurate judgment about analyzability during the consultation or initial contacts?

6. What is the nature of the clinical evidence offered in support of the views of the authors we studied? How does our own clinical evidence compare with that of others? How did we make use of our clinical data, from the psychoanalysis of a number of cases, to reach the conclusions we will report in this monograph?

3.

Case Material

Case Report I

Miss W was a twenty-seven-year-old unmarried research assistant who sought analysis with the encouragement of a former psychotherapist who had helped her over a bout of depression and difficulty in getting along with co-workers some years earlier. She complained of recurrent depressive periods, of an increased use of nonprescription drugs to help her sleep and lift her spirits, of poor relationships with men, and of a fear of being hurt by others. She also said she generally felt lonely, dissatisfied, and uncertain as to what she wanted out of life. She admitted she was a compulsive eater at times, but only after a long time in her analysis was she able to describe her actual symptom of episodic bulimia followed by self-induced vomiting. She made a neat, attractive appearance and though slightly plump did not look overweight. She spoke earnestly and haltingly and seemed solemn and ponderous rather than overtly depressed. Her statements about herself were framed in clichés and tended toward generalizations and vagueness, and she expressed concern about the "normality" of what she revealed.

During the initial sessions she told about her unhappy early life and of her present dissatisfactions. She seemed childlike and gave the impression of being somewhat restricted in the exercise of her intelligence, imagination, and capacity for self-expression. She supposed that male patients naturally got preference in regard to scheduling since "they have greater responsibilities than women." At the first interview she said she was disconcerted because the analyst looked too much like her father. Later it turned out that this "uncanny" perceived resemblance was based merely on her vague recollection of a photograph of her father as a young man which she had seen years earlier.

She was the younger of two girls. Her parents came from apparently conventional middle-class families residing in a small Midwestern industrial town. Her father was a restless soul who before his marriage had had a reputation for financial irresponsibility and was thought of as something of a black sheep. Miss W had been told by her mother that she was supposed to have been a boy, and she had always been convinced that her father was deeply disappointed that she was not his hoped-for son. She believed that this might have contributed to his subsequent readiness to abandon the family.

During her second year of life her father left for the first time. Financial troubles and restless impulsiveness were implicated as the cause of his defection, but the patient was never entirely sure of the actual reasons or circumstances, which were treated as shameful secrets by the mother and all other relatives. For the next year-and-a-half there were a number of moves, joinings, and separations. When she was four-and-a-half years old he disappeared once more. She was told she cried daily for him for a long time.

Mother and daughters then lived with other relatives for several years, which were recalled by Miss W as bleak and unhappy. There ensued another happy reunion in California, where her father had in the interim relocated himself. The patient remembered this period, which lasted for about three years, as idyllic, despite the fact that there was considerable friction between the parents. She referred often to the beautiful surroundings and sunshine as accounting for her happiness, and had longed for warm weather ever since that time.

The father left once more, this time for good. The patient and her sister subsequently made several summer visits to him, each time attempting to get him to return with them, though he was soon living with another woman. There were sketchy memories of these visits, but analytic material revealed that the children were conscious of, and disturbed by, the sexual situation in the father's new household. Shortly after the patient reached puberty, all contact with her father was lost for good, and she professed throughout her analysis to be uncertain whether he was alive or dead.

The mother worked as an executive secretary and supported her children without assistance from the father but became rather irritable and demanding. The girls were expected to cook and clean house, and the patient was often alone. Her habit of consuming sweets to console herself dated from those years. Other early signs of disturbance were an intolerance for separation from her mother, which was noted when she entered nursery school, kindergarten, and first grade, and difficulty mastering schoolwork. This was described as confusion, anxiety, excessive concern about getting instructions wrong, and a propensity to make foolish errors. The older sister, on the other hand, was an excellent student, very dominant and confident and the acknowledged leader of the pair, on whom Miss W was always very dependent.

In adolescence the patient often quarrelled with her mother. She was frequently enjoined not to disturb her sister, who tended to be sickly. Though interested in boys, Miss W did not go out on many dates while in high school, as she was rather shy and inhibited. After her graduation she undertook special training in research skills rather than attempting to go to college. Upon completion of this preparation she went to work in a city some distance from her home. She was restless and changed jobs often but claimed she did so each time for better pay and conditions. Unlike her father, she was very responsible about her work and also sent money home to her mother to help her meet expenses.

She quarrelled with roommates and co-workers because she tended to feel easily slighted and hurt and thought she was less favored in comparison to others. She also frequently had a hard time understanding or taking account of others' needs. She had a few brief, unsatisfactory affairs with men who were not very caring or were emotionally unavailable. She was inappropriately crushed when one man she had dated only casually married another woman. Her sister pursued higher education and achieved professional status, married well, and had several children.

The patient was generally robust and enjoyed good physical health, in contrast to her sickly sister. Miss W had, however, had hypochondriacal worries from time to time. She always consciously felt very attached to, and admiring of, her sister, but there were strong hints in the history she gave of an intense rivalry. One such was a period of intense worry that her sister had a fatal illness, based upon a misinterpretation of the nature of a minor ailment from which the sister had suffered when they were both adolescents. The patient remained in close contact with her mother, who never again seemed to have much interest in men after the marital breakup. The mother became quite obese and continued to work at her job, which apparently afforded her considerable satisfaction. The patient also had had intense fears that her mother might die when she became ill on one occasion when the patient was in her early teens.

Course of the Analysis

The patient had considerable difficulty from the very first in speaking freely and spontaneously. Her connection of the analyst with her image of her father affected her strongly. She was convinced he could not be interested in her and would abandon her as the father had done, and she presented herself poorly, in part in order unconsciously to invite this outcome. She felt unfavorably compared to others as one who "broke the rules," "made mistakes," and "couldn't learn right." She was also suspicious and critical of the analyst and others, and feared this would offend, though she had no apparent awareness of the aggressive component of these behaviors. So essential was it to try and make a favorable impression that she could only offer "associations" to her early dreams which were derived from her recollections of various interpretations of symbols she had read in books about psychoanalysis or dreams. She had to give "correct" answers and hide what she considered "wrong," i.e., embarrassing or impolite thoughts of her own.

She was entirely preoccupied with what she imagined the analyst thought of her and also wished very strongly for him to advise her on the conduct of her life and instruct her, as well as give approval to what she said and did. She did not tolerate very easily his handling of her requests and questions as analytic communications and felt hurt and angry at these frustrations. She twisted his comments to conform to her wish for advice and approval, and at the same time to serve her tendency to experience him as critical and judgmental. Despite repeated attempts to clarify the nature, extent, and origins of these distortions, they persisted for many months. It was very clear that she related to the analyst intensely as if he were the longed-for literal replacement of her lost father, although elements of the transference also reflected aspects of her relationships to her sister and mother at times.

So powerful was her wish to be close to the analyst that she attempted to rent an apartment in the building where his office was located, an act which he learned of inadvertently from the building staff. Miss W could not seem to understand the importance and potential value of discussing, i.e., analyzing, such impulses. Her intense curiosity led her to try to find out all that she could about the analyst's personal life, and she continued at the same time to conceal her thoughts about him during her analytic sessions. The persistence of this behavior, in particular, keeping secret her thoughts concerning the analyst, did not serve only defensive purposes; it also satisfied her unconscious wish to punish and frustrate her father and at the same time to punish herself by provoking rejection through creating the unfavorable impression she consciously worked so hard to prevent from occurring.

In spite of these obstacles to free communication and to "learning" how to work in the analytic setting, the outlines of her history and her conflicts did gradually emerge. It became apparent early on, and remained true to some extent for the entire duration of her treatment, that the analyst actually learned far more about Miss W's experiences and mental contents than seemed to be the case on a day-to-day basis. His feelings of pessimism, frustration, and doubt about the viability of the treatment reflected the surface withholding and the apparent inability to respond and behave more like typically cooperative analysands. Her exaggerated curiosity and inhibition of learning were connected to the conflict over learning more about the father, incorporating both his silence and secrecy and the mother's shame-determined policy of not discussing him forthrightly and of enjoining the girls to maintain the same façade of pretense and silence. There were also elements of the conflicts she experienced in respect to understanding the exact nature of the relationships in the extended family with whom she lived for some years, in the father's second household, and, by extension, in all other sexual relationships as well.

In the first dating relationship she undertook after commencing analysis, she impulsively began sexual intimacies almost immediately, tactlessly questioned the man about himself, yet failed to learn even simple facts about him—never finding out what his job was, for instance. She acknowledged a conscious fear of developing sexual feelings about her analyst, and so she welcomed the opportunity to divert them onto another man. She was, however, extremely guilty about sleeping with this individual and redoubled her tendency to turn the analyst's comments on the subject into judgmental ones. After some weeks it became clear that the boyfriend was a rather hostile, suspicious, accusatory, and quite possibly paranoid person, and she broke off the affair. Afterwards she ruminated endlessly about who had been at fault, which obviously repeated childhood concerns about her parents' marital failure.

As the attachment to her analyst grew still more intense, she reacted strongly to separation from him, not talking much before and after the interruptions, and consoling herself during the breaks with sweets as she had done since childhood. She seemed unable to find words to describe or define her feelings or nuances of meaning. She rarely spontaneously identified anyone in events she described, nor did she provide those details of setting and sequence which ordinarily enable a person to follow and comprehend what he is being told. It was as if she could not empathize with the listener and recognize that data must be provided if one cares to be understood by another. It appeared as though she unconsciously wished to create in the analyst the sense of ignorance, confusion, frustration, and loneliness which had characterized much of her childhood experience. As the first summer separation approached she became more depressed, withdrawn, and silent, emphasizing the mechanism of doing to the analyst what had been done to her by "leaving" first, as well as re-experiencing her own helpless and depressed responses to abandonment.

A visit to her sister during the summer break was the stimulus for the emergence of material about that relationship when the analysis resumed. She envied and resented what she perceived as her sister's better endowment and more favored treatment, and this was enacted in the form of increased friction with her roommates. The current household situation came to resemble the earlier relationships among the patient, her mother, and her sister, but Miss W was so overwhelmed by guilt and shame that she had tremendous difficulty in acknowledging her own rivalrous attitudes and hostile wishes. She became caught up in her embittered sense of desperation and disappointment, which dominated the transference. She resumed self-medication and increased her over-eating, stopped dating, and became more overtly resistant to talking about her past. She also acknowledged a fear of discussing sexual thoughts which appeared in conjunction with her dreams, and in particular those which might involve her analyst. One day, when she had an early morning session, she was standing inside the glass street door of the analyst's office building when he arrived, and in that session reported a dream in which she had been standing and looking out of a window. This led to her recollection of the story she had been told of standing by the window crying for her father after his disappearance, and the interpretation of the transference connections led to a temporary reduction in tension. She then met a man whose first name was the same as that of her sister's husband and plunged into an affair. The transference suddenly shifted form, with the analyst perceived as an interfering, disapproving mother. She soon elected to leave her roommates and live alone but shortly thereafter became disappointed in her new boyfriend, who was distant, withdrawn, and elusive. She became angry, critical, and demanding with him, which led to a breakup, and had thoughts of doing the same to the analyst. This produced great apprehension that instead she would be dismissed as a punishment.

A dream in which she had a baby and was disappointed that it was a girl ushered in much productive material, including the first meaningful discussions of her feelings of inadequacy and inferiority in the context of a comparison between the sexes. The ideas about having been supposed to be a boy emerged, along with her theory about her father's disappointment in her. In the transference she became stubbornly and defiantly silent and continued to alternate between thoughts of punishing the analyst by rejecting him and fearing his retaliation. Positive sexual longings were effectively blocked by the increasing negativism and sadomasochistic atmosphere which had come to dominate the analysis.

Summer plans to share a vacation cottage with other single friends brought out material which further clarified the complications of her envious, competitive relationship with her sister and its attendant guilt. She saw her sister unconsciously both as the more beloved girl and as the better-endowed son, favored by both father and mother. The approach of summer also brought out material pertaining to the preadolescent summer visits to the father, and she chose to pursue the most unapproachable man in her vacation community, while rudely rebuffing all those who showed any interest in her. Once more she became silent and withdrawn as the analytic break approached, and she again entertained thoughts of moving to a distant place and breaking off the treatment.

In the fall of the third analytic year the transference became still more intense and difficult to manage. Her repetition of the wishes, fantasies, and reactions stemming from her childhood attachment to her elusive, unsatisfactory father could not be consciously acknowledged. Such interpretations evoked storms of rage and denial, followed by depression and withdrawal. She insistently demanded tranquilizers and other drugs, railed at the analyst for being cold and unsympathetic, and steadfastly rejected all his efforts to demonstrate that these responses were related to the issues in focus in the analysis. She idealized land-lords and superiors at work, misperceiving them grossly and inappropriately, expecting them to treat her as a favored and beloved daughter, only to experience crushing disappointment time and again when they failed to live up to her highly un-realistic expectations. Over and over again she felt betrayed and hurt and then sank into a chronic state of sullen resentment. A complex mixture, difficult to disentangle, of these positive oedipal disappointments (further heightened by the birth at that time of her sister's child), with elements derived from the maternal transference, came to dominate the clinical picture. Her feelings of deprivation and rage directed at the mother expressed preoedipal wishes and conflicts in which oral and anal fantasies and modes seemed to predominate, but these seemed also to reflect in regressive forms some aspects of a powerful negative oedipal configuration which had been strengthened as one consequence of the disappointment in the father after his departure when she was four years old.

She became increasingly resistant and provocative, withhold-ing, and silent. She simultaneously threatened to leave and sought to induce the analyst to dismiss her. She seemed utterly incapable of joining in any effort to examine the sources of this behavior, which threatened to destroy the analysis. The analyst, more than at any other period, had to struggle with counter-transference irritation and frustration and the inhibiting effect of the need to keep these feelings from showing. A sense of hopelessness, feelings of guilt at analytic "inadequacy," and compassion for her obvious and unrelenting misery were all prominent in his self-awareness. After many weeks of this near stalemate, it began to appear that the situation was unresolvable by analytic means, and consideration was given to terminating the analytic endeavor and recommending instead some alter-native form of therapy. As these possibilities were discussed with Miss W, she reacted as though the decision had already been reached, confessed her sense that she had always believed she would be a failure like her father, blew up, and attempted to quit on the spot. This was headed off for the moment. She then added that her conviction that the analyst literally resembled her childhood memory of her father had made it impossible to discuss openly the sexual attraction she had felt from the very first day. This was followed, not by relief and increased openness, but rather by a total lapse into silence which lasted for days.

After a supervisory consultation it was concluded that the analysis seemed unworkable, and the possibility of termination was once more brought up with Miss W. This time she flew into a rage and left the office in the middle of the session. She returned a few moments later to ask if she could in essence have another chance. She resumed work, and very much in the sense of a confession, told of her shame and guilt at masturbating, and of the overwhelming need to censor such thoughts. In the same session she revealed for the first time her secret bulimia and self-induced vomiting. From that dramatic moment, which appeared later in retrospect to signify unconsciously a magical undoing of the crushing abandonment by the father, and a wished-for "second chance" with him, the analysis took a different course.

For the first time she could get herself to continue to speak without demanding constant verbal rejoinders. Although neither her silences nor her tendency to withhold embarrassing thoughts disappeared completely, the degree of both, and the vagueness and lack of detail which had been so frustrating, notably diminished. In the ensuing months the masturbatory conflicts and fantasies and their representation in oral terms were gradually explored. Details of her eating pattern, fellatio experiences, oral impregnation theories, and corollary ideas of acquiring a penis of her own through oral incorporation, as well as fears of retaliation and damage, emerged. In the context of a new affair with a man who had considerable potency difficulty, a tangle of confused and conflicting material surfaced. Distortions of her body image, convictions of having excessive, "masculine" strength and size, as, for example, unusually broad shoulders and powerful hands, contradictory ideas about his and her own genital conformation, adequacy, and damage, and her various beliefs that one or another sexual position or practice was essential or favorable to provide satisfaction dominated her thoughts. She especially preferred to sit upright while he lay supine, which represented her unconscious wish to have/be an erect penis herself. She identified with the analyst and bullied her boyfriend into admitting his sexual problems and accepting treatment. She insisted on reading psychiatric papers and books and concentrated on her friend's problems instead of her own.

Her fantasies of having been castrated appeared next, accompanied by irregular menstruation. She shamefully admitted using phallic objects as masturbatory aids, and spoke at length of her hypochonriacal fears of bodily (and emotional) damage. Only indirect hints at sadomasochistic masturbatory fantasies could be detected at this juncture.

She expressed for the first time the idea that her sexual difficulties, including anorgasmia, could be cured by having sexual relations with the analyst. She next elaborated her conviction about his wife, whom she imagined to be ideal: beautiful, brilliant, accomplished, and undoubtedly a physician as well. There then appeared the first frankly masochistic fantasy of being injured by a bus and hospitalized, thus gaining the care, interest, and attention of many physicians of both sexes.

Primal scene material and sadomasochistic interpretations of sexuality appeared in increasingly recognizable forms, as fighting, forced entry and then as producing mutilation and pain. Their relationship to her frigidity, and to her inability or refusal, or both, to respond to interpretations in the analytic situation thus became clarified. During the next year the genetic sources of her primal scene fantasies and confusions, including experiences in the home of the relatives with whom she had lived, and in that of her father and his girlfriend, came to light. Her reluctance to surrender her idealized version of her ne'er-do-well father was finally acknowledged.

Further sources of bodily confusion came up amid recollections of her menarche, with themes of injury, denial, restitution, and condensation of genital with anal fantasies and preoccupations. Shame and related phallic and anal exhibitionistic wishes and conflicts could be explored, with gradually greater recognition and acceptance of her lifelong masculine strivings and feelings of inadequacy and envy. Her next boyfriend was clearly a narcissistic choice, and she attempted to utilize him to satisfy her own frustrated longings. She became infuriated when he refused to permit her to masturbate him. Her difficulty in perceiving men with realistic accuracy, since they had to be flawless or grossly defective, or both, was now seen to be in keeping with both her preoccupations with possession of a phallus and castration and her disparate images of her father.

Anal images next dominated the material; childhood and adult experiences including enemas and intercourse *per anum* contributed to the fantasies that helped form her distorted views of feminine inferiority, which in turn reflected an equation of the vagina with the anus. This material also helped explain her shame reactions and her problems with impulse control, which played a contributory role in her stubbornness and negativism in the analytic situation. Masochistic daydreaming was revealed. Its pattern followed the general formula: "If I suffer greatly and remain patient and uncomplaining, I will eventually be rewarded." These fantasied rewards varied at different times, but most seemed derived from the wish for father's return and related wishes to gain the longed-for penis and baby. Interpretation of these ideas was experienced as tantamount to ridicule and explicit frustration of them; she reacted with rage and symptomatic exacerbation which clearly revealed the oral and anal sadistic aspects of her conflicts. Belittling and contemptuous ideas about men were expressed, and what can only be described as furious overeating, unconsciously intended to acquire by force what she felt had been withheld from her, was prominent for some time.

Homosexual material, derived from childhood closeness with the sister, was in evidence, but analytic work with it took place in an atmosphere of anger, shame, disbelief, and reluctance to discuss and comprehend these ideas. Withdrawal and projection were resorted to, as was usually the case when disturbing matters came up for serious examination in the analysis for the first time.

In the fourth year of work the theme of being cheated appeared in many forms, stemming at first from a discussion of adjusting her fee. Finally her own disowned impulses to cheat others in order to obtain what she wanted could be discerned. This led to further elaborations of her sadomasochistic orientation, this time around clearly recognizable beating fantasies. She acknowledged enjoying "taking things to the brink of disaster," and the excitement of imagining she could provoke the analyst and others into losing control of their emotions. She alternated these ideas with prolonged periods of self-administered verbal beatings, which took the form of unrelieved self-accusations and self-criticism.

At this time an experience which served to organize much of the material emerged from repression. This was the memory of a traumatic tonsillectomy performed when she was four by a surgeon who was a friend of her family. She had a postoperative hemorrhage, allegedly caused by her crying, and had to be returned, conscious, to the operating room for further treatment. She recalled being coaxed to open her mouth and then being hurt by the procedures carried out. Dreams and hypnopompic imagery confirmed the importance of this event, which contributed both to her orogenital condensations and her sadomasochistic concerns. Her silence in the analysis also represented an invitation to the analyst to "coax" her to open up.

During the latter part of that year she met a new man, warmer and nicer than any of her previous boyfriends, and became able for the first time to have orgasms during coitus, though she still preferred those practices which enabled her to feel more or less dominant and in control of the sexual situation. She came gradually to recognize both that her own problems had contributed greatly to her previous sexual dissatisfaction and that she had now improved substantially as a result of the analysis. This was reflected also in the fact that co-workers, friends, and family were by then responding to her as warmer, nicer, more considerate, and easier to get along with most of the time. Phobic reactions to insects and animals had all but disappeared. Rigid orderliness which bordered on compulsion had relaxed somewhat. She revealed that she had been aware of these changes for some time and had concealed them as best she could from the analyst. This turned out to be determined in part by her inhibitions against showing herself off, in part by the old pattern of spiteful revenge, but a new element was also added. Improvement meant thinking ahead to the end of the analysis and thus facing the eventual loss of her relationship to the analyst, and she preferred to put this off.

When her then-current affair began to wane, she came to recognize that she was usually preoccupied almost exclusively with what she did or did not get from the other person. She was not concerned with what she in turn could give to her partner and in fact she felt she was quite unloving and uncaring toward them. Once more, connections to the past, specifically to her loss of her father's love, emerged as determinants of her childlike, essentially narcissistic attitudes toward her relationships.

If the first phase of the analysis was stormy, inchoate, and discouraging to the point of despair, the second was essentially one of confused, tangled, and intertwined themes and fantasies, stubborn and difficult defenses, and slow progress. The third and final phase was much more like analytic work with other severely troubled neurotic patients. Themes were clearer, she was a more consistently cooperative partner in the work, defensive reactions were less strident and of shorter duration, and the transference issues were more easily recognizable and resolvable than was true earlier in the treatment. Nevertheless, at one point quite late in the treatment, when she was expressing her longing for a satisfactory relationship with a man, she brought forth with utter seriousness the idea that the analyst should be able to find her someone suitable. After all, she reasoned, he knew her well, knew her needs, and could evaluate other people. It made perfect sense to her that, like a parent in olden times, he should select a mate for her!

The major thematic innovation of the final phase was the revelation of the nature, strength, and complexity of Miss W's tie to her mother. Fantasies of actually finding a man to marry made her aware of her guilt at the idea of leaving her mother and of outdoing her. Ideas of true independence, expressed in the transference, brought out her rivalrous death wishes, and consequent guilt, retreats, fears, and self-punitive worries

and defeats. The men she met were still less than fully satisfactory. Some recrudescence of the longing for, and attachment
to, the oedipal, idealized father preceded a period of sad, guilt-
tinged conflictual material about giving up her love for her
father in favor of some new, better man.

Reactivation of the loving attachment to her mother, with a
full panoply of wishes to marry, give, and receive babies in the
negative oedipal constellation, and a fuller, clearer expression
and acknowledgment of her intense, murderous rivalry with
her sister were all features of the fifth analytic year.

Oral and anal sadistic incorporative and destructive wishes
at both prephallic and phallic levels were expressed, and their
relationship to envy, self-punitive fantasies and behavior, and
her weight problem were sufficiently worked through to permit
her to successfully and reasonably diet and maintain her weight
loss. A more attractive, feminine appearance brought forth
competitive, exhibitionistic material, particularly in relation to
her obese mother. In this connection, a dreaded fantasy "came
true" when her mother became seriously ill and the patient had
to leave her job and her analysis for a few weeks to go home
and nurse her. On her return she was able to report that she
had managed well, had not been too upset, and had made a
startling and reassuring discovery. Her mother and all the other
relatives she saw were, she had noted, still preoccupied with the
family "tragedy" of the ne'er-do-well father, emotionally bound
to his memory and the impact he had had on all their lives. She
herself, through analysis, had gained a clearer perspective and
greater freedom from the past than any of the others, her
mother included.

Another summer visit to her sister stimulated further clarifications of her ambivalent feelings and wishes, and of the degree and nature of guilt reactions these engendered. The trip
itself went well, and upon her return she reported for the first
time a clearer, more objective, and realistic view of her sister
and her life. Her "bossy" qualities, nervous tension, some defensiveness, and a not-so-ideal marital relationship were observed on this occasion, in keeping with the reduced degree of
envy, bitterness, and sense of inferiority on Miss W's part.

During the prolonged termination phase proper, she worked through her conflicts about "deserting" her mother to make a life of her own. In the transference, the analyst sometimes represented the father of her romantic fantasies, for whose love the patient imagined competing with her mother, and at other times was seen as the mother, loved and hated both, from whom she could not tolerate permanent separation.

In summary, her periods of regression were of briefer duration and lesser intensity, her capacity to bring forth new material was greater, and her depression was more likely to be in evidence during her analytic sessions and much less apparent in her daily life. Her relationships with others had improved to the point where her sympathy, advice, and judgment were sought out by friends, and her capacity for realistic assessments and planning was strikingly better. She appeared like a severely neurotic individual who had profited greatly from analysis, albeit one with residual limitations and difficulties.

She had better relationships with men but was not completely satisfied. She felt ready for commitment and marriage but saw this as still in the future. She planned, after termination, to move to a Sunbelt city in the Southwest, comparable to the one where her sister lived and unconsciously related to the childhood memories of the happy time in California.

Diagnostic Considerations

Those features of this case which led us to feel she was a borderline patient may be summarized as follows: Her difficulties had been severe in many areas of functioning for many years; they were evident in sexual maladjustment, superficial relationships with others, serious educational inhibitions, depressions, and abuse of drugs. Her reality testing was markedly deficient, both in and outside of analysis, as was evident in her tendency to misjudge social situations, and her marked incapacity to empathize with the needs and feelings of others. She insisted on attempting to convert the analytic relationship into one of real gratification. Her misperception of the character of her lovers and her anatomical and sexual confusions were particularly striking. She was egocentric and could be callously indifferent to others at times, and was easily hurt and quietly but stubbornly enraged when her wishes were frustrated or her narcissism otherwise injured. She had many symptoms and pathological character traits, some of which only emerged after some time in analysis. These included phobias, episodic bulimia, and self-induced vomiting, abuse of various medications in an effort to alter moods and relieve tension, compulsive rigidity barely masking chronic anxiety, frigidity, depression, and poor impulse control, excessive dependency on her sister, suspiciousness, and irritability, as well as a number of somatic complaints which were of emotional origin. The transference was immediate and intense, as noted, and much of it was consciously concealed. Her productions, even relatively late in the analysis, seemed more fragmentary, contradictory, and confusing than is usual with analyzable patients. She always found it difficult to examine her wishes concerning the analyst and her reactions to him. Her withholding and provocation during the early period of the analysis were a problem for the analyst, whose counteraggression led sometimes to impatience, reflected in a tendency to overinterpretation, or alternately, to inhibition of his activity. Her slow progress gave rise to frequent doubts about the advisability of continuing the treatment, although strong wishes to rescue her were simultaneously also present in the analyst. Her prevailing mood until the final two years or so was of depression, with irritability which sometimes had a paranoid tinge. Control of aggression toward others and a pronounced tendency toward self-destructive activity were a major poblem as well.

Case Report II

Dr. X was a twenty-three-year-old single, Jewish medical student when he began his ten-year analysis. He entered treatment because he was failing his second year of medical school and was depressed and upset about his parents' impending divorce. He had been living at home while attending medical school when his parents separated and his father left the home. He became depressed and could not concentrate, and his relationship with his mother began to deteriorate. He started to fight with her verbally, especially when she seemed gentle or loving, which he experienced as her being overprotective and babying him. He left home and took an apartment of his own, but his depression and poor school performance continued. He felt his life would never be the same because of his parents' impending divorce, and he ruminated about future occasions which would be ruined because his parents would not be together to share them with him.

During the initial interviews he displayed little awareness of what had happened to him. He did not understand why he could not study since he very much wanted to be a physician. He did not know what treatment could offer him, but he accepted his mother's advice and came to see an analyst who had been recommended by his mother's former analyst. The patient stated that he had never had many friends and that he had been unhappy as an adolescent. He started to date in college and had had only one steady relationship, and that had lasted only for a few months. Almost as an afterthought and without much emotion, he said that the only one he had ever loved in his life was his dog, who had died when he was a teenager.

Dr. X was born during World War II and did not see his father, who was a physician, until he was three years old. He had a brother two years older than he who was married and attending graduate school in another state. The two boys lived with their mother and her parents while their father was away during the war. He spoke little of his grandparents. His mother's analyst described the maternal grandfather as a rather tyrannical man, and that analyst felt the patient's mother had married a man similar to the grandfather.

The patient had few memories prior to the age of five or six. He vaguely recalled looking into his parents' bedroom and seeing them lying together after his father's return, when the family moved into their own apartment. Dr. X's mother became pregnant when he was about four years old. She carried the baby to term but the infant, a girl, died a few hours after childbirth despite the efforts of the father, who was present at the delivery. Dr. X had no memories of his mother's pregnancy or of any events surrounding the birth and death of his sister.

Although he recalled some fighting with his brother, he did not feel any rivalry with him. He always thought he was "as big as" his brother and did not fear him. He had nightmares between the ages of five and six of monsters and animals coming to harm him. The patient developed recurrent ear infections at age six. These necessitated treatment with injections of penicillin, which were administered into his buttocks by his mother while his father held him down. He recalled being terrified and fighting both his parents.

He subsequently went through a prolonged period of being naughty at home and at school. In contrast to his brother, he was the "bad one" and felt unjustly punished by his father. He began to indulge in cruel treatment of animals, such as "bopping" frogs on the head with an oar while rowing a boat at a summer place, drowning salamanders in the toilet, and killing insects in sadistic ways. He would also mistreat his beloved dog when he became frustrated and angry.

Two memories from about age eight were vivid to him. He remembered feeling terribly guilty when his parents bought him a bicycle, and walking off the tennis court in frustration and rage after his father criticized him. He vowed never to return to tennis and kept his vow for one year despite his father's attempts to placate him.

When he was ten, his mother enrolled in graduate school, and he dreaded the evenings when she would be gone because his father frequently punished him for misbehavior. He would fantasize killing himself, thereby punishing his parents, because he was being picked on. During these years his father took care of the family's medical needs, and he frequently chided the patient for fearing the pain of injections or treatment for minor illnesses.

As Dr. X approached adolescence, he was sent to private school because his parents felt the neighborhood public school was not good enough. He felt that this deprived him of the opportunity to make close friendships either at home or at school. He had only one good friend, a boy who had had polio, with whom he usually got into trouble at school. During his teens he was shy with girls, especially because he was ashamed of his acne. He felt his father criticized his diet and his care of his skin, as well as the way he walked.

Dr. X did not masturbate until the age of twenty while at college. He recalled a few nocturnal emissions but believed he had no desire to masturbate during his teenage years. During the initial interviews he revealed no sexual fantasies.

During college things improved for him. He was able to make friends and began to do well academically. During the summers he worked in his father's hospital as an orderly and operating room aide. He wanted to be a physician like his father, whom he admired. He was not aware that his father had been having an affair when the family thought he was attending professional meetings. He also was completely unaware of any discord between his parents, although the mother had entered analysis because of the deterioration of the marriage.

Dr. X's brother had also been headed toward a career in medicine, but had changed his mind and completed a Ph.D. in science. The patient was secretly glad that only he was to fulfill his father's wish that his sons would be physicians.

The father was described as a tough, coarse, and unsympathetic man, but one whom the patient admired and feared. He remarried shortly after the divorce. His father was opposed to his being in analysis but consented to pay for it while the patient was in medical school. The mother completed her doctorate and was teaching. She rarely dated but enjoyed her career. She seemed to the patient to be overprotective, and he felt she wanted to be too close to him.

At the beginning of the analysis Dr. X said he enjoyed playing tennis, poker, and visiting the race track. He followed horse racing avidly and despite the fact that he was careful not to gamble heavily, his interest had become a sore point between him and his father. During college he was active in drama and was a good singer. He still had some regrets that he did not pursue singing as a career. His relationships with women were characterized by his rejecting them as soon as he perceived that they were interested in him.

Course of the Analysis

The first few years of the analysis dealt mainly with his relationship to his father. His conscious attitude toward him was one of respect and admiration. He depended on his father for advice as well as for assistance in shopping for clothing. He even planned to have his father remove a small cyst he had developed. The analytic work, however, gradually showed him his strong resentment toward his father, who was often insensitive, mocking, impatient, and sarcastic. It was upsetting to the patient to feel angry at his father. He did not experience this upset as guilt or fear at this point, but as a sorrow that he would not have a good relationship with him. It became clear that he feared his anger would end their relationship forever. He always imagined that confrontations between people would make them unable to be friends again.

He decided to postpone his surgery, which was later performed by another physician. He gradually became less dependent on his father, but it was not until he became an intern that he assumed the burden of paying for his treatment. He keenly felt his father's disapproval of his poor work in medical school, and he realized that his failure was in part an unconscious expression of hostility toward him. Later he realized that it also was a self-punishment for oedipal wishes which had been revived at the time of the parents' separation. He also feared his father's disapproval of his poker playing and interest in horses and even imagined his being angry if the patient went out with a woman instead of studying.

The idea that by failing medical school he could frustrate and disappoint his father and thus exact some revenge was to be one important element of the transference. Unlike those transference reactions of borderline patients which are stormy, impulsive, and dramatic in their intensity, this patient's transference feelings were hidden and silent. He acted as though he was wary and mistrustful of the analyst and the treatment, although he denied having such feelings. He said rather early on, when the analyst made some attempt at understanding his transference feelings, that he was not going to have *any* feelings toward the analyst. As the treatment progressed it became a source of humiliation to him that he would not be able to maintain that position and he would have to acknowledge strong feelings toward his analyst, after all.

He treated his mother as though any contact with her was taboo, and he was apprehensive about seeing or talking to her. He always felt she was trying to get "too close" to him. For a number of years during the treatment he consciously thought that his mother might want to sexually seduce him. Although this was not a delusion, it was a belief of great intensity which he could counter with more rational explanations of her behavior. On one occasion he was to pick her up and drive her to a family affair. She suggested that he could come right after tennis and change in her apartment rather than having to go home before coming to get her. On another, she invited him to dinner on an evening before a holiday when she knew he could stay later than usual. He was suspicious of her motives for both of these suggestions.

His relationships with women took on a repetitive form. He would seek someone out and feel attracted to her. As soon as she became interested, he began to fear she was trying to "tie him down," or restrict his freedom. He could not believe that a woman might like him or wish to marry him out of love. One woman encouraged him not to use a condom during her "safe period" when he expressed some dissatisfaction with condoms. He then believed she was purposely trying to get pregnant to force him to marry her and he did not feel that any possible desire to marry him involved affection for him. He experienced women as trying to trap him. He once said that he feared that a woman "would suck me up into her as though she were a vacuum cleaner." Because of these fears, which were similar to those he felt about his mother, he would reject women and flee from them.

Although his work in medicine was progressing satisfactorily, he had few friends and kept aloof from everyone. In groups he feared to speak up because if he made a mistake it would be a terrible humiliation, especially if he had led everyone to believe he knew the answer. Scenes of much competition with his father were now remembered and recounted. His father used to quiz him as a child, and this continued through the first year in medical school, when they would argue about anatomy to see which one of them was right.

He began to reveal extremely rivalrous feelings with his peers. He became preoccupied with his competitiveness. He always felt that a colleague or an attending physician would prove him wrong and thus humiliate him. He was completely unaware of his own wishes to be victorious over and scorn other men. He revealed that he could not stand it if anyone passed him when he was driving a car. He imagined the man laughing to himself for having passed the patient. He would, in turn, speed up, sometimes disregarding his safety. For a number of years of analysis he did not mention his brother and insisted, if this was brought to his attention, that he did not think his brother played an important role in his life.

As the treatment progressed, transference issues became more prominent and stimulated the emergence of the conflicts described. If he had any emotion about the analyst, he would experience it as a humiliation and a "giving in." He imagined the analyst taking satisfaction at having broken him down and overcoming his determination to have no feelings at all about him. In this sense he saw the analyst as needing this power over him and deriving sadistic pleasure in his humiliation. Whereas the relationship of these feelings to his attitude toward his father was apparent, the patient was as yet unaware of his own sadistic impulses. He would imagine his analyst gloating triumphantly if he would make an interpretation or add a comment to what the patient himself had said.

He continued to come to treatment, never missing a session, while feeling more and more that in the end the analyst would make him feel like a helpless baby with needy feelings. He also felt he was being made to feel "small" and stupid. He became angry if the analyst made what he considered to be an "authoritative" remark. He began to feel very suspicious of his analyst's motive for treating him and suspected that his analyst wanted to get something from him or do something to him, although he did not know what it was.

It was in this context that he revealed that he had an obligatory masturbatory fantasy. He had not talked much about sex except to say he had satisfaction, although he worried about his performance. He now said that in order to have an orgasm while having intercourse or masturbating he had to have a specific, repetitive fantasy. An older woman has enticed him into being with her, although she does this in a subtle way. He allows himself to be like a baby with her by having her hold and pet him and masturbate him. However, the woman says she will continue to caress him to orgasm only if he will become a little girl. He consents and reaches climax. As a little girl he is conscious only of wearing a dress, and not aware of any genital change. It was an essential part of this fantasy that the woman has planned the entire seduction and that it is she who wants him to be a little girl.

Dr. X experienced terrible shame about this fantasy. He had no idea about its origins or what it might mean, other than to feel it was very perverse. He now recalled previously repressed memories from his childhood. As a small boy he used to imagine the woman in the next apartment enticing him or forcing him into her apartment and doing sexual things to him, such as manipulating his genitals. He also fantasied women tying him down and playing with him sexually. A dream from childhood, around the time he was getting the injections, was remembered. A woman holds him face down on an ironing board and puts shaving cream into his rectum.

Another dream from about age ten which had previously been reported became more understandable. He is in a kind of locker room with tile on the floor. A woman surgeon has just castrated him and he looks down and sees the sutured wound. He has diarrhea. Additional associations to the dream led to the recollection that his mother administered an enema to him while he lay across her lap staring at the bathroom tile.

As the analysis dealt with his fears of being castrated, mutilated, and turned into a girl, he recalled that he used to try on his mother's clothes at about age thirteen. He would run through the house naked if no one was home, enjoying the feeling of the air on his skin, and then put on his mother's underwear and her dress. He would look in the mirror but could not remember what he was thinking. He did not recall sexual arousal and did not masturbate during these episodes.

The patient had clearly trusted the analyst enough to tell him about what had been a continuing source of great shame, but along with this trust came a renewed suspiciousness of the analyst's intentions. Up to this point the patient had reacted with almost no feeling to the analyst's vacations, weekends, or occasional cancelled sessions. After one summer vacation the patient returned and came forty-five minutes late. During the five minutes remaining he told the analyst that after their last session he thought he would miss him. The next session was characterized by the patient denying that this feeling was meaningful and expressing his fear that the analyst would be sadistically pleased at having broken down the patient's will. During that summer he had had a dream in which he is lying on the couch naked and his analyst is masturbating him. He thought to himself in the dream, "So this is why he is treating me!"

This dream also paralleled a current relationship with an older woman who was willing to caress and masturbate him without having intercourse. He was thus living out his fantasy. It was important to him, however, and therefore not entirely satisfying, that she was not, as far as he could tell, doing this out of any ulterior motive but was trying to be nice to him. He was shocked by this dream because it made him wonder whether his suspicions about the analyst doing something to him had anything to do with his fantasy. He had previously rejected any ideas of homosexual feelings and, indeed, was especially suspicious when a friend had put his arm around him.

During the fourth and fifth years of analysis his defenses of projection and isolation of affects and his fears of being humiliated intensified. He became increasingly fearful of his own aggression but did not feel himself to be angry despite considerable enjoyment when watching sadistic films. He always imagined being the victim of others.

His transference feelings became very intense. He was convinced that the analyst had ulterior motives to ensnare him and humiliate him. He felt his analyst would force him to give in—to admit his childish needs or to admit that the analyst was correct and he was wrong. Then his analyst would have overpowered him and made him weak, small, and stupid. Although he was aware of the relationship of these fears to his masturbation fantasies, he did not want to admit that his analyst was important to him or that, for some reason, these were *his* wishes and needs which were being expressed.

In addition to this he wanted to defeat his analyst and make the latter feel stupid and small. He began to take satisfaction if his analyst did not understand something or would grope for words. He wanted to mock his analyst although he feared doing so. His relationships in the hospital now seemed on the verge of collapse. He imagined being everyone's enemy and feared he would say things to offend. He accused the attending physicians of being sadistic and of trying to humiliate him even though by now he was aware that he identified with sadists in violent films.

He began to feel that if he got better and changed it would be a victory for his analyst, and he doubted whether he wanted that to occur. All interpretations were warded off and mocked, and there was a prolonged period of stalemate. He could not believe that it was more important to him to make his analyst feel small and stupid than to have himself change and get better.

Finally, his analyst, after many months, asked him whether he thought they should stop or that he should seek a consultation. His initial response was one of victory. "I never thought I'd hear you say that." He then began to cry and plead with his analyst not to discontinue. He acknowledged that his wish to humiliate his analyst was stronger than his desire to change, but he felt that if he stopped he would lose the one friend he had. Subsequent to this he did not experience the terrible humiliation he had expected, nor did he suspect his analyst of deceiving him by threatening him.

There was, however, no dramatic change in the work, but a gradual and significant one. He began to acknowledge painful longings to be loved and cared for. He felt, for the first time, wishes to be cuddled, caressed, and loved by a woman which he did not have to project onto her. Now oedipal wishes and memories became pronounced, and with them intense fears of

being attacked by other men. Fears of castration for masturbation were experienced.

At this point a number of dreams and associations led to a
reconstruction by the analyst of the mother's depression after
his newborn sister died. This was subsequently confirmed by
the mother. An important motive for his erotic fantasy of a
woman wanting him to change into a little girl was that he could
be the little girl she had lost and grieved for. If he were a girl,
he would undo her depression and relative withdrawal from
him.

He now recalled many feelings of loss of love and of separation from his mother. He had a number of dreams of being
in a cavity representing her womb. Being a girl was also an
attempt to undo separation from her. The fantasies of being
tied down by women served the same purpose and were also
projections of his own possessiveness and desire to control
women.

A number of changes began to take place. He became less
fearful of his mother and more capable of spending time with
her. He had two relationships with women which were more
sustained. On occasion he was able to perform sexually without
his fantasy. The analytic work proceeded better. Despite the
intensity of his feelings, he was now able to see the "as if" quality
of the transference. The observing part of his ego was in evidence as he became more aware of his intense infantile needs
and longings and his defenses against them.

As memories of oedipal fantasies and fears of castration became more prominent, he began to experience more and more
pleasure in doing medical procedures which involved surgery.
He realized that to be a little girl also meant that he would not
have to fear castration. In addition, if he were a little girl with
his mother she would not be harmed by his aggressive wishes
toward her. If he were a girl he would not have a destructive
phallus.

He had a fantasy that his father dies and his second wife
afterwards invites the patient to dinner and seduces him. Rivalrous fantasies were now accompanied by guilt and fears of
retaliation. He realized that he derived unconscious pleasure

from his father leaving the home and leaving him alone with his mother—the very thing which had precipitated his depression and failure for which he sought treatment. His fear of his father when he was a child was now remembered. The father, the monster of his childhood nightmares, was thought to be the one who had killed the baby sister, although Dr. X had been told his father had made heroic efforts to save her. He thus projected his own wishes to kill the sister on to the father but also represented his father as the murderous castrator to be feared.

As the analysis progressed he finally began to talk about his brother. Feelings of intense rivalry and envy emerged and with them a picture of his brother being the favored one. He experienced rage and disappointment toward his parents, especially his mother. He dreamt about being trapped in a closed space—the center of the earth—and had a nightmare about a penis floating in a closed space filled with fluid. His association to the latter was a memory of his mother reading him a book about the fetus floating in amniotic fluid in the womb. This evidently occurred during her pregnancy, and a fantasy of identification with his dead sister emerged. This seemed to be derived from guilt feelings over death wishes toward the little girl and played a part in his fears of entrapment and castration.

During the eighth year of analysis he met a woman and began to feel close to her without having to flee. This coincided with his increased ability to see his mother more realistically. He delayed going into private practice out of a sense of guilt over achieving his lifelong goal. He also had fears of other physicians resenting his success. He defended himself against his competitive strivings by declaring that he was still a boy and did not feel capable of getting married and establishing a practice.

As the termination of his analysis became a real possibility, he clung more tenaciously to his analyst, finding it difficult to think of leaving him. During this phase it became more clear that his mother's depression and her inability to understand his needs and frustration as he was growing up had profoundly affected him. His father, too, though in a less subtle way, had ignored his unhappiness and difficulties. Dr. X became more able to recognize the rage he had felt and the defenses he had developed to deal with the thoughts and feelings associated with it.

He married the woman he had been living with and was able to secure a position in a different town. Almost to the end of the treatment he hoped his analyst would actually become a father to him—love him and care for him, not just as an analyst! This would reassure him that his marrying, going into practice, and leaving the analyst did not destroy their relationship.

This long treatment had changed Dr. X considerably. Defenses such as projection, denial, reaction formation, and isolation of feelings were now less necessary or at least used by the ego in a healthier way. He had not only gained an understanding of himself but he was capable of feeling closer to people, both male and female. The feeling that he had never loved anyone in his life but his dog left him when he realized how hateful and rageful he had felt. He was no longer depressed and his sexual fantasy, although still used on occasion, was no longer obligatory for orgasm.

He became more tolerant and accepting of his longings, needs, and sexual fantasies. Feelings of humiliation and helplessness were decreased considerably, and he was more comfortable with his rivalrous thoughts. Perhaps most importantly, his view of people became more realistic and less colored by his own projections, fears, and misinterpretations. He felt that his childhood and adolescence, once seen as so unhappy and painful, had had their good times as well. Finally, he was able to accept his parents' difficulties with more understanding.

Diagnostic Considerations

This patient was considered to be borderline because of the pervasiveness of the psychopathology, which involved almost every area of his functioning. He demonstrated many features which corresponded to the composite clinical description assembled from our review of the literature.

His pathology invaded his entire character structure and was of a relatively stable degree with no severe regression to psychosis. His reality testing was impaired, especially in the areas of his object relations, where he viewed women as trapping and ensnaring him. He also, for many years, thought his mother might actually wish to seduce him. His object relations were also characterized by marked suspicion and mistrust. He had few friends and always felt he would be humiliated or scorned by men. His life history revealed the presence of chronic depression, isolation from friends, and sexual functioning which required for orgasm a particular obligatory sexual fantasy.

Although there was no breakthrough of "psychotic fragments" or primary process thinking, his suspicions about his mother's intentions were persistent and severe and he had many quasiparanoid feelings. In contrast to other borderline patients whose transference reactions are characterized as immediately intense, impulsive, excessively clinging, or openly hostile, this patient's transference was revealed in, and hidden by, a rigid, unfeeling, unemotional façade. The defensive quality of this behavior became clear in the course of treatment.

Narcissistic manifestations were evident in the patient's prolonged periods of being alone and withdrawn. The defensive nature of this characteristic came to be understood as well. His affects were overcontrolled, leading to an appearance of rigidity of his personality. There was a marked inability to accept the "as if" quality of the transference. He tried to elicit countertransference feelings of helplessness, defeat, and humiliation in the analyst of the sort which had marked his own suffering as a child.

All of these features persisted for a long time during treatment; nevertheless, after much analytic work, considerable alteration had occurred, so much so that by the end of treatment the designation borderline no longer seemed to apply to him, as contrasted with how he had appeared for so many years.

Case Report III

The patient, Miss Y, was a twenty-four-year-old single, white Protestant publisher's assistant who entered analysis two years after she was graduated from a small Midwestern liberal arts college. When her treatment began, her major complaints were feelings of depression with severe self-loathing ("I feel like a piece of shit"); obesity with bulimic episodes; severe pervasive anxiety with fears of cancer and death; vaginismus and frigidity; and multiple phobias. Her object relations were sadomasochistically oriented with persons of either sex, usually with herself as the passive dependent partner. Her heterosexual experience was almost nil, and her sexual fantasies were mainly homosexual.

The patient was the older of two daughters born in a small Midwestern city during World War II. This was the home of her maternal grandparents, and she, her mother, and maternal grandparents lived together into her second year while her father was away in the war. This time was described throughout her analysis as a particularly happy one, during which time, she had been adored by the grandparents, whom she felt were her real parents. She was the "queen." Her father returned when she was fourteen months old and moved the family to a nearby city, and a younger sister was born when she was twenty-eight months old. At this point, she turned almost completely to her father, who dominated her life from then on.

Her mother, who was working during her first year while they lived with the grandparents, functioned in a childlike way in her own parents' home and continued her childlike, dependent behavior with her husband. She submitted to his overbearing demands but was felt by the patient to be infantile, narcissistic, smug, critical, and emotionally ungiving, so that in her quiet way, her moods dominated the lives of both children as well as her husband.

Father, on the other hand, was an overpowering tyrant. A nearly psychotic, anti-Semitic small-town pharmacist, he terrorized both daughters with his rages and his preoccupation with potential harm coming to them from sitting with their legs crossed, shaving their legs, eating certain foods, and a multitude of other irrational beliefs. In addition, he was overwhelmingly seductive, lying naked in bed with them into their teens, checking their breast development, and, in the case of the patient, weighing her naked almost daily to check for possible eating indiscretions. He demanded open access to bathrooms and bedrooms well into his daughters' college years.

There had been an unwanted pregnancy prior to the patient's birth which had been ended by an illegal abortion, which both parents had agreed upon for "economic reasons." The patient had known about this from early in her childhood.

Her younger sister was described as being like her mother: thin, beautiful, cold, smug, and rejecting. In fact, however, the patient had actively tortured her, had played homosexually seductive games with her, and had actively rejected her. The patient's masturbation fantasy involved getting a small, dark-haired girl, who looked like her sister, very "hot."

At the age of three-and-a-half, the patient had an hernia repair which played a prominent role in her analysis. She recalled kicking at the doctors both on the stretcher and in the operating room. She was told that her father had to be thrown out of the operating room, where he had intruded out of his extreme anxiety. Later, she felt that he had "betrayed" her when he removed the stitches, himself.

When she was four years old, the family, which had moved back to the grandparents' house, moved away for the second time to a nearby city. There is some likelihood that her mother became depressed at that time because of the separation from her own parents.

The second grade was a problem year for the patient. Her sister entered school and became a rival there. The patient responded by giving up her thumb-sucking and beginning to overeat. At this point, obesity became a central issue in her life, and it remained so up until the time of her analysis. Her parents responded to her overeating by threatening her with punishment, watching every bit of food, and weighing her daily. Weight gain through latency and adolescence was accompanied by beatings, yelling, restriction of sweets and starches, and the assurance of physical disease and spinsterhood. Thinness was equated with happiness. The patient was aware, however, that this issue hid behind it all her other guilts, particularly the homosexual and sadistic play with her sister.

She became an excellent student, and school provided a welcome distraction from her anxieties at home. She developed crushes on a number of her female teachers, who responded positively to her attentions. At the same time, she was filled with heterosexual romantic fantasies involving teachers and other men. One particular fantasy, that of a robber coming to school and selecting her from the other girls and then going down a slide with her, came up in the analysis and will be discussed below. Many of her latency-age fantasies, however, reflected her numerous fears. These included tunnel and bridge phobias, fears of being shot, bomb fears, fears of disease, and recurrent death fears for herself and her parents. Intense fears of her mother dying occurred after a favorite fourth-grade teacher died. She remembered praying to God to keep her mother alive so that she would not be left with her father. Around this same time she had a screen memory of father choking her mother and carrying her to the bathroom during the night.

Throughout latency and adolescence she was jealous of her sister's successes. Sister was believed to be thinner and prettier, and she could use her sullen moods to manipulate her parents. She was socially successful with girls and boys and was good at dancing and athletics.

When the patient reached high school she had her first dating experience. Her parents disapproved of the young man involved. With him she had her only sexual experiences prior to college. These involved his petting her to quick orgasm. She was occupied only with her own sexual pleasure and her fear of being discovered and had little or no feeling for him. Her only true "love" during these years was a female teacher. She would think about her all the time, admire her comments, and would ride by her house in the hope of seeing her. Her glowing reports of this teacher made her parents so jealous that they tried to forbid her from continuing the relationship.

When she went away to college, she became quite disturbed. Although she was popular on campus, she became depressed and gained forty pounds, blaming all of her unhappiness on the structure of campus life. She transferred the next year to a smaller liberal arts college nearer her home city. Her academic success continued, and for the first time, she developed a crush on a male professor. However, when he approached her sexually, she retreated and encouraged him to pursue a girlfriend of hers. When he did so, she became depressed but lost forty pounds to "become beautiful for him." However, he did not respond to her, and she fled from him to two young women, one of whom was extraordinarily kind, warm, and loving and the other of whom was brittle, hard, and very cruel to the patient.

She entered therapy during this time with a woman therapist at the school. She was seen as kind and loving. The patient spent many of her sessions crying and was relieved that for the first time, she could tell someone how unhappy she was. When the therapist moved away, she was sufficiently concerned about Miss Y's depression and possible suicidal intent that she referred her to a psychiatrist in a nearby city. She saw him for one year in once weekly psychotherapy. The doctor reminded her so much of her father that she could only cry and belittle herself, denying her rage at him. Upon being graduated, she came to New York to look for work and at the recommendation of her psychiatrist, sought analysis.

Course of the Analysis

The patient was a tall, sandy-haired, attractive, moderately overweight young woman who dressed casually and was smiling and pleasing during the initial interviews. She spoke easily with strong affective tones and related well to the analyst. When she began on the couch, she felt enormous pressure to be fully open about everything with no sense of privacy. Farting and toilet scenes appeared frequently in her thoughts, and she would struggle with her embarrassment and shame over presenting this material. The transference was instantly intense. The analyst was seen as a strong, God-like doctor who would rescue her from her crazy father. On the other hand, in the first session on the couch, she hallucinated his laughing at her. His silence was seen as cold and critical and his interpretations only confirmed her worst fears that she was a "faker" and that all that she had said previously was "worthless." Often she assumed that her analyst's curiosity was perverse. At one moment she would offer glorious hymns in praise of him, while at another, he would be seen as weak and ineffectual, like a dog whom she could force to sniff her genitals. The alternative presentations of herself or her analyst as exalted or degraded could occur within moments of each other during the same session and persisted throughout much of the analysis.

Nonetheless, she continually was able to bring in relevant material and dreams with which she could work, whenever the state of the transference permitted. Pleasant memories of her father at age four emerged, as well as the pleasant fantasy of being chosen by the robber at school. She was able to date during this early period of treatment but retained her intense involvement with her two girlfriends from college, both of whom had also moved to New York.

However, later during this first year, the transference took on an ever-increasing sadomasochistic intensity, so that it became almost the exclusive focus of the analytic work. She would deliberately and defiantly withhold material, hoping and fearing that her analyst would scream at her and lose control and hit her. He was her Nazi jailer, and she was his Jew victim. Then the roles would reverse. She demanded advice on all sorts of subjects and saw him as extremely withholding. Suddenly, she would shift into a more seductive mood, talking of love and marriage, telling jokes, quoting poetry, and expecting the analyst to respond to her. Then, she could shift back to her sadistic mood. Anger would mount during an hour because it was "like a hamburger—you take one bite and you become aware it will be all gone." Interpretations focused on the repetition of her relationship with her father, including both her idealization and her rage, but she distrusted the analyst's remarks because father, too, could talk rationally, only to explode in a rage a few moments later. Degradation and teasing of herself and the analyst took place daily, often alternating with feelings of mutual love and praise. Night-time phone calls to demand answers to questions or relief from panic were common. Threats to quit or to transfer were routine. Rage that the analyst was not omniscient compounded the problem.

The only effective interpretation during this time was to point out how she was tormenting and torturing her analyst much as her father had done to her. Although this produced guilt and rage, it began to make her think of herself as a torturer and not only as a victim of her sadistic analyst/father.

During the times the analyst was briefly away, she denied any feelings of loss but felt "dry and dusty inside," compared to a warm, full feeling of "cookies or coins in her hands while in her grandmother's bed," which she felt when she felt close to her analyst. Both before and after the separations, she was excessively withholding and defiant.

During her second year of analysis, whatever work was done was done against this backdrop of the sadomasochistic paternal transference, which had now begun to focus around her rage at genital differences. Dreams were of female men and masculine girls, a picture of herself with a "peony" growing out of her vagina, twin female infants with ugly genital rashes, herself as a phallic Dracula rising from the waves. Much of her rage was associated to her appendectomy, which was seen as a castration in which her father had colluded. Her obesity had a number of new meanings in this context. Fat women may be sexually free and open with their mouths and their vaginas. On the other hand, an obese woman could be masculine since a large "pad of fat" would "cover her hole." Thin women could be penetrable and vulnerable to men, or they could be cold, narcissistic, hard, and phallic.

In keeping with this conflict, her behavior in the analysis deteriorated further, and she felt increasing pleasure at her sullen silences and her threats to sit up or walk out. She belittled her analyst endlessly, and many telephone calls were made openly to annoy him. Attempts to interpret this behavior failed, and the telephone calls were finally interdicted. Her immediate feeling was that she was "butchered" and "castrated," and memories of her surgery came up again in her associations. Her rages were intense when she was premenstrual. A dream which expressed the conflict clearly was as follows: She was riding in a bus with a man but preferred the man behind her. She lifted her skirt and farted in his face.

In the third year the struggle continued. Romantic and sexual feelings were followed by rage and anxiety. For example, when sexually excited during an hour, she left and had the following fantasy: A gunman sneaks into the office and threatens to shoot her analyst. She seduces him by saying her analyst is terrible and she only goes to him because her father forces her to do so. The gunman is taken in by the ruse. She kicks him in the balls, and her analyst admires her. A few days later she became enraged at her analyst and fantasied shooting him in the balls, saying "Now, try to laugh." When reporting some of her romantic and sexual feelings, she got up off the couch, saying she had heard the next patient buzz to come in. This was an hallucination.

During this year, continuing confusion between the sexes came up in associations suggesting primal scene material: An old farmer falls in love with her, but his wife comes along to win him back by showing him her beautiful breasts. She has hair around her face like a beard and her thighs and legs are thin, like those of her father.

Despite the intensity of her ambivalence toward men and her own confusion about her sexual identity, she was able to date and pet for the first time and was able to relax sufficiently to use a tampon during her menstrual period.

During this time her close, loving, girlfriend from college became pregnant and delivered a daughter. The patient became extraordinarily possessive of her friend and enormously jealous of the baby girl. While watching her friend nurse the baby, she felt her face to be covered with mucus and found herself making sucking motions with her lips. She was extremely angry and jealous of her friend's husband as well. With loving sadness, memories of her mother in the hospital with her baby sister emerged.

These events also led to primal scene material. She began to talk of listening for sounds from her parents' bedroom indicating that her mother preferred her father. The old screen memory of father carrying mother to the bathroom and choking her came up again. Another memory which seemed unreal to her, of being at a beach on a boardwalk near a slide recurred, but now she was convinced that the boardwalk rails were the slats of her crib. The slide by the boardwalk, which also appeared earlier in the robber fantasy, became the sexual position of her parents during orogenital activity, most likely with her father's rear in the air. As this fantasy/memory emerged she began to cry and felt she was going to urinate on the couch.

At this point in her life her girlfriend who had had the baby, announced that she was moving away from New York and leaving her husband. The patient became enraged at her and recalled her fears that her mother would abandon her or die during her childhood. In addition, she began to have erotic fantasies about her girlfriend's husband. She was also enraged with her analyst for allowing all of this to happen.

Despite all of the regressive feelings which emerged in the analysis, her life outside of the analysis continued to mature. She moved into her own apartment and began to cook and clean for herself. She was able to take the first steps toward a postgraduate degree while continuing to work at her job. She survived numerous rejections while looking for a new job, and when she finally found one she was very successful at it. She began to date somewhat more frequently and had an occasional affair.

Her transference neurosis, however, became even more bitter and negativistic after her girlfriend and her daughter left the city. Her analyst was the bad father who allowed the good mother to disappear and die. Her rage and her grief were intense, and she often refused to stay on the couch, refused to talk, left the office on a few occasions, and called in the night to berate her analyst and to grieve for her friend. Her bitter isolation remained refractory to any intervention, and she constantly threatened to change analysts. After months of apparent stalemate, the analyst began to consider her demand as a reality and raised the question of a consultation. The patient responded with surprise, incredulous that her analyst could give her up and could stop trying to "control" her. This transference fantasy was clearly connected to her father, who had had to be the only omnipotent, controlling force in her life.

The analyst's countertransference feelings reached a crescendo during this time, certainly contributing to his raising the issue of a consultation. From the beginning of the analysis he had felt bullied and buffeted around by her shifting moods. Her negativism and withholding would provoke his anger, only to be followed by her softening and showing some progress. In addition to her change of mood, the analyst was often guilty about his anger and responded to his own guilt with rescue fantasies and an increased determination to see the analysis through to the end. Then he would be attacked or disappointed again and would respond once more with hostile fantasies. There was no question that the analyst was thus experiencing what the patient had felt at the hands of her father. All of these feelings reached their most intense pitch after her friend and surrogate mother abandoned her.

This transference crisis finally softened, and there emerged clearly for the first time in her analysis transference feelings which were associated to her mother's critical attitudes. She felt the analyst had quietly disliked her throughout the treatment. He was smug, cold, and critical and found most of her traits objectionable. Her manners, her walk, and her speech were crude, and she was generally clumsy and obese. She became self-conscious about her hands and extremely guilty about her sexual activity. She was sure that her mother was a sexual prude. During this period in her analysis, she would run to the dentist after sexual activity, convinced that her teeth were rotting, and was always shocked when he found nothing wrong.

At this point, more detail of her primal scene fantasy emerged. She recalled again the bathroom scene fantasy of her mother being choked and now began seeing male genital arrangements in dreams, including a man's stiff, waxy body. One day she came to her analyst's waiting room and saw a new, attractive, blond female patient. She became jealous and enraged with the analyst for collecting pretty young women, including those who bleached their hair, with their "dark roots" showing. After days of rage, she began to consider the analyst's comment that the "dark roots" might be a fantasy. She then dreamed that she was in her grandparents' house. A bomb dropped and she saw a flash of light, which she associated to the sun coming up showing her parents' bed opposite to her crib. A dream followed in which a man is dying and she gives him mouth-to-mouth resuscitation with a tube-shaped machine that has a bulb hanging underneath it. She began to eat and chew more at this time. Finally, she had an image of her father's light sandy hair pressed against her mother's dark pubic hair, with his back arched in the position of the "slide," confirming her previous memory. She also became sure that this scene was a contributing factor to her bomb phobia. Her conviction had been that mother was being bitten and hurt, but she now began to think that her mother was having pleasure. She felt jealous and dreamed, "Mother had dropped dead or was shot by a gun or blowgun. Father, sister, and I are sitting in the kitchen and mother's spirit appears. I invited the spirit to sleep with father, who is lonely, but the spirit cannot, and instead asks me to sleep with father." She awakens with anxiety. In another dream she is having intercourse with a man and her father approves. She thinks that her mother is dead, but mother appears looking thin and beautiful.

With the reworking of the oedipal material, her life began to change even more. Her lesbian masturbation fantasies continued to be present, but now she believed that they were preferable because they were anxiety-free. At this time she began to become seriously involved with a somewhat passive young man with whom she was orgastic if she were on top of him, rubbing on his thigh, but she was also beginning to have vaginal sensations. However, during their first intercourse, she was so anxious that she hallucinated that her phone was ringing, jumped from her bed convinced that her parents were calling, and visually hallucinated her parents' car and her father outside of her building entrance. As she calmed down, she realized that it was the phone ringing next door, a different car, and the doorman standing outside.

Beginning with the fifth year of her analysis, the treatment began to become increasingly manageable and much more like that of a neurotic patient. Her complaints about her analyst gave way to fantasies that his wife had died and she would have to console him and his two daughters. She began to show herself in a more appealing way, using her intellect and humor consistently without fleeing behind a barrage of negativism and anality.

Despite this positive change, she became increasingly more obsessional in her productions and finally confessed to her analyst that she had continued to fear him, no matter how much she had been able to tell him. She was convinced all along that both of her parents had indeed been crazy and continued to feel that that might be true of her analyst as well. She could never tell what he was thinking. He could conceivably be a maniac who could murder her, despite all the evidence to the contrary, and she could never dare to leave him. Even at this point in a calm session, she heard comments by him to be judgmental and critical. At that point her analyst began to explain to her more fully some of the thinking behind his interventions. If he commented on her homosexual fantasies or her eating binges, he had a reason other than condemnation. This method seemed to reassure her further, and she began to tell in more graphic detail about her parents' craziness, particularly her father's rages. She was extraordinarily anxious in presenting the details and had feelings that she was spinning off the earth. Her father seemed murderous to her. He pulled her hair and slapped her face. He had assured her that her teeth would rot if she drank soda; that her legs would be cancerous if she shaved them; that any medication would ruin her liver; that stooping would dislocate her spine; that sitting crosslegged would cripple her. When she was twenty-one years of age he beat her with a strap and called her a "whore" for wearing a slip, and her sister was beaten and called a "whore" for trying out make-up. Her mother watched all of this passively, perhaps vicariously enjoying the father's sadism.

Working on her fears that her parents and her analyst were crazy was accompanied by a continuation of progress in her life outside of the treatment. She had dated a few men and was more sexually relaxed. At this point she decided to and did marry her passive but very loving boyfriend, despite her anxiety over the decision and her ambivalence toward him. She did not feel that she was able to face the intense competitive feelings that she was likely to feel with a stronger, more aggressive partner. Her decision to marry spurred feelings of phallically conquering her boyfriend, her mother, and her analyst. "I'd have no problem if I were a man—even my weight would be okay." "I'd walk right over to you and shove my tit in your mouth like a penis." She wanted to cuddle the analyst, to give him two big full cannisters of ice cream. Her negative oedipal wishes and her own oral needs for her mother fused with images of her warm, giving grandparents. At this point in treatment she became orgastic during intercourse for the first time.

Her attitude toward men softened even further, and she felt unambivalent romantic feelings toward her analyst, her father, and her college professor. The analyst's wife, her own mother, and even her beloved girlfriend began to appear as ugly, old, and depreciated. For the first time she told her analyst that her mother had a big pot belly and had had it for years. She remembered how she had felt thinner and sexier than her mother as she entered adolescence. Her images of herself as ugly and obese clearly expressed guilty, defensive, self-loathings which had her mother's body superimposed on her own. In this context, her masturbation fantasy of seducing the dark-haired woman/sister/mother was seen as a denial of her hostile and competitive wishes toward these rivals.

However, the intensity of her sexual and competitive feelings continued to frighten her. She began to sit up on the couch to see if her analyst was "in a rage" or "totally disgusted" with her. By the end of her seventh year, she insisted on "sitting up," ostensibly to check her analyst's responses and to see if she could believe them. Underneath lay her desire to defeat her analyst/father and to reverse their roles. In a dream, "A machine is pumping gas into the house and father is choking and looks like he's dying." Associations showed a reversal of the earlier primal scene theme in which mother is choking. Following this dream she performed fellatio, which was rare for her, and felt that her teeth were rotting, and then felt like Dracula, who could be a woman draining men of their life's blood.

As the working through of these conflicts continued, she was able to deal with her analyst with less intrusion of the bisexual, sadomasochistic fantasies. Termination was planned, and she was able to ambivalently conclude the treatment. She was able to marry the passive man she had been living with. The relationship was stable and she no longer felt herself to be a victim, but she was quite guilty that she was too overpowering for him, which seemed to be so. Nonetheless, their sexual relationship was satisfactory and she was often orgastic.

The final clinical result showed that she had made considerable improvement. She no longer had periods of depression nor did she have strong feelings of self-loathing. Her capacity for feeling genuine pleasure had markedly increased. She lost weight and maintained her new level, albeit with difficulty, by repetitive dieting and regular exercise, something she had never been able to do prior to her analysis. Her anxiety had disappeared almost completely as had her fears of cancer and of dying. Professionally, she was able to advance at her job, was able to obtain a graduate degree, and was even able to do considerable creative work. She had also been able to develop deeper relationships with both men and women and had become a sensitive, supportive friend.

Diagnostic Considerations

We considered this patient to be borderline for the following reasons: she showed multiple symptomatology which compromised her functioning, including severe pervasive anxiety approaching panic; severe depressive moods with self-loathing; multiple phobias; hypochondriacal preoccupations; obesity with bulimic episodes; reading and writing inhibitions; severe sexual inhibitions plus vaginismus and frigidity; and pervasive homosexual fantasies. Her moods showed extreme lability. "Acting out" was often necessary for tension discharge. Projective mechanisms were prominent and paranoid ideation was common. She exhibited a considerable degree of regression, including primary process and hallucinatory material which was intermittently present at times of extreme stress. Finally, transference reactions developed almost immediately in the treatment and were unusually intense and persistent despite the analyst's interpretative efforts.

Case Report IV

Miss Z entered analysis in her mid-twenties, shortly after having been graduated from college. She had come to New York to look for work and to start analysis, the latter step having been recommended to her by her psychiatrist in her home city. He had seen her during her vacation visits home from college, when she had been quite severely depressed. Her major complaints in her initial interviews were her depression, her inability to form a good relationship with a man, overeating with periodic binge eating, and a compulsive gesture of pointing her index finger to her temple whenever she thought of harm occurring to a member of her family.

She was the oldest of three children and the only daughter, born in a nearby city. Her father was a dentist who never practiced his profession but who ran the family-owned department store. He was a bitter and resentful man who felt that he had been cheated by life, since he had to work in the family business while his younger brothers went on to professional prominence. He took out his anger on his passive, less intelligent wife, who was a "southern belle," deeply attached to her own mother. His sarcastic and nasty humiliations of his wife were an everyday part of the patient's early life, and these scenes became even more prominent during her late latency years and early teens. Her parents separated while she was away at college, and her father died during her analysis.

The patient seemed to have been her father's favorite, which was a mixed blessing. He would compare her favorably to her mother and would act seductively with her, but he often would be angry at her and humiliate her. During her latency, he extracted her loose teeth, amid excitement and giggles, and he would supervise her homework accompanied by his screaming and her tears. When she was in her mid-teens, as he was about to embark on a business trip, he grabbed her and kissed her passionately on the mouth. During these years he had become a heavy drinker and was quite depressed and paranoid.

When the patient was three-and-a-half years old, her mother became ill with "spots on her skin." The family took her to a famous medical center for diagnosis and treatment. The patient returned home, at first with a housekeeper whom she barely knew. They were then joined by her father. Mother underwent a splenectomy and did not return for about a month. During her absence the patient became increasingly attached to her father.

When she was four-and-a-half or five years old, while her mother was pregnant with her first brother, her father was drafted into the army and was sent to the west coast. Both parents were terrified that he would be sent to Korea. The patient was a bewildered participant in the almost daily, anxiety-laden phone calls between her parents. Father was not sent overseas, returned for one day at the birth of her brother, and then returned home permanently five months later. After her brother's birth she began to beat her dolls and would frequently make her brother cry if her parents were about to leave, so that they would delay their leaving and pay attention to the children. However, she shortly thereafter became a "little mother." Around this time she began to cling to her mother, had obsessional concerns that harm might come to her mother, and was terrified when the parents went out. At the same time, she clearly felt herself to be "daddy's girl."

She reached puberty at twelve years old, and her youngest brother was born when she was thirteen years old. She remembers feeling that, even more so than with her other brother, this child was "her baby." She ate a great deal at this time, gained weight, and felt "full." She began to masturbate almost daily, using thigh pressure, without conscious fantasies. Around the same period she began to be aware of her father's excessive concern with her health. When she had oral surgery, he was in the recovery room, and she saw a look of panic on his face. When she had chest pain he examined her chest, allowing her to show him her developing breasts.

During high school her social life was extremely limited. She had few dates and lived vicariously through the social lives of her girlfriends. She did develop a romantic crush on President Kennedy and played hookey to go to Washington in order to meet him. Subsequently, she read extensively about him and his family. Her compulsive gesture, the index finger to the temple, may have been related to his assassination.

When she was in college she began to date regularly. She would be extremely seductive when she first met a man. This would quickly be replaced by extreme clinginess. Between her second and third years of college, while away at summer school, she had a moderately severe depressive episode during which her binge eating began. During her last year of college she had her first intense sexual experience, mutual orogenital relations. Afterwards she was convinced she was pregnant and became sufficiently upset about it to frighten the young man as well.

Course of the Analysis

The patient was a short, plump, stylishly dressed, boyish woman who was timid and coy in the initial interviews. She was guarded and evasive and presented only factual material. Almost immediately thereafter, she began to convey her "preoccupations" with an air of intense drama and emotion, usually anxiety and anger. She would call her boyfriend in another city five or six times in the space of a few hours. She did not understand why she was calling and could only say that she needed "reassurance." Often she felt so desperate that she would have friends make the call and hang up. She had begun to have intercourse with her boyfriend, and every month she was convinced that she was pregnant, despite the fact that she used adequate contraception. She experienced nausea, breast enlargement, and fullness in her abdomen. On many occasions she had pregnancy tests taken. She was also preoccupied with the possibility of developing cancer, particularly breast cancer secondary to her contraceptive pills or leukemia secondary to X-rays. She also worried about infections and allergies. In addition, she was constantly concerned about her weight and consulted many diet doctors who prescribed pills, which she did not take since she considered the doctors to be "quacks."

Shortly after treatment began, she was dropped by her first boyfriend. Almost immediately, she took up with another passive young man, and she followed the same pattern with him as with the previous boyfriend. They would have intercourse once a week, and her compulsive telephoning would begin, even though she was aware of the fact that she did not particularly care for him. Every month the pregnancy fears would dominate all her thoughts.

From the beginning of the treatment, her transference reactions were intense. She felt that her analyst was not interested enough in helping her and was not concerned enough about her possible pregnancy, her medical illnesses, or her weight problem. She would call her analyst as she did her boyfriend. She would dangle the diet pills from the "quack" doctors in front of him, while cursing him for not caring enough for her to protect her from these doctors. Any interpretation was felt as an accusation to which she would respond, "So, what's wrong with that?" At the same time she was frightened that her analyst would "dump" her as a result of her provocations and would frequently try to give him gifts in order to placate him.

At the end of the first year of treatment she created a crisis over a possible pregnancy. It coincided with her analyst's leaving on vacation, and she responded by dragging her boyfriend from one hospital emergency room to another, convinced she was pregnant. Finally, despite the fact that all tests were negative, she convinced one doctor to give her pills to bring on her period. When her period began, she was sure that she was having a miscarriage.

Any attempt at interpretation or reconstruction relating her pregnancy fears to unconscious wishes to be pregnant, or possibly connecting them to her separations from her mother at the time of her splenectomy or at the time of her mother's pregnancy while her father was in the army, were met with lack of interest or fury that her analyst was denying her "real" problems. Despite these manifest responses, by the beginning of her second year certain conflicts had been clarified. She became aware that her own anger precipitated her frantic phone calls as she worried that her boyfriend's well-being was endangered by the intensity of her feelings. She also realized that frequently she ate to "stuff down her anger." These insights led to a disappearance of the "finger to the temple" gesture which was seen as an attempt to "blast the thoughts out of my head," as well as to punish herself. Her fears of being abandoned and her arranging disasters for herself at work were also seen as self-punishments.

She became increasingly depressed and tearful during this time and expected and wished that her analyst would ridicule and humiliate her as her father had done to her mother and herself. She worried about becoming increasingly involved in the analysis. She did not want to give her analyst the "satisfaction," and she also feared becoming very depressed, as she had been during her semester at summer school. Her fantasies became more anal and sadomasochistic. Once she dropped her ring off the couch and said she wouldn't look for it, insisting that her analyst do it for her. She explained later that she wished/feared to show him her buttocks, coupled with a wish to fart in his face. This was symbolically enacted when she paid her bill. She rushed into the office and shoved a wad of dirty bills under her analyst's nose.

During this second year, the repetitive telephoning, the binge eating, the monthly pregnancy fears, and the fears of side-effects from her contraceptive pills continued unabated. Interpretation focused on all of these as a defense against having more feelings in the analysis as well as a self-punishment, in the form of somatic fears, for her rage at the analyst. This was in turn connected with her mother's abandonment at the time of her splenectomy and her father's abandoning her when drafted. During this year it became clear that she called her mother three to four times a week, long distance, which was costly far beyond her financial capacities. This constant contact with her mother continued throughout her analysis.

Also during this time, her boyfriend's mother died. She became so inappropriately demanding and clinging that the usually mild-mannered young man ended their relationship. She responded by joining an expensive dating service and then began coming to the sessions dressed "fierce" and "like a whore" to show the analyst what she really was. She began to arrange for her old boyfriend to come to her apartment and have sex with her in a way which she felt was "lewd and humiliating" and which she did not sensually enjoy. At the end, she would arrange a pretext to be given money. Often this "prostitution fantasy" would take place before the session and would lead to a number of unproductive sessions. These episodes replaced the compulsive telephoning, except for her calls to her mother.

Coincident with the "prostitution fantasy," her overtly castrating and depreciatory attitudes toward men emerged. "I want to break his balls" was a common remark. Within the transference she became aware that her behavior was unconsiously intended to castrate the analyst by rendering him impotent. She begged to be "dumped" by him out of guilt, while at other times, she fantasized seducing the analyst and driving him to suicide for his inability to control her. After that, she would commit suicide out of guilt! At this time, while she was out on dates, she would feel the same intense anger toward her escort and then would arrange to feel debased and humiliated at the end of the evening.

By the beginning of the third year of analysis, affectionate and lovingly sexual feelings began to emerge in the transference. She missed her analyst over the summer and felt badly for being so uncooperative. However, these feelings were accompanied by anxiety and "feeling shitty." If she dressed nicely, or "sexy," or "slinky," she would feel uncomfortable walking to and from the couch out of fear that the analyst would find her attractive. A productive "good hour" made her anxious, and she often would provoke arguments and become abrasive. She was able to see the defensive and gratifying nature of the fighting as reminiscent of her adolescent battles with her father. To control her mounting tension, she said, "Let's get something straight. I hate you; you hate me. Let's keep it that way." On one occasion the analyst smiled at her ending remark, and the next day she lost her purse on the subway. She became more aware of her mother's permissiveness in allowing her and her father to be too close. These sexually fearful attitudes existed side by side with progressively more blatant sexual fantasies toward the analyst.

Over the Thanksgiving holiday, while she was at home, her father had a myocardial infarction and died twelve hours later.

She felt badly that she had not been able to tell him how much she loved him. She cried for a week, and then she attempted to cope with his death by an increasing concern about money, a more conscious wish to have a baby, and an increased clinging to the analyst and any other father figure.

The money that her father left her was all she would ever have of him. It became clear that this was associated to her father leaving behind a baby when she was five years old. In the months after his death she dreamed of a "minnow" being stuck in her nose which had to be taken out. Associations led to her father showing her the eggs inside a pregnant fish. Shortly thereafter she dreamt she was four-and-a-half months pregnant and liked it. Interpretation of her pregnancy wishes no longer met with any objections.

Her openly loving and sexual feelings toward the analyst made her feel even more intense pain and anger when he went on his winter vacation. Impulsively, she made arrangements to move to her home city for the following year but was so overjoyed on his "safe" return that she cancelled them. She moved to an apartment near her analyst's office, announcing that he was now the "center of my life." She developed a conviction that he would not leave on his summer vacation because she needed him. Her analyst interpreted that she was reliving her father's departure for the army, which had been reawakened by his recent death. Although she responded with tears and occasional despair, she continued to re-enact the conflict with her dates. After having sexual contact with men, she would arrange to be humiliated and then would become full of anger and recriminations. The analyst interpreted that she felt she had more "control" over her life by prearranging these scenarios than she did when she lost her father as a child, than she did now as an adult, or than she had over her analyst during treatment. She did not completely accept this interpretation, but evidence of her belief in her ability to control by magical means came to the fore. Optimistic thoughts had to be hidden from the gods. Anxiety and pessimism would prevent disaster. Even as an adult she "monitored" her brother's airplane travels, as she had tried to keep her mother in her sight during her latency period.

Prior to the analyst's summer vacation she read a novel in which a woman whose husband is dying performs fellatio on the doctor and swallows his semen. Associations led to her father passing on his color-blind gene and his bad temper to his children, and then to the analyst's never giving her a gift. The desire to have a baby from her analyst was clear to her. Over this summer, she became involved in a tempestuous affair with a married Don Juan while overseas. She loved him and hated him, and with him she was able to achieve orgasm during intercourse for the first time. However, he returned to his family in the United States and did not contact her. She was not able to locate him but began repetitiously to call his parents, recreating her desperate need for her father after his death and the similar feelings she had had for him while he was in the army. She searched desperately for her new lover. A dream confirmed his role as a paternal symbol. In the dream she located him in the town where her father's brother lived and where her father had had his first coronary.

During this first year after her father's death, her love/hate feelings toward him and toward her new lover who abandoned her reflected the love/hate intensity in the transference. Any imagined slight led to weeks of petulance and rage, followed by the old fears that the analyst would dump her and now by the fear that her anger would kill him. Once she called the analyst's home and a woman answered the phone. She was enraged and said quite seriously, "I thought I was the only one in your life."

In her rage she would occasionally dress as a prostitute and tell her analyst, quoting the feelings of a call girl in a book, "Baby, you haven't even touched me." At the very time that her prostitution fantasies were being expressed, pregnancy wishes and her wish to have a baby were also in the forefront. However, the pregnancy wish was expressed in terms of orally castrating her partner to become pregnant. Her eating binges occurred at these times, and she felt "pleasantly full." She was delighted when a friend told her daughter to bite off the head of any man's penis if the man tried to molest her. At the same time she threatened to steal a magazine from the waiting room which had pictures of human embryonic development in it. With her increasingly conscious awareness of her pregnancy wishes and fantasies, her fears of cancer, leukemia, and infections disappeared in short order. Her pregnancy "fears" disappeared also, but now she was disappointed each month when she was *not* pregnant.

Around this time she began to have intercourse with a new man who was loving and assertive. She liked being passive and feminine but found herself trying to control him, "doing her old thing," by telephoning, demanding his company, and blowing up about minor issues. During intercourse there was similar behavior. She would grasp her partner so tightly with her thighs that he would become uncomfortable and anxious. When questioned, she reported that her masturbatory practices and fantasies had changed during her analysis. She now placed two fingers in her vagina and clasped her thighs around her hand with maximal pressure, with the fantasy that a man is performing cunnilingus on her and she is suffocating him. She began to act out the fantasy of getting her analyst/baby inside her and crushing him and punishing herself at the same time. Mainly, she tormented herself by binge eating, which she blamed on herself and on the analyst, and by mismanaging her funds so that she had little for herself and was always late with her fee.

Following months of this behavior, directly erotogenic (sexual) masochism became prominent. It was heralded by a dream where a man pursues her trying to pull out a loose tooth. Memories of her father pushing out her deciduous teeth returned, as did the exciting memories of their numerous fights over homework. She was now fully aware of how sexually exciting they were. She also recalled that when she was an adolescent she provoked her piano teacher to hit her hands with a ruler. Just prior to the analyst's vacation, she located her former lover, the Don Juan. She flew to his town where she found him living alone and psychotic with grandiose delusions. Nonetheless, she provoked him to rape her, which excited her greatly. She returned to her analyst saying she was going to marry this lover but calmed down over the ensuing week and did not return to see him.

Just before the summer, she began to work for a man who was associated with her paternal uncle. She became his "smart little helper," a stance which she remembered taking with her father. In the heat of these feelings, she decided to lose weight for the man and gave up her binge eating. This symptom was replaced by a period of sexual promiscuity during which she was aware of hating both her partners and herself; she also engaged in "binge telephoning," calling any of her ex-lovers and angrily hanging up when they answered. During this time her favorite boss was fired and she became depressed and lethargic about working at all, or pursuing her graduate course, unless she could relate to a boss/father.

After several months of this behavior, her acting out decreased, and she revealed to her analyst a relationship with a young man who treated her with respect and consideration and who liked her. She found herself being shy with him and sexually timid. Months went by before they had intercourse, which they both enjoyed. She did not enjoy talking to him on the telephone, limiting their contact to "essentials." She could not believe that he cared for her so much. Did he not see what everyone else knew, i.e., that she was not worth getting involved with? At this point she resurrected one of her old lovers and played one man off against the other in her mind. When she was with her loving boyfriend, he seemed kind and gentle and she wanted to marry and have a home and children. When she was with the other man, he was seen as seedy, sinister, and mean and could give her the pleasant pain she craved. However, when she re-enacted her old prostitution fantasy with him, it was no longer exciting. Her new boyfriend began to show a lovingly forceful side which she found quite "masculine" and similar to the memories of her father. Naturally, it was around a separation from her analyst that she decided to live with him and, upon the analyst's return, announced her plans to marry him in a few months. She oscillated in her desires to marry and set up a polarization between her analyst and her lover over her analytic fee. She wanted to withhold a fee raise which would come after her marriage, and many dreams and fantasies had to do with anal retention of the analyst's baby/penis, with associations to her father's leaving her money when he died and her wanting her father's baby when he went into the army. She did marry and after her honeymoon oscillated between her anger at her analyst over her fee and anger toward her husband for not giving her a baby. When the summer break came she decided to stop her analysis with the clear recognition that more work needed to be done, although she was happy with her plans to have a home and a baby.

In retrospect, the analyst recognized two important unanalyzed elements in this treatment. Her telephone calls and "monitoring" of her mother continued throughout the analysis, and it seemed impossible to focus the patient's attention on her mother, because of the intensity of the paternal transference. In addition, it seemed clear that any progress and understanding could be accomplished only if accompanied by suffering. This masochistic stance was never directly approached during her analysis, although it seemed clear from some dreams that the guilt was associated to rage at her mother and destructive wishes toward her siblings.

Diagnostic Considerations

This patient was considered to be borderline for a number of reasons. She had multiple symptoms: depression, severe anxiety, eating binges, hypochondriacal preoccupations, and sexual unresponsiveness. Her social life was severely constricted, and she lived largely in a fantasy world or vicariously through others. When she did draw friends into her orbit, they were used to help her to act out her fantasies and fears about pregnancy and abandonment. The men who did enter her life were interchangeable and were used as partners in her sadomasochistic fantasies. Her masochistic identification with her mother was obvious, but in the transference, she identified with her sadistic and abandoning father as well. She was exquisitely sensitive to separation and loss, and much of her symptomatic behavior corresponded to impending or actual separations from her analyst.

The transference was immediate and intense. The sense of

an analytic process often seemed beyond her as she demanded that her analyst actively participate in her pregnancy fears and her desires to lose weight. Well into the treatment, she moved into an apartment near his office, since he was "the center of my life." She was offended and upset when a woman answered the phone at his apartment.

During much of her treatment her analyst found that her provocativeness stimulated angry feelings, and both sadistic impulses and the temptation to abandon her were coupled with rescue fantasies and guilt.

Reality testing was severely compromised in a number of areas. Most obvious was her preoccupation with pregnancy fears, which reached such intensity that she could go from emergency room to emergency room trying to convince the physicians to participate in her beliefs. More than once she was able to convince an unbelieving sexual partner that her fears were legitimate. Certainly, in the transference, reality testing was extraordinarily faulty for an unusually long time. Her conviction that her analyst wanted to torture her, and her conviction that she was the center of his life and that she could seduce him, lasted almost to the end of treatment. Her hypochondriacal preoccupations were firmly believed until finally analyzed as self-punitive responses to her rage and castrative wishes.

4.

Object Relations

Every thorough evaluation of a patient involves a comprehensive study of the patient's current relationships to the people
in his life—as well as of those in his past. Our Study Group
spent considerable time discussing the object relations of our
patients in an attempt to describe and delineate the special
characteristics and qualities which are typical of, or prominent
in, borderline patients. We were trying to find common features
which would differentiate this group from psychoneurotics, on
the one hand, and psychotics, on the other.

We began our deliberations by trying to describe the nature
of the ego functions in our borderline patients. One of the
members of our group, Dr. David Beres, had included object
relations in his list of ego functions in his paper "Ego Deviation
and the Concept of Schizophrenia" (1956). We soon realized
that object relations themselves partake of so many ego functions as well as those of id and superego that it seemed more
appropriate to consider this topic not simply as an aspect of ego
functioning but rather as a more complex and multidetermined
aspect of psychic functioning.

In recent years there has been a growing interest in "object
relations theory," especially as applied to borderline and psychotic patients. Sometimes object relations theory is contrasted
with the familiar structural theory, and it is felt by some that
it offers a more useful way to view the development of psychopathology in sicker patients. One of the purposes of this
chapter will be to discuss this complex issue. Our major task in
this section, however, will be to describe and outline the object

relations of our four analyzed borderline cases and to attempt to understand the development of their object relations from early childhood to adult life. We will also contrast and compare our findings with those of Kernberg, whose work on borderline patients emphasizes the importance of psychoanalytic object relations theory.

Various Object Relations Concepts as Applied to Borderline Patients

During the discussions of the Kris Study Group it became apparent that many analysts used different terms and concepts from various object relations theories and applied them to borderline patients. Some analysts, utilizing the developmental framework proposed by Mahler and her co-workers (1975), stressed the idea that borderline patients had failed to adequately progress through the separation-individuation phase. Others emphasized the belief that these patients had not established a clear distinction between their self representations and object representations, viewing this process in the manner described by Edith Jacobson (1964) in *The Self and the Object World*. Those analysts who were especially impressed with the narcissistic features of our patients would talk about their relating to people as "self-objects," using a term introduced by Heinz Kohut (1971) in his work on narcissistic patients, despite the fact that he clearly distinguished them from borderline cases.

There are also those analysts who rely heavily on the work and theories of Melanie Klein (1946). They emphasize that the setting up of internal object relations in the infant's mind begins quite early and leads to specific introjects derived from projective-introjective processes. However, by far the most commonly accepted application of object relations theory to the study of borderline patients by analysts has been derived from the work of Kernberg (1975, 1976). He suggested that these patients suffer from a specific kind of "pathological internalized object relations" derived from the splitting of all-good and all-bad self and object representations.

We will now briefly review the ideas of these various authors and theorists to see in what way their views may be applied to an understanding of borderline pathology.

Mahler's formulation of a gradual phase of separation-individuation, which constitutes a transition from earlier autistic and symbiotic states to a later integrated capacity for object constancy and stable self and object differentiation, has become widely accepted by analysts. Her child observation studies have led her to divide the separation-individuation process into four successive subphases: differentiation, practicing, rapprochement, and consolidation of individuality. Her view is a developmental one and places great emphasis on both the child's innate endowments and the capacity of the mothering figure to respond to the many needs of the infant and toddler. Serious interferences with a mother's ability to respond to her child's needs may lead to impairments in the child's ability to master the phase-specific tasks which are subsumed under the heading of separation-individuation.

More recently Mahler emphasized that a particularly difficult developmental period occurs around eighteen months of age, during the "rapprochement crisis." Because of the interference with the separation-individuation process which may occur at this time, as well as the observations of the arousal of intense ambivalence or "splitting," she has concluded that many of the pathological manifestations of borderline patients may be a regression to, or a fixation at, this period of life (1971). However, in the same paper Mahler was careful to point out that, "My intention, at first was to establish . . . a linking up in neat detail, of the described substantive issues with specific aspects of borderline phenomena shown by child and adult patients in the psychoanalytic situation. But I have come to be more and more convinced that there is no 'direct line' from the deductive use of borderline phenomena to one or another substantive finding of observational research" (*ibid.,* p. 415).

The most concrete use of Mahler's observations as applied to the development of borderline pathology is to be found in the writings of Masterson (1972) and Masterson and Rinsley (1975). These authors proposed that the borderline condition is derived from failures during the process of separation-in-dividuation and, more specifically, from fixations at the rap-prochement phase. They believed that these failures lead to a specific configuration of internal object relations. According to Rinsley (1977, p. 57):

> The object relations unit of the borderline turns out to be split into *four part units,* each comprising a *part-self repre-sentation* and a *part-object representation* together with an as-sociated affect. These two part units represent, respectively, derivatives of the two principal themes of interaction with the borderline mother, that is, the mother's maintenance of her libidinal availability in response to her infant's cling-ing, regressive behavior, and her withdrawal of her libi-dinal availability in the face of the infant's efforts toward separation-individuation [Rinsley's emphases].

Jacobson's work (1954, 1964) stressed the importance of the gradual differentiation of the self- and object-representations. She proposed that we view the infant's early mental images as being in an "undifferentiated" state. At this stage there is no clear differentiation between himself as a separate entity and the outside world. He may not as yet be aware that his own tension states come from his own body or that his gratifications and easing of psychological tension are afforded him by some-one other than himself. Gradually, however, there must be a building up of mental images of the self and the outside world along with sensory perceptions of the self and the other. This later stage, however, is one during which the self-representation and the object-representation are likely to be distorted as a result of projective and introjective mechanisms.

Those analysts who emphasize the importance of introjective and projective mechanisms in the borderline condition refer to fixations at this stage of self-object differentiation proposed by Jacobson. Jacobson was careful to suggest, not that self-object differentiation should be thought of as taking place only during some specified period of a few months of childhood develop-ment, but rather that it occurs gradually over the course of the first three years of life. She did stress that wishes to fuse or merge with the object might persist and result in failure of self-object differentiation. In her paper "Contribution to the Metapsychology of Psychotic Identifications" (1954), she wrote that in states of schizophrenic regression the patient returns to that stage of "undifferentiation" of self- and object-representations whereas patients with psychotic depression regress to a phase where the self- and object-representations, although still differentiated from one another, can easily be introjected and projected, leading to gross distortions in object relations. But whereas Jacobson referred to regressive revivals of this phase of development, Kernberg, who has relied heavily on her concepts, believes that borderlines remain fixated at this stage of unintegrated or "split" self- and object-representations (see below, pp. 96-97).

Jacobson also emphasized that during states of regression in schizophrenics and psychotic depressives, as well as borderlines, there is a breakdown of identifications. The identifications in borderline patients and patients with psychotic depression undergo a regression to that phase of development when "total" or "magical" identifications take place. Imitations, rather than true identifications in the ego, become more prominent. According to Jacobson, this predisposes the borderline patient to identity disturbances, typical examples of which are the "as if" characters described by Helene Deutsch (1942).

Many authors have stressed the narcissistic features of borderline patients and therefore have turned to Kohut's work (1971) in an attempt to better understand their development. Kohut was dissatisfied with what he considered to be Freud's emphasis on the dichotomy between narcissism and object love. He stressed that the child's narcissism need not be altered or channeled only into object love but finds a separate pathway into healthy self-esteem and self-esteem regulatory functions (an idea already partially expressed by Freud in the third chapter of his paper "On Narcissism: An Introduction" [1914]).

Kohut's theories, although referred to as a "psychology of the self," are not usually included under "object relations theory." Yet his ideas do have to do with the development of the self- and object-representations as they are influenced by the parents' empathic responsiveness to the growing child. According to Kohut, parental failures in this capacity interfere with the necessary internalization of self-esteem regulating functions. As a result of these failures of what Kohut called "transmuting internalizations," the patient's self representation is characterized by marked disturbances in the regulation of both self-esteem and states of tension. The development and persistence of the "grandiose self" as well as the "idealized parent imago" represent an effort to deal with this defect. In addition, these failures lead to disturbances in the patient's relationships to objects and, therefore, a distortion of the object representation. People are used primarily to enhance the patient's self-esteem, to help him reduce his states of tension, and to "mirror" or support his notion of his "grandiose self." Kohut called this type of object representation characteristic of the narcissistic patient, the "self-object."

Although, as we have said, Kohut distinguished borderline from narcissistic patients, many analysts have utilized his ideas of failure in parental empathy to understand the development of narcissistic features in borderline patients. Kernberg feels that certain patients with narcissistic personality disorders are actually borderline patients since they meet his other criteria for this diagnosis.

Klein's work (1946, 1948) does not deal directly with borderline patients. Nevertheless, it is relevant to review briefly her ideas here because her conception of the development of "internal object relations" has influenced object relations theory in general and the work of other authors of the British school, as well as that of Kernberg. Klein's concepts of the development of object relations concern the setting up of introjections in the child's mental life during its first six months of existence. Her theoretical postulates are based on the need for the child to deal with the death instinct which threatens its own life. Very early the death instinct must be projected *outward* (or, as she prefers it, into the object) and the object-representation, whether it be a breast or a primitive notion of mother, is experienced as threatening and persecutory. She speculated that the threatening and persecutory breast is then introjected, leading to an image of a "bad internal object." The libidinally available image of mother is also introjected, producing a "good internal object." She maintained that these "introjections" lead to an already established "object relation" at three months of life which she called the paranoid-schizoid position. At this stage the defense mechanisms of splitting, projective identification, primitive idealization, denial, and omnipotence are operative. It is important to note that whereas Kernberg rejected Klein's adherence to the importance of the death instinct, he emphasized that it is precisely these same defense mechanisms which are operative in borderline patients. Although Kernberg did not place their use as early in life as three months of age, he believed that it is because of the persistence of such mechanisms that the child cannot integrate the all-good and all-bad self- and object-representations.

Kernberg (1975, 1976) has written the most comprehensive account of the object relations of the borderline patient. He attempted to integrate the ideas of Klein, Jacobson, Mahler, and some of the authors of the British school, as well as take into account Freud's theories of development and the clarifications in ego psychology brought forth by Hartmann (1939, 1964).

Most recently (1976, p. 59), Kernberg organized his ideas into a:

> general theory of (1) the origin of the basic 'units' (self-image, object-image, affect disposition) of internalized object relations, (2) the development of four basic stages in their differentiation and integration, (3) the relationship between failure in these developments and the crystallization of various types of psychopathology, and (4) the implications of this sequence of phases for general structural developments of the psychic apparatus.

Kernberg stressed that we must arrive at a better integration of drive theory and object relations theory. "Libido and aggression represent the two overall psychic drives which integrate instinctive components and the other building blocks first consolidated in units of internalized object relations" (p. 104). Thus he indicated that the processes dealt with respectively by drive theory and object relations theory should not be contrasted or utilized to conceptualize different forms of pathology but must be thought of as being interrelated with one another in psychic development.

His basic stages in the development of object relations are as follows:

Stage 1: Normal "Autism," or Primary Undifferentiated
            Stage

This phase covers the first month of life and precedes the consolidation of the "good" undifferentiated self-object constellation. Failure or fixation of development at this stage is characteristic of autistic psychosis.

Stage 2: Normal "Symbiosis," or Stage of the Primary Un-
            differentiated Self-Object Representations

This phase extends from the second month of life to about six or eight months of age. There is a relative incompleteness of the differentiation of self- and object-representations from each other and a persisting tendency for defensive regressive refusal of "good" self and object images when severe trauma or frustration determines pathological development. Pathological fixation of, or regression to, stage 2 is characteristic of symbiotic psychosis of childhood, most types of adult schizophrenia, and depressive psychosis.

Stage 3: Differentiation of Self- from Object-Representa-
            tion

This stage begins around the eighth month of life and reaches completion between the eighteenth and the thirty-sixth month. It ends with the eventual integration of "good" and "bad" self-representations into an integrated self concept, and the integration of "good" and "bad" representations into "total" object representations. Failures in development during this stage lead to the development of the borderline personality organization. During this stage an early constellation of defenses is brought into operation, centering on splitting or primitive dissociation and fostering the other early defenses of denial, primitive idealization, projective identification, omnipotence, and devaluation.

Stage 4: Integration of Self-Representations and Object-Representations and Development of Higher Level Intrapsychic Object Relations-Derived Structures

This stage begins in the latter part of the third year of life and lasts through the entire oedipal period. The typical psychopathology of this stage is represented by the neuroses and "higher level" character pathology. Repression becomes the main defensive operation of the ego.

Stage 5: Consolidation of Superego and Ego Integration

This is an advanced stage of development with the gradual evolution of ego identity.

There are a number of points which should be emphasized about these stages of development. In addition to the relationship of his views to the work of Mahler and Jacobson, Kernberg adhered to the general idea that the earlier in life trauma or impaired care-taking occurs, the more serious will be the psychopathology which is developed. For example, "Pathological fixation of or regression to stage 2 of development of internalized object relations is clinically characterized by the failure in—or loss of—the differentiation of ego boundaries, which is characteristic of symbiotic psychosis of childhood, most types of adult schizophrenia, and depressive psychoses" (p. 60).

It is also important to note that Kernberg specifically attributed the development of borderline pathology to *failures in development* in stage 3, which begins around the eighth month of life and reaches completion between the eighteenth and the thirty-sixth month. In his earlier writings (1966, 1967) he seemed to indicate that borderline pathology is related to failure occurring prior to the eighteenth month of life, when mechanisms of splitting are operative.

Kernberg believes that schizophrenics either regress to, or are fixated at, the stage of merging of self- and object-representations, whereas borderline patients do not regress to this stage but maintain unintegrated or "split" self and object representations. According to him, it is this lack of integration which leads to "identity diffusion" and causes chronic pathology of what he calls "internalized object relations." He believes that the borderline's object relations always bear the stamp of this early developmental failure. As a result of the arousal of excessive aggression early in life or of an excessive innate aggressive drive, the child who later becomes a borderline is permanently unable to integrate realistic conceptions of the self and the object. Therefore the patient frequently sees people as all-good or all-bad or may see himself in this way. Kernberg postulated that such "splitting" occurs early in mental life as a consequence of the immaturity of the mental apparatus, i.e., the inability to integrate cognitively the many characteristics of the object and the self. Later, however, in order to preserve the integrity of the "ego core," this split is maintained for defensive purposes and remains as a fixed part of the borderline's concept of himself and others. There is a lack of integration of the various aspects of the self-representation and a corresponding lack of integration of the aspects of the object-representation. The defense of splitting involves the use of other primitive defenses such as projective identification, primitive idealization, denial, and omnipotence. Object relations are consequently distorted by these defenses, and these distortions persist into adult life.

We cannot, of course, review all of the authors who have contributed to an understanding of object relations theory or those who have specifically applied their formulations to borderline patients. To do so would involve an entire monograph in itself. For example, there is Winnicott's conception of the "false self" and the "true self" (1965) as well as the work of Masterson and Rinsley discussed above. We have tried to include, if only briefly, those authors whose ideas came up most frequently in the Kris Study Group. However, there was another psychoanalyst whose views on object relations played a central role in our thinking about borderlines, and that was Freud himself. A brief survey of his contribution is in order now not only because we feel he had important things to say about object relations but because our conclusions about our patients were very much derived from Freud's concepts as well as from those of the psychoanalysts who elaborated upon and extended them.

Freud's Views on Object Relations

It is of some interest that Freud's conception of object relations and structuralization is often not cited in the current literature on object relations theory. Jacobson, of course, followed him, and Kernberg included this aspect of Freud's work in his historical overview of object relations theory (1976). But for many it is as though object relations theory applies only to the very early months of the child's life and concerns itself only with the earliest introjections. For others, it appears that object relations theory applies only to prestructural and certainly preoedipal phases of development. It is often overlooked that the entire *Indeed* structural model is very much based on object relations.

It is true that Freud did not specifically write about "object relations" and did not designate part of his work as an "object relations theory" of development. Nevertheless, many of his works dealt with precisely these areas of psychic life.

In his papers, "Three Essays on the Theory of Sexuality" (1905) and "Instincts and Their Vicissitudes" (1915b), Freud was developing his fundamental concepts of drive theory, as well as the unfolding and maturational sequence of the libidinal drive. However, at no time (and this is reflected in all of his writings, including the case histories) did he lose sight of the important role of the object toward whom the drive is directed in influencing the development of these very same drives. Deflections in the aims of the drives, as well as displacements of the drive onto other objects, are the result of the complex interaction between the child and his parents with all of its attendant gratifications, frustrations, disappointments, fears, and demands of reality.

The immature child will cathect his early objects in terms of oral wishes and fantasies since this is one of the primary modes of interaction at that time. This is not to say that the presence of oral fantasies, in and of themselves, is indicative of primitive or archaic modes of ego functioning since such fantasies obviously persist throughout development and into adulthood, as is evident in wishes, behavior, language, and dream life.

The anal phase of development is characterized not only by the predominance of libidinal and aggressive fantasies derived from the pressure of these drives and their derivative mental representations, but by the interaction with the object toward whom the drive is directed. Issues of power, compliance, withholding, and the beginning sense of autonomy are important elements of this phase.

During the phallic and oedipal phases the vicissitudes of the sexual and aggressive drives are influenced again by the nature of the child's experience with his parents. It is this phase of development, the oedipal, that Freud believed to be the crucial one for the development of the personality and for neurosogenesis.

It is perhaps his understanding of the resolution of the oedipal complex that enabled Freud to conceptualize the structural model presented in *The Ego and the Id* (1923). This might be considered to be Freud's most explicitly stated "object relations theory." The identifications which occur during and after the oedipal phase are lasting ones which result in traits of character and the building up of stable self-representations. The idea that traits of character are, then, "precipitates of object cathexes" is already an important statement of object relations theory. During this time, the introjections which occur also lead to significant structuralization of the psychic life.

It was in this same book that Freud most clearly wrote about the development of the superego. The superego itself is seen as the "heir to the Oedipus complex." This structure, based as it is on introjections of parental values as well as upon the degree to which sexual and aggressive drives must be neutralized, is an outcome of the "object relations" of the child. We emphasize this once again because it so often appears that the concept of introjection is limited to the very early months of life in many of the articles which deal with object relations theory.

Even before the publication of *The Ego and the Id,* Freud wrote a profound paper that also deals with object relations. In "Mourning and Melancholia" (1917b), Freud was trying to relate the normal state of mourning to the pathological state of severe depression. He stated that the subject in mourning or depression often views himself in the same critical way as he had previously viewed the lost love object. Rather than behaving like the lost object by taking on his characteristics, the subject views himself as having the same negative traits as the object even if this is not truly the case. Although this process is sometimes not explicitly related to "object relations" theory, it surely should be, because what is described are perceptions of the self which actually refer to traits of another person. Whether one calls the process incorporation, introjection, internalization, or identification is still a matter of controversy and definition; but the clinical phenomenon is clear enough. Loss of an object is often followed by an identification or a self-perception that one is like the object. In the case of mourning, Freud postulated that it represents an effort to preserve the attachment to the object; in the case of melancholia, where the self-perception concerns critical or bad traits, it is an effort to deal with the hostility toward the object—a matter of ambivalence and guilt.

We feel it is also important to add that Freud introduced another kind of "object relations" theory in the Schreber case (1911a) and in the paper "On Narcissism: An Introduction" (1914). He outlined a developmental progression of libidinal cathexis beginning with the state of autoerotism, proceeding to a state of narcissism and only then going on to that of object love. The main point of this sequence is that there is a gradual shift in the investment of libidinal cathexis from the self-representation to the object-representation. As mentioned in Chapter 1, Freud utilized this concept to compare the schizophrenic's regression to an archaic narcissistic state with a stage of normal narcissism in infancy. This developmental scheme, then, is another form of "object relations" theory which proposes a progression from an overcathexis of the self (narcissism, the regression in the schizophrenic) to a valuing of, and interest in, the object (as in loving, caring, and consideration of the other). Freud was fond of describing the state of falling in love as an example of total depletion of narcissistic libido and a total overvaluation of the object. In doing so he acknowledged that both states, i.e., total overvaluation of the self and total overvaluation of the other can be examples of serious disturbances in object relations and that some proper balance must exist between the libidinal investments of the self-representations and of the object-representations.

It is not exactly clear how Freud distinguished between the state of autoerotism and that of primary narcissism. In the Schreber case he stated that in paranoia there is a regression to narcissism whereas in schizophrenia there is a further regression to autoerotism. Later, he was to say that schizophrenia is a return to the objectless state of narcissism. He was groping with the idea that very early in mental life there is no clear distinction between the self- and object-representation (just as it was difficult to distinguish what was inside and what was outside). We would understand his formulations to refer to what we today call, following Hartmann (1964), the undifferentiated stage. Only gradually is there a clear distinction in the child's mind between the self and the other, and the first object of libidinal cathexis is the self or the child's own body. Early in life, the mother or her body parts (as well as the child's own body parts) upon which the drive may be satisfied may be conceived of as representing the total object.

When some analysts talk about borderline patients viewing objects only as " part objects"—for example, only as a satisfying breast—they are trying to describe something about the urgency of the drive and the indiscriminate nature of the persons who can serve as gratifiers of the drive. They are pointing to the

persistence of infantile traits which usually are related to fixations and regressions to earlier modes of relating as well as to
inadequate distinctions between the self- and object-representations.

It is not difficult to see, when viewed from an object relations
point of view, that another aspect of this libidinal sequence of
cathectic investments described by Freud is the change from
the object being seen and experienced only as need satisfying
to the object being seen in a more discriminating way—which
Hartmann has called the "constant object" or the "whole object."
The sequence of developmental progressions from undifferentiation of self and object to need-satisfying object to constant
object was elaborated upon by Jacobson (1964) and Mahler et
al. (1975) and applied to aspects of the psychopathology of
borderline cases. Similarly, the sequence of the gradual distinction between self- and object-representations and the specific failures of this developmental process in borderlines was
studied by Kernberg (1975).

We will conclude this brief summary of Freud's contributions
to "object relations theory" by emphasizing that at least two of
our major conclusions about the object relations of borderline
patients are derived from our understanding of Freud's concepts. One of these findings is that our patients made profound
identifications with their very disturbed parents, leading to
pathological character traits, thought processes, and symptom
formation. The second is that *oedipal conflicts* played an important role in the development of the object relations of our patients. Their concepts of themselves and others as well as the
nature of their superegos were profoundly influenced by the
failure to resolve these oedipal issues in a satisfactory way. We
are not contrasting these two conclusions with those which emphasize the importance of preoedipal factors in development.
Freud himself made it clear, later in his career, that he understood that preoedipal developments cast their stamp on the
oedipal period, and that they may leave a permanent record
of their influence on character, object relations, and symptom
formation. Nevertheless, we believe that oedipal phase conflict
is often neglected or minimized in the literature which deals
with the development of borderline psychopathology.

Some General Considerations

First, we would like to stress that these brief reviews of the
literature should make clear to the reader that object relations
theory should not be contrasted to structural theory as though
they were separate, or as if the latter refers only to oedipal
phase development whereas the former concerns pregenital
phases. Of course it is understood that structuralization of id,
ego, and superego is a gradual process and that very early in
mental life one cannot speak of a clear distinction between self-
and object-representations. Identifications do not refer *only* to
those which occur at the resolution of the oedipal phase. There
are early identifications which can be considered to be introjections that promote psychic structure. As Beres pointed out
(1956), "Freud (1921) described identification 'as the earliest
expression of an emotional tie with another person' (p. 60) and
in 1923 he speaks of 'a direct and immediate identification
[which] takes place earlier than any object cathexis' (p. 39)." In
evaluating the type of object relations which characterize the
borderline patient, we would emphasize that whereas important
introjections and identifications take place quite early, equally
important and relevant ones contribute to structure formation
and personality development later in childhood as well.

Another major issue we would like to take up is how we derive
our understanding of the mental life of the child from the study
of normal and pathological adult life, and, correspondingly,
how our conceptions of early mental life, some of which are
derived from childhood observation studies, influence our understanding of adult psychopathology. It was one of Freud's
great achievements that he derived his concepts of infantile
psychosexual development from the analysis of neuroses in
adults. He was able to reconstruct not only the mental life of
the three- to five-year-old oedipal child but also the earlier oral
and anal phases of development. He utilized these ideas to stress
maturational sequences in libidinal development, object relations, reality testing, and structuralization. When he turned his
attention to the psychoses, he reconstructed an early narcissistic
phase of development from the symptoms of megalomania,

hypochondriasis, and end-of-the-world fantasies (1911a). That is to say, he utilized the observations he was able to make on the regressive states of psychoses to reconstruct the child's mental development.

In 1954 (p. 1), Bak, addressing himself to the psychopathology of schizophrenia, wrote,

> The methodological pitfalls of reconstructing biological phases of maturation through extrapolation from adult pathological phenomena into a genetic frame are well known. It is our basic approach that in pathology we deal with regressive phenomena, but we should certainly keep in mind that owing to the complexity of the disease process which affects the ego and its functions to a varying degree and only in parts, the genetic aspect can only be observed together with the alterations of the above mentioned structures. We refer especially to the relative integrity of some autonomous ego functions (Hartmann), the varying degrees of integrity of perception, and of the super-ego, which while undergoing regression *necessarily bring about an entirely different picture from the one we may hypothesize in early infancy when these functions and structures have not yet come into existence* [italics added].

Despite this warning, Bak himself, throughout this paper and later (1971) utilized the regressive state of schizophrenics to add to our conceptualizations of primary narcissism, the undifferentiated phase, early object relations, and the laying down of self- and object-representations in infancy. This is in the best tradition of psychoanalytic theorizing and has been followed by many authors, including Hartmann, Jacobson, Mahler, and Kernberg.

As we have mentioned, Jacobson (1954) distinguished the regression in acute schizophrenic episodes from those of acute psychotic depression on the basis of the degree of self-object differentiation. Bak (1971) did the same in contrasting the regression of the schizophrenic to that which takes place in the severe perversions. Now we have the same process of theory building taking place regarding borderline patients. From a study of the manifestations of the adult psychopathology in borderlines, various authors are not only deducing the fixation points of these disorders but are attempting to add to our understanding of the mental life of the child. Just as Freud was able to derive an understanding of the anal phase of development from the character traits, symptoms, and fantasies of obsessional patients, current theorists are describing the development of early object relations from the study of the psychopathology of adult borderline patients. In addition, there is the hope that the results of observation studies of infants and toddlers which are done with an "analytic eye" (Mahler) will dovetail with the conclusions drawn from adult patients.

Nevertheless, we believe it *is* important to mention Bak's warning that we cannot equate or establish an identity between various states of regression and a corresponding time period in childhood to which these regressive states refer. Melanie Klein, studying psychotic and neurotic children, maintained that the child at three months of life has a full range of fantasies leading to complex introjections—the paranoid-schizoid position. Masterson and Rinsley, studying the behavior of borderline adolescents and their families, noted the frequent difficulty these young people have in separating from their mothers and the attitudes that their mothers display which rewards clinging dependent behavior and punishes or withholds love for autonomous, independent strivings. They then surmise from these manifestations that exactly the same problem existed during the separation-individuation phase, leading to the fixation of the patients' object relations which they describe. But they seem to disregard the fact that these could not possibly be the only problems of borderline patients, nor do they address themselves to the likelihood that those difficulties which may have occurred early in development inevitably affect subsequent development and may well lead to even more intense oedipal-phase conflict.

Kernberg's work impressed us as much more comprehensive, detailed, and thorough and takes into account, as does Jacobson's, the entire sequence of drive and object relations development as well as the development of the ego. Nevertheless, he too, as can be seen in his section on the stages in the development of object relations (1976, p.59), followed a similar approach. Specifically, pathological fixation of, or regression to, stage 2 (two to eight months of life) is characteristic of symbiotic psychosis of childhood, most types of adult schizophrenia, and depressive psychosis. Failures in development during stage 3 (eight months to thirty six months of life) lead to the development of borderline personality organization.

It was our conclusion, based on a detailed study of the analyses of our four cases, that we could not specify that the crucial etiological determinants for the development of all borderline patients took place between the ages of eight months to eighteen months. (See below, chapter 8.) Specifically, we could not say that the object relations of our cases directly represented the outcome of fixations at, or regressions to, this period of life. Indeed, we were impressed with the degree to which the pathologic features of the object relations were *also* derived from later stages in development. We also felt that the borderline group of patients represented such a heterogeneous category that to point to a specific fixation point in all of these types of cases was not possible.

We now examine in detail the object relations of our cases and hope that these reviews and comments will be helpful when considering our conclusions.

The Object Relations of Our Borderline Patients

Our own conclusions about the object relations of borderline patients are based primarily upon the observations of the Kris Study Group in regard to the four analyzed cases. However, we also drew upon our own and the group's experience with other borderline cases as well. Our major conclusions are in general agreement with those of other workers. Some of them have been given too little emphasis in the literature. Our main points are the following:

1. Oedipal-phase conflicts played an important role in the disturbance of the object relations of our patients.

2. Identifications with very disturbed parents played a prominent role in personality development and object relations.

3. There was a marked persistence of sadomasochistic wishes and their associated conflicts, which were derived from every phase of psychosexual development. These strongly influenced the nature of our patients' relationships to others and their concepts of themselves.

4. These patients show a greater degree of fluidity of ego boundaries, i.e., less stable differentiation of the self- and object-representations than is found in neurotic patients.

5. These patients displayed marked narcissistic features which pervaded their relationships to others.

6. Severe reactions to separations and loss, as distinguished from problems in self-object differentiation, were prominent.

7. Superego conflicts were severe. The structure of the patients' superegos was of course influenced by their object relations, and as development continued, their superego functions played an important role in determining subsequent relations to others.

Although these conclusions will be discussed separately, they are all interrelated and influence one another.

1. The Role of Oedipal Conflicts

All of our patients showed evidence of severe oedipal problems. It is therefore not accurate to view borderline patients as suffering primarily from pregenital conflicts. Rather it is important to try to understand how the pregenital conflicts influenced the oedipal phase. This is of course true for neurotic patients as well, but we were impressed by the profound degree of disturbance in the resolution of oedipal conflicts in our borderline patients. These observations seem to be neglected in the current literature on borderlines, especially in the work of Masterson and Rinsley, and to an important degree in Kernberg's writings as well. Kernberg stated that borderlines show a premature entrance into the oedipal phase, apparently in an effort to master the problems caused by splitting and the resultant ego weakness. It was not possible for us to demonstrate from our analyses that our patients experienced typical phallic conflicts before the age of two or three. What was clear, however, was that the sexual conflicts were pervaded by conflicts from earlier levels of psychosexual development.

The persistence of severe oedipal triangular conflicts with marked frustration, jealousy, and sadomasochistic interactions is characteristic of borderline patients. These conflicts are undoubtedly influenced by pregenital disturbances in the same way as a little girl's oedipal relationship to her father bears the stamp of her earlier relationship to her mother. However, in some of our cases, trauma during the oedipal phase itself seriously interfered not only with the resolution of the Oedipus complex and the formation of the superego, but with the nature of subsequent object relations. These phallic phase traumas will lead to regressions which may or may not rest on profound pregenital disturbances.

For example, in Case II, the patient's mother gave birth to a little girl who died a few hours later. This event, occurring between the patient's fourth and fifth birthdays, was not only a trauma itself but led to a marked depression in his mother with profound effects on the patient. His attempt to cope with his mother's withdrawal led to an obligatory masturbatory fantasy of a woman *wanting him* to change into a little girl, i.e., the little sister for whom the mother was grieving. Although this was not the only motivating factor for this fantasy, it was an extremely important one. It influenced his sexual life, his fantasies of being feminine, and played an exceedingly important role in his perception of women. He constantly saw them as trying to seduce and entrap him, no matter what their actual intentions were.

In Case I, the patient's father repeatedly abandoned the family. Her relationships with men were, to a considerable degree, influenced by the fear of abandonment and by fantasies concerning the reasons for it, e.g., that she was not the male child she imagined her father wanted. During her first session the patient actually believed the analyst looked like her father, so strong was the wish to reunite with him. After two-and-a-half years of analysis a stalemate seemed to have occurred, but the patient requested another chance to continue, whereupon she confessed her masturbatory practices and fantasies and revealed her secret bulimia and vomiting. The latter turned out to be related to oral impregnation fantasies and desires to gain a penis through incorporation.

Case III had overtly oedipal dreams during the course of analysis. She dreamed that her mother had died and that mother's spirit returned and asked her to sleep with father. She manifested intense transference oedipal longings and corresponding feelings of hatred and jealousy toward her rivals. The negative oedipal constellation was also important. She had a number of homosexual fantasies and longings to get father out of the house in order to be alone with mother.

Case IV also demonstrated intense romantic wishes to be with her father, who had left her when she was four-and-a-half or five years old. She was extremely jealous of her two younger brothers, and many of her hypochondriacal symptoms were traced to oedipal pregnancy fantasies. She recalled in the analysis her sexual excitement when father pulled her deciduous teeth. The transference was intensely erotic and romantic, and she felt terribly jilted when she once called the analyst's home and a woman answered. She said she thought she was the only woman in the analyst's life.

2. Identifications

We found that all of our patients had made strong identifications with their disturbed parents. These identifications frequently served a defensive function, as in identification with the aggressor, but it is apparent that identifications with parents are involved in many aspects of personality development which do not serve primarily defensive functions.

We were most impressed with identifications with certain sadistic aspects of the parents' behavior. Case III was a typical example of this. She identified with her almost-psychotic father in his sadistic torment and abuse of her and treated her analyst in the same way. It was also true that she frequently saw the analyst himself as the crazy, sadistic father while she was the helpless victim. This identification with her father, which included her accepting some of his "crazy" ideas, was not necessarily one formed very early in life. Much of this behavior of her father became apparent to her during the oedipal phase and continued well into her adolescence, when he examined her and humiliated her.

Case IV would tease, torment, and torture her analyst much the same way as her father had treated her mother. In thus identifying herself with her father and behaving like him, she was identifying with the aggressor. Simultaneously she identified with her mother in her deep-rooted conviction that she was dumb and stupid and that she was being dominated by her analyst. It is clear that identifications with both parents were important factors in her character development.

In Case II, the patient had a strong identification with his father, whom he perceived as a cruel man who would criticize and humiliate him. His fantasies that he was like his father and that he would humiliate and criticize other men were mainly repressed and projected. He had to struggle a great deal to keep them in control.

We could not confirm the idea that identifications seen in borderlines are necessarily of a "primitive" or magical kind; nor would we say that they undergo the kind of regression postulated by Jacobson. We felt that identifications were fantasies that one is like another person. The patient's actual behavior, thoughts, and feelings might or might not correspond to that of the parents. We found many reasons for the presence of these fantasies and behavior. They served both libidinal and aggressive needs, were involved in defensive functions, or played a role in superego and character development.

We did not find it easy to distinguish the type of identification seen in our patients from those formed in neurotic patients. What was most obvious was that at times our patients acted toward the analyst and others in the same way as their disturbed parents had behaved toward them.

3. Sadomasochistic Conflicts

Our four cases exhibited many sadomasochistic features, both in their fantasy lives as well as in their behavior. Their sexual lives and their relationships in general were permeated with aggression—either directed outward, or toward the self, or both. Since they so often dealt with their aggression by projection, they frequently feared objects and tended to use more massive or rigid defenses against these fears and the impulses which generated them. The presence of severe sadomasochistic conflicts were associated with derivatives of anal-phase conflict. We were impressed with the presence of severe ambivalence, rigid reaction formations, and magical thinking. We felt that "primitive idealization" and devaluation (defenses emphasized by Kernberg) were related to the intensity of the ambivalence. Although it was certainly true that intense ambivalence toward objects would sometimes result in their viewing some people as all-good or all-bad (currently defined as splitting by Kernberg and others), we did not find this feature to be present in *all* of our cases. Case III showed the most marked ambivalence and often showed the characteristic vacillation of good and bad self- and object-representations described by Kernberg. As we have noted, she would for periods of time see her analyst as a bad, sadistic tormentor and herself as the innocent victim. This perception could suddenly shift, even within a session, and she, herself, would feel like the torturing sadist. Her analyst always tried to understand and interpret to her what had happened to cause this shift, i.e., what was happening in her mind to change the dynamic interaction between wish and defense. Our other patients who were borderline did not necessarily exhibit this vacillation although their ambivalence was quite marked.

The sadomasochistic features which permeated their lives often specifically found their most marked expression in their sexual behavior. Fantasies or fears of being devoured, enslaved, or utterly controlled were encountered frequently. This caused them to have great anxiety about their sexual lives, whether they feared that they would be hurt or that they would hurt their partners, or both. Castration fears and fantasies in both sexes were therefore heightened, often leading to strong inhibitions or perverse acting out.

Case IV constantly provoked her analyst to attack her. As an adult she became sexually excited at the idea of her father pulling her teeth. She recalled the sexual excitement she felt when he would get angry and yell at her while she was doing her homework. In the course of the analysis she provoked a psychotic boyfriend to rape her.

Case II constantly believed his analyst wanted to humiliate him and had a dream that he was lying on the couch and his analyst was masturbating him. In the dream he thought "So *this* is why he is treating me." He always looked for an ulterior motive in his analyst which would confirm for him his belief that he was being taken advantage of. His main belief, that women would ensnare and entrap him, was also in part derived from sadomasochistic fantasies.

As Case I progressed, she began to have and to reveal frankly masochistic fantasies. Her masochistic daydreaming mainly took the following form: "If I suffer greatly and remain patient and uncomplaining, I will eventually be rewarded." Beating fantasies emerged and in the fourth year of analysis she remembered a traumatic tonsillectomy performed when she was four which became interwoven with castration and primal scene themes.

Sadomasochistic struggles could be played out not only with another person but within the patient's own personality, with one of the "parties" taking on the attitude of a cruel sadistic parent while the other was a cowering, helpless child. Sometimes physical illness or somatic pain was interpreted in this way, as though the patient were being tortured—often as a punishment for voracious appetites or uncontrollable impulses.

4. Self Object Differentiation

Turning to the issue of self object differentiation, we can say that we did not observe the severe, gross psychotic distortions that one sees in schizophrenic regression. Our patients did not experience conscious, panic-laden feelings of confusion between themselves and the outer world. However, insofar as projection was a very prominent defense mechanism, they often distorted their perceptions about themselves and others. At times they believed they were capable of great empathy, but in reality, what they imagined other people were feeling was derived primarily from projections of their own feelings.

It is often emphasized that borderline patients primarily project aggressive drive derivatives on to others. M. Klein stressed this in relation to the schizoid-paranoid position. Kernberg also stressed that splitting is a defense primarily used to protect the ego because of the preponderance of aggressive conflicts. We certainly found that projection of aggression onto others and the consequent fear of objects was very prominent in our patients. However, we also found that many other impulses were projected that also led to distortions in object relations. Frequently encountered examples of such other impulses were envy, greed (oral appetites), homosexual impulses, and other sexual needs as well. Impulses to control and enslave others were also projected, as were harsh superego attitudes.

The intensity, fixity, and pervasiveness of projection went along with, or was a corollary of, a failure to differentiate clearly between the self and the object. However, this was not a global manifestation. Sometimes it occurred mainly in one area where a particular set of wishes and fears were very prominent. Case II was not always aware of his intense competitive strivings and their connection to his relationship with his father and brother. He was aware, for example, that whenever he drove in a car, he was annoyed when anyone passed him, but he was not conscious of wanting to win out over and humiliate other men. He often feared that other men wanted to do this to *him*, but it took a long time to understand his own competitive and, at times, sadistic wishes to humiliate, trample over, and destroy other men.

Case III frequently felt her analyst was in a rage with her. At those times she was completely unaware of her own rage. She frequently made mistakes in social situations because she believed that other people's feelings were her own or vice versa. Case IV also showed intense projection in the transference, and at moments she would not know who was the sadist and who was the masochist.

Despite our finding of these problems of poor self object differentiation in certain areas of our patients' lives, we were reluctant to attribute them to *specific* fixation points of childhood development. Whether one utilizes the ideas derived from Mahler's work or those of Jacobson and Kernberg, it appears to us to be difficult to be precise about the etiology of disturbances of these kinds (see Chapter 8). We presume, however, that severe conflicts during the first few years of childhood *must* affect self and object differentiation, but we believe that this developmental process continues throughout childhood and may be affected by events or interactions which occur later in development as well.

5. Narcissistic Features

We were all struck by the profound degree of narcissism in our patients. That is to say, they were more than usually concerned with gratifying their own needs rather than relating to other people in a more mutual, give and take, manner. As a matter of fact, it was difficult for them to conceive of relationships as being mutually satisfying. More often, they feared that another person would take advantage of them. For example, Case II believed that his analyst wanted him to submit and give in so that the analyst could derive satisfaction, usually of a sadistic nature. Case III saw her analyst as selfish and using her for his own purposes. She would react to anything the analyst did or said as a narcissistic slight to her. She also quite consciously felt he should only be doing things for *her*. She would frequently call her friends on the phone and speak endlessly about her own problems with no conscious sense that she was taking up their time. We understood these feelings as projections of the patients' own wishes in the transference.

The patients often demanded or unconsciously expected that the analyst and others would gratify their libidinal desires in the most concrete way. Words and interpretations were clearly not sufficient—real gratification was what was wanted. Case I wanted to rent an apartment in the building where her analyst was located and later insisted he actually find a man for her to marry. Case IV demanded that her analyst drink a toast with the bottle of champagne she had brought to her hour on New Year's Eve.

However, people in their lives were used not only for libidinal gratification but often for self-esteem regulation. These patients needed to be approved of, praised, and admired to a greater degree than the neurotic patient, who, of course, has such wishes as well. Often our patients would react to frustrations on unwelcome interpretations with such great hurt and disappointment that analytic work seemed doomed to failure. Narcissistic withdrawal or outbursts of rage were not uncommon. Interpretations were likely to be experienced as criticisms, wishes on the part of the therapist to hurt or humiliate them or to have power over them, or both. Consequently they made people (including the analysts) feel that they had to be careful not to hurt them. These patients could only tolerate people behaving as they wished them to do. Thus, they exercised a certain degree of control over everyone.

We felt that each and every psychosexual phase exhibits not only libidinal and aggressive satisfactions, disappointments, and frustrations, but also narcissistic hurts and wounds. In contrast to Kohut, we did not find it helpful to view narcissistic problems as necessarily involving failures of parental empathy or to consider narcissism as having a separate line of development from object-related libidinal and aggressive maturation. These are inextricably intertwined and we felt that the consequences of instinctual *conflict* are involved in producing narcissistic personalities. Often we found that narcissistic traits were attempted *solutions* to conflicts rather than separate from and unrelated to instinctual conflict. We found ourselves, then, in closer agreement to Kernberg than to Kohut about these issues, and we would stress the apparent overlooking of conflicts over aggression as a limitation of Kohut's approach.

6. Separation Problems

Most borderline patients show, especially in the transference, severe problems concerning separation. Our patients were no exception to this. In the histories of our patients there seemed to be a great deal of actual object loss in childhood. We do not believe, however, that actual object loss or separations are necessary to produce profound fears of separation. Mahler (1975) made it clear that the nature of the day-to-day interaction between child and caretaker may be more important than actual separation experiences in determining such reactions.

We would stress that separation fears in and of themselves are not necessarily related to early trauma or defective early mothering. Fears of loss of the object and loss of object love are also very prominent during the later, oedipal phases of development. Sometimes it is difficult to distinguish, when these patients are in analysis, the oedipal from the oral and anal roots of separation fears.

Case I would frequently react to separations from her analyst by not talking to him before and after these intervals. She would also frequently console herself during separations by eating sweets. These represented to her both oral longings and secret sexual satisfactions in his absence. Case III acted out in a more dramatic way. She would call the analyst many times in the face of separation and demand that he speak with her. She would be enraged and furious, come late for her sessions, and then blame the analyst for her state of distress. Case IV moved to an apartment near her analyst so that she could be close to him without feeling there was any need to explore this behavior. She also believed that he would not go on vacation and leave her. She frequently threw herself into an affair immediately after the analyst went on vacation. Frequently these patients unconsciously experienced separations as punishments for not being good, which sometimes paralleled their actual experience in childhood.

7. Superego Conflicts

We found in reviewing the literature that superego conflicts seem to be neglected in discussions of the object relations of borderline patients. If one follows our review of Freud's thoughts about structuralization, it seems obvious that borderlines would have marked superego difficulties. However, Kernberg seemed to stress that borderlines do not experience guilt in the same way as the neurotic patient, citing the fact that the fixations in their "pathological internalized object relations" occur prior to the development of the superego as a solid structure. To be sure, we tried to distinguish between conscious feelings of "internalized" guilt and those of fear of bodily damage or persecution. This distinction, so often cited even in regard to neurotics, is not an easy one to make.

We were impressed with the importance of guilt conflicts and the defenses used in relation to these conflicts in our borderline patients. Some of these patients, when they were unconsciously feeling that they had taken too much from the analyst, i.e., when they feared he could not tolerate their greedy, draining demands, would attack the analyst to try to make him feel guilty. Actually, it was the patient who was feeling guilty about what he was getting or what he had stolen from the analyst. These ideas would sometimes be expressed in a more regressive form, with feelings of guilt being experienced as fears of being hurt or punished.

These patients' superego conflicts pervaded their object relations. Their severe guilt feelings led to inhibitions and frequent depressive episodes. Case III was so guilty about her first sexual experience that she hallucinated a telephone ringing, rushed to a window, and imagined that her father was outside the building. She also had the feeling that her teeth were rotting whenever she had sexual fantasies. This idea was derived from the feeling that she ought to be punished for her oral castrative wishes. Case IV had active prostitution fantasies in which she would get punished by being humiliated for her sexual desires. Her hypochondriacal fantasies were in part rooted in guilt feelings over her oral pregnancy wishes as well as wishes to orally castrate her partner. The more she could acknowledge her oedipal pregnancy fantasies, the less she imagined she had cancer, leukemia, or infections. These "fears" were anticipations of punishment as well as self-punishments. Case II began to fail in medical school when his father left him alone with his mother at the time of their separation. He was thus punishing himself for the gratification of his life-long wish to have his mother for himself. Toward the end of his analysis he delayed going into private practice out of a sense of guilt over achieving his cherished goal. He had the fantasy that if he finally became a doctor in practice, it would lead to his father's death or his castration.

Conclusion

We have found ourselves in agreement with many authors who have described the object relations of borderline patients. We were more cautious than many, however, in attributing the development of these disturbed object relations to a specific pregenital phase of development. We have made note of the difficulties involved in deducing the early developmental processes in the child from regressive states or from psychopathology, although we acknowledge the importance and validity of this approach.

Although we have learned a good deal from the study of object relations as elucidated by Mahler, Jacobson, Kohut, Klein, and Kernberg, we also wanted to emphasize the relevance of Freud's contributions to object relations theory. In accordance with his views we wish to stress some findings that seem to be relatively neglected in the literature about borderline patients. These have to do with the importance of oedipal conflicts in determining the nature of the subsequent object relations, and the influence of identifications with disturbed parents in the development of the borderline personality. In addition, we found these patients to exhibit profound sadomasochistic conflicts, poor differentiation between self- and object-representations, significant narcissistic features, marked separation problems, and prominent superego conflicts.

5.

Reality Testing

In the course of the clinical discussions about each of our study cases, various members of the Kris Study Group would point to evidence of faulty reality testing in respect to certain aspects of these patients' behavior or judgment, within as well as outside of the analytic situation. At first no special effort was made to define what was meant by the term; it was apparently assumed that this familiar clinical observation was understood by all colleagues without a more precise delimitation of what it was intended to convey. However, we gradually became aware that it was being applied to different kinds of data. Sometimes it was how the patient acted in life situations being described in analytic sessions; sometimes it might be behavior in the sessions themselves; at still other times it referred instead to the analysts' views of their patients' reported thoughts, judgments, perceptions, or interpretations of themselves, their analysts or other people and situations they had encountered. Furthermore, the degree of failure or defect in reality testing was seen to be quite variable, as was its tendency to persist or recur. We came to realize that our implicit assumption that reality testing is describable simply as either impaired or intact was quite inadequate. The actual situation is more complicated; gradations exist, and the circumstances and conditions in which impaired reality testing makes its appearance vary from patient to patient. An attempt was made to study what factors influenced this complex and unstable function. Before describing what we observed and concluded, it will be helpful to review briefly some of the background of this difficult clinical concept.

Freud's Theory of Reality Testing

Freud's early ideas about reality testing are implied in Chapter VII of *The Interpretation of Dreams* (1900) in the outline of his theoretical schema of the early development of the mental apparatus. He wrote that hallucinatory wish fulfillment is not able to bring about stable satisfaction of instinctual needs, and what he called the "roundabout path" of seeking a more gratifying "perceptual identity" from the outside world, rather than from within, gradually develops as the infant's experience and capacity permit. Only in a footnote added in the 1919 edition does he make explicit that *reality testing*, a way of deciding whether things are real or not, is essential to this development. It is quite clear that this addition filled in what Freud had already assumed; what he now called reality testing referred to the distinguishing of a perception of the external world from an inner, hallucinatory wishful image.

He first introduced the term "reality testing" in his paper, "Formulations on the Two Principles of Mental Functioning" (1911b). He referred back to his earlier exposition and added a description of the "secondary process" which emphasized what is real. In a key passage he then stated, "A new principle of mental functioning was thus introduced; what was presented in the mind was no longer what was agreeable, but what was real, even if it happened to be disagreeable" (p. 219). The operation of the reality principle gradually encroaches upon the previous hegemony of the (newly renamed) pleasure principle, although this encroachment is less complete in the area of sexuality than in other aspects of mental life. Reality testing, then, is a developed capacity which may serve the functioning of the reality principle.

Freud went on to elaborate that this newly acquired capacity led to further adaptations in the psychical apparatus. In retrospect we can now recognize this as a preliminary formulation of the ego functions which provide the underpinnings of reality testing, though, as Hartmann (1956) pointed out, this paper antedates the beginnings of ego psychology by a dozen years. Freud specifically emphasized the following adaptations:

heightened importance of the sense organs, and of *consciousness,* which now discriminates sensory qualities rather than merely pleasure-unpleasure; the functiton of *attention,* a kind of active seeking out of sensory impressions; and *memory,* which is a way of recording the results of such psychic activity. To these is added the objective, discriminating function of *judgment,* which Freud contrasts with *repression;* the latter, Freud said, operates rigidly in accord with the dictates of the pleasure-unpleasure principle. Their combined operation leads to decisions about the truth or falsity of ideas, which is another way of saying whether or not they are "in agreement with reality" (p. 221).

In the course of the major refinement of his ideas contained in the series of metapsychological papers of 1914–17, Freud again addressed himself to the problem of reality testing. In "A Metapsychological Supplement to the Theory of Dreams" (1917a) he wondered how hallucinatory images in dreams (and sometimes elsewhere as well) are able to overpower reality testing. He took as his point of departure an idea first expressed in "Instincts and Their Vicissitudes" (1915b), namely, that perceptions of external events can be distinguished from perceptions from inside the organism according to whether or not they can be made to disappear by muscular action. His reasoning continued that the system *Cs. (pcpt.),* to which at that time he ascribed the reality testing function, "must have at its disposal a motor innervation which determines whether the perception can be made to disappear or whether it proves resistant. Reality testing need be nothing more than this contrivance" (p. 233). Interestingly, he went on to postulate that withdrawal of cathexis from the system *Cs. (pcpt.),* perhaps because the reality is unacceptable to the ego, is a mechanism which succeeds in abolishing the possibility of reality testing, thus stating clearly the case for defensive interference with reality testing even at this early stage.

In sum then, what Freud referred to in 1917 as the work of reality testing, i.e., the distinction between perceptions and ideas, seems to mean in actuality the distinction, in regard to the site of origin of a given mental stimulus, between outside and inside the organism. This is an idea which continued to occupy a central place in his thinking on the subject from then onward. Reality testing subsumes whatever psychological means are available for drawing these distinctions, and it is evidently a complex process which is subject to modification under specified conditions. For example, mourning is one such condition, and Freud applied his newly revised formulation to that problem in "Mourning and Melancholia" (1917b), which was written literally at the same time as the "Metapsychological Supplement to the Theory of Dreams" (1917a).

A further reconsideration of his ideas, after the introduction of the structural theory, is to be found in the paper on "Negation" (1925). His restatement points out that reality testing appeared to him then as a question of whether "something which is in the ego as a *presentation* can be rediscovered in perception (reality) as well. It is, we see, once more a question of *external* and *internal*. What is unreal, merely a presentation and subjective, is only internal; what is real is also there *outside*" (p. 237). Subsequently he added that "the reproduction of a perception as a presentation is not always a faithful one; it may be modified by omissions, or changed by the merging of various elements. In that case reality testing has to ascertain how far such distortions go" (p. 238). Once again he pointed to what clinical experience had repeatedly demonstrated, that perceptions of the external world are vulnerable to defensive alteration under the influence of drive derivatives and unpleasurable affects. This is another way of saying that reality testing may be overpowered by the need to modify impressions of reality which, for whatever reason, seem unacceptable to an individual's consciousness.

Subsequent Contributions

Ferenczi, in 1913, elaborated on Freud's paper on the two principles in his classic, "Stages in the Development of the Sense of Reality." He addressed the question of the development of the reality principle, wondering whether it is imperceptibly gradual or proceeds in a series of steps, and if the latter, whether the various stages can be recognized or their derivatives demonstrated in mental life. Evidently he believed the last to be true, for he used findings regarding the conviction on the part of obsessional patients concerning the omnipotence of their thoughts, feelings, and wishes as a basis for elaborating an extensive hypothetical series of developmental stages. These begin during intrauterine life, which he called a *period of unconditional omnipotence,* following which the infant successively passes through periods of *magical-hallucinatory omnipotence, omnipotence by the help of magic gestures,* and finally the use of *magic thoughts and magic words.* Only after this progression can the reality principle be said to be established, though even at that stage it does not completely dominate adult mental life, either in normals or in neurotics. Ferenczi made the point that these stages are to be thought of as stages of ego development (whatever he may have understood by that term in 1913) and that these were to be distinguished from stages of libidinal development. However, he added, perhaps regression takes place in both areas of mental life, and a schematic plotting out of the regressions on both axes might be useful in explaining the variety of neurotic outcomes encountered clinically.

Federn (1952) utilized a different explanatory model in his assumptions about reality testing. He suggested that what he preferred to call the "sense of reality" becomes the means of distinguishing internal from external stimuli. This qualitative experiential distinction is a function of the "boundaries of the ego" acting as if constituting a psychological organ of perception. He carried the concretization of this analogy further by proposing that variations in the energic investment of the hypothesized ego boundaries explain such symptoms as experiences of derealization. Although most present-day analysts do not make much use of Federn's ideas, nor do they for that matter rely upon economic explanations to account for symptoms, there does persist a tendency to speak of reality testing as though it is a function performed by a piece of psychic apparatus—a complicated measuring and recording device of sorts. Its "components" may be those elements enumerated by Freud in 1911, that is, sense organs, consciousness, attention, memory, and judgment, but it is as though these are implicitly conceived of as arranged in some contraption like a scientific instrument. This may be imagined to be working properly or not as an entity; or perhaps instead it may be thought of as possessing an inherent degree of accuracy which is less in sicker patients, greater in healthier ones. One implication of the adoption of a concrete model of how reality testing is performed is the notion that it functions globally rather than discretely, variably and with highly individual dynamic specificity. The latter view is much more in accord with clinical observations, as has been noted. Yet another implication which seems to be favored by an assumed "organ" of reality testing is that difficulty with reality testing, at least of a more severe nature, is reflective of an inherent "weakness" or "defect" in this apparatus, which may be derived from constitutional sources or from early traumatization, or both; in any case it comprises in effect a deficiency state which is referred to simply, and we think misleadingly, as "defective reality testing."

Modell (1968) explicitly disagreed with the notion that reality testing works in a all-or-nothing way. He offered a complex, ingenious theory based upon "two organs for the structuring of reality." One is represented by genetically determined autonomous ego structures which are impaired only if there has been a very serious deprivation, such as an almost complete absence of an adequate maternal environment, in the course of development. The second is a structure formed by each individual that requires for healthy development a form of "good enough" mothering which permits the child to acquire the capacity to tolerate adequately the painful separateness of objects. The functioning of this second structure is what one usually observes clinically, according to Modell, as its pathological manifestations are able to mask the potential ability of the autonomous structures to provide accurate data of reality. His ideas thus illustrate the aforementioned tendency to attribute problems with reality testing to hypothetical difficulties in the earliest stages of development.

It has continued to be true that all analysts agree on a common-sense basis that newborns cannot have the capacity to test reality, and that this ability only develops gradually as children grow to maturity. Although theoretical reconstructions of the growth of the mental apparatus may not necessarily utilize the stages which Ferenczi imagined, they all assume that some fundamental steps occur at the very earliest stages of ego development. Emphasis is generally placed on the acquisition of the capacity to distinguish outside from inside, to which, as mentioned above, Freud first paid attention in "Instincts and Their Vicissitudes" and the "Metapsychological Supplement to the Theory of Dreams."

In more recent years the trend has been to address this problem in terms of the development of self-object differentiation, as in the work of Jacobson (1964). Thus Freud's postulated purified pleasure ego stage, in which good equals inside and bad equals outside, is interwoven with the idea that the earliest distinctions between self-representations and object-representations are bound to be extremely tentative, fluid, and unstable. Introjective and projective mechanisms are assumed to operate so as to make self- and object-representations at first correspond to the good-bad distinction, and then only gradually are the perception and registration of other kinds of self- and object-representations of increasing complexity, variety and stability made possible by the maturing of the ego organization. It is because of the interconnectedness of these patterns of early mental structuring that the capacity to make consistent, accurate distinctions between self- and object-representations has become one of the criteria by means of which reality testing is often measured.

The most substantial explication of the complexities of the concepts of reality testing and the reality principle, in the light of ego psychology, is to be found in the work of Hartmann. In "Notes on the Reality Principle" (1956), he pointed out that the notion of the reality principle is used in two different ways: (1) The idea of taking into account, from the standpoint of adaptation, the "real" features of an object or situation, and (2) the tendency to shift activities away from immediate needs for discharge. He also added that pleasure may be inherent in the activities of the functions that subserve the reality principle. He elaborated Freud's point that the reality principle constitutes a modification of the pleasure principle, not a supplanting of it. The development of the ego leads to a reassessment of pleasure values. It does not modify the id, of course, but affects the interaction of the systems. In other words, what changes are not the essential characteristics of pleasure-unpleasure, but the conditions under which each occurs. For example, a major compensation for instinctual renunciation is the expectation of a gain of approval from parents, i.e., the substitution of one kind of pleasure for another. Thus instinctual renunciation, originally unpleasurable, can become pleasurable as the ego develops and more sophisticated interactions become possible.

Hartmann also noted that "the reality principle includes both knowledge or reality and acting in regard to it" (p. 252). It did not concern him especially, but we might well take note that reality testing per se would seem to pertain only to the first aspect, if it is to be delineated from the more general concept of the reality principle. He added the cautionary note that there is not a simple correlation between the degree of objective insight and the degree of adaptiveness of the corresponding action which follows upon it. He went on to observe that what may be adaptive in one respect may well interfere with adaptation in another.

It is already obvious that such sophisticated analysis of the situation in respect to an individual's relationship to reality renders simplistic and untenable the notion that reality testing can be described globally. Hartmann then moved on to the heart of the matter when he showed that even knowledge of reality is subject to inevitable distortions. He observed that in respect to concept formation, habits of thought and emotion, language, even to some degree perception, the developing child's mind is much influenced by his relationships to objects as a consequence of his great dependence on them. While "a 'realistic' object can be of great assistance to the child in discriminating fantasy and reality," (p. 256) the pleasure to be gained from conforming often "means the acceptance by the child of erroneous and biased views which the parents hold of reality" (p. 256). He described the likelihood of tensions between a knowledge of *scientific,* i.e., *objective reality,* and of *social reality,* whether the latter term implies the microcosm of the family or the larger social world of the culture in which the individual child lives. In sum, he pointed out, there are two distinct pictures of reality which oppose "the concept of 'objective' reality which Freud mostly used; the one, as we know, corresponds to what we usually, in a simplifying way, call magical thinking; the other, to a view in which not validation but intersubjective acceptance is used as a criterion of reality" (p. 259). This consideration should weigh heavily in the evaluation of reality testing capacities in individuals raised in highly pathogenic environments. As will appear later, our work with the patients we studied testified to both the correctness and the importance of this caveat.

Still another contribution to the subject is that of Frosch (1964, 1970). He described a group of patients he called "psychotic characters" who are equivalent to what we and others refer to as "borderlines." He believed their difficulty with reality is less severe than that of true psychotics but more severe than that of most neurotics. He emphasized the ready reversibility of their distortions. In an effort to delineate more clearly the exact nature of the disturbance, he proposed that these patients' problems with reality be considered as having three separate although interrelated aspects; their feelings of reality, their relationship to reality, and their reality testing. His patients showed significant alterations in their feelings of reality, which are subjective symptoms that Frosch characterized as altered ego states, such as depersonalization and derealization. He also stated that they have trouble in relation to reality while retaining relatively intact reality testing. To illustrate this distinction, he mentioned a patient who had experienced a sensory hallucination but who recognized that it had been a projection of an internal stimulus once it became apparent that others had not shared the sensory experience.

We agree with Frosch's opinion that borderlines suffer from disturbances in respect to reality which are quantitatively different in severity from those of psychotic patients, on the one hand, and of neurotic patients, on the other. However, we found his attempt to distinguish between relation to reality and reality testing unclear and difficult to apply to our own clinical material. Furthermore, we could not confirm his observations in certain important respects. For one thing, we did not consistently find a ready reversibility of distortions, misperceptions, misjudgments, and projections. Our data suggested that borderlines do show failures in reality testing, although not as severely as the psychotic patients. In contrast to Frosch's experience, we did not often encounter the phenomenon of disturbances in feelings of reality in our study population.

Whereas some of the Kris Study Group members continued to regard alterations in the feelings of reality as more likely to be associated with more severe degrees of pathology, others of us were not convinced that there is a direct relationship. Most of the group agreed that it is best to think of these feeling disturbances as constituting complex symptoms which require analysis to disclose their specific meanings for each patient. Arlow (1966, 1969a) demonstrated that the altered feelings about the reality of the self or environment may comprise part of the manifest content of the symptom and are not necessarily a consequence of profound changes in the actual capacity of the ego to make the discriminations and judgments which otherwise constitute reality testing. An analogous argument in respect to feelings of identity and problems of identity was advanced by Spiegel (1959) and by Abend (1974).

Arlow also contributed an important addition to our understanding of the problem of reality testing in another paper (1969b) "Fantasy, Memory, and Reality Testing." His central point was that there is inevitably interaction, on a continuous basis, between perceptual input registering external reality and what he called "fantasy thinking." He utilized the analogy of two film projectors simultaneously showing images on opposite sides of a translucent screen. The integration of these differing sources of data is an ongoing ego activity, the result of which provides the only possible judgments about what is real. Fantasy thinking, it must be noted, is largely unconscious, and it is centered around the crucial instinctual concerns of childhood mental life, and their associated conflicts and derivatives. It is therefore a source of wishful and defensive distortions in the final amalgamated products of the ego's integrative efforts. Thus it appears that Freud's concept that reality testing must discriminate between inner and outer sources of stimuli poses a task which cannot be accomplished in any absolute sense. This suggests that it is not so much a question of defective reality testing as opposed to intact reality testing, but rather of assaying the nature and degree of the deficiency. The clinical issue becomes that of evaluating how significant are the distortions, and of ascertaining the circumstances in which the extent and impact of disturbances in reality testing are most likely to be evident. Stein's (1966) paper, "Self-Observation, Reality and the Superego," specifically calls attention to the role of superego components in the genesis of certain problems of reality testing, further underlining the complexity of the issues involved, as well as the high degree of individual specificity which ought to be anticipated in attempting to understand a given patient's difficulties in this area.

Although Freud's idea that a break with reality serves to distinguish psychoses from neuroses did not stand up without qualification to careful clinical assessment of an analytically sophisticated nature, it has persisted as a rule of thumb of descriptive psychiatry. Certainly, observation of grossly psychotic patients, and even many borderline patients as well, readily confirms that they suffer from far more extreme forms of disturbed relationship to reality than do less sick individuals. This observation, along with the assumed relationship between severe mental illness and very early trauma or maldevelopment of the mental apparatus, has served to reinforce the presumption that reality testing as an ego capacity is critically influenced by the events of the earliest stages of psychic development. To most analysts these assumptions seem very plausible, as do the theoretical descriptions of early development of the mental apparatus. It is worth noting, however, that it is very difficult if not impossible to document such relationships from analytic data. The *a priori* assumption that *all* serious disturbances of reality testing always, of necessity, indicate that there was severe trouble in the period of self-object differentiation, for example, may not be correct. Such an assumption is potentially misleading if it distracts from analysts' attention to other problems which may exert a powerful influence on reality testing as well. Our own data strongly suggest that disruptions such as severe castration anxiety, occurring later in development, may also contribute to quite serious degrees of damage in capacity to test reality, and furthermore, that significant improvement in this aspect of ego functioning may be one favorable result of successful analytic treatment. Accordingly, analysts should approach this clinical problem with caution in respect to their own assumptions about it, and with an open mind as to its clinical significance.

The Approach of the Kris Study Group

In our clinical discussions we tended to use the concept of reality testing in a less sharply delimited way than is suggested by Freud's specification that it refers only to distortions of sensory perception. We did not confuse it, as some do, with the reality principle, at least not in respect to that aspect of it which Hartmann described as the tendency to shift activities away from immediate needs for discharge, even though our patients certainly gave evidence of that behavior. *We used "faulty reality testing" to indicate the clinical judgment that our patients' views of the world were often quite unrealistic.* In this we do shade close to Hartmann's other specification of the reality principle, the capacity to take into account, from the standpoint of adaptation, the "real" features of an object or situation. We retained more emphasis on the capacity to perceive and register the real features of the world of objects, upon which the stricter definition of reality testing rests. We believe many other analysts are also inclined to use reality testing as a term which assesses their patients' ability, or inability, to view situations, other people, and themselves in accordance with objective reality. In any case, what is of primary importance for our present purpose is that the reader be able to understand the nature of the clinical material which led to our judgments about these borderline patients' reality testing.

To illustrate the kinds of data which we took to indicate difficulty with reality testing we chose the following: One patient regularly misunderstood social and professional situations, and grossly misjudged other people (Case I); another was so convinced of the reality of her hypochondriacal fantasies that she repeatedly sought medical examinations in spite of all interpretations and her own cumulative experience; this patient also had occasional hallucinations (Case III); yet another berated and threatened her analyst and insisted on his gratifying her wishes in activities with him despite "understanding" the nature of the treatment relationship (Case IV); the fourth patient persisted in a belief in his mother's seductive wishes, despite his own more logical judgments, and severely mistrusted his analyst for years while continuing to come to him (Case II).

These distortions were often prominent in highly charged areas, those which Hartmann has pointed out are more commonly vulnerable to subjective deformation in all persons and not just the severely ill. Yet we had the collective conviction that these borderline patients had greater difficulty in this area than did most others. In some or all cases, we were impressed by the degree of unlikelihood of their beliefs, or the gross illogicality of their thinking. We felt that the inappropriateness of their understanding and behavior was much more striking than that usually encountered in the analysis of neurotic patients. In all cases, the tenacity with which these unrealistic ideas persisted, even in the face of analytic attention, was considered much greater than usual. This was especially notable in the transference, as witness the examples listed above.

While thinking and judgment, as well as perceptual activity, are involved in most of the pathological situations mentioned above, we consider it appropriate to describe them as manifestations of trouble with "knowledge of reality," to borrow Hartmann's term. We found it helpful to elaborate rather than adhere to the condensed formulas which contrast ideas and perception, inner and outer worlds, in the following way: All the disturbances noted are manifestations of the impingement of unconscious forces on the capacity to perceive, think, and judge with realistic objectivity. This is of course merely to say the same thing in other words, but it makes it more evident that we are dealing with a familiar and ubiquitous phenomenon, the interference with ego functions by unconscious conflicts. What we call reality testing is a compound ego function which involves perception, thought, memory, and judgment as component functions, as Freud recognized as early as 1911. When one formulates the problem of faulty reality testing as we have done here, it is clear that normals and milder neurotics display it in many ways; there is little doubt that a microscopic examination of every analytic session would yield numerous examples. With borderline patients, the extent, degree, and persistence of the distortions seem demonstrably greater; in short, we seem to be confronted again with a quantitative difference rather than a special defect with a specific origin and etiology.

As a practical matter analytic work generally requires that attention be concentrated on unraveling the exact nature of the distorting influences and the purposes served by their action. Once again this is not in any way remarkable, since clear reference to the wishful and defensive motivation for disturbances of perception is to be found as far back as "A Metapsychological Supplement to the Theory of Dreams" and was undoubtedly familiar to Freud long before that was written. The more complex question of what factors rendered these sicker patients more liable to marked disruptions of reality testing than others is more difficult to address.

We do not feel we can offer an organized hypothesis concerning this question with confidence that it is supported adequately by clinical data. We have, however, made certain observations which seem to us to bear on this important and interesting problem. We were impressed by the degree of pathology in respect to reality testing which seemed to be present in the families of our patients. Certainly social reality was very much discordant with objective reality for these patients. Not only was there pressure to accept idiosyncratic ideas and standards of behavior, but pathological models of modes of ego functioning concerned with reality testing were part of the psychological environment of each of these individuals throughout development.

All of our patients displayed significant utilization of projection in their defense patterns. A fuller elaboration of this feature of their pathology is to be found in the section of this report devoted to the defenses, but we mention the clinical finding at this point because it bears on the question of the origin of their damaged capability to test reality. There can be no doubt that projections of instinctual wishes and of superego attitudes, both of which we observed with great frequency in all of our patients, have the effect of distorting the perception and interpretation of objective reality. As noted earlier, many analysts regard a strong propensity to use projective mechanisms as indicating that serious difficulties were present at an early stage of psychic development, and this is linked to the proposition that faulty reality testing is, *au fond,* a consequence of such early disturbance. We would not be prepared to discount the proposition that difficulties at very early developmental periods are often important pathogenic factors, perhaps even the crucial determinants in producing these more severe impairments of reality testing. We are not convinced, however, that the finding of extensive use of projection alone affords sufficient clinical grounds for making this assertion. We concluded that we could not isolate early disturbances as causative, either of the prominence of projection or of faulty reality testing. We found ample evidence of severe trauma throughout development and would prefer to say that the proposal that the existence of major problems in reality testing always indicates pathogenesis in the first eighteen months of life should be regarded as unproven, although not necessarily incorrect.

We also noted that the improvements which became apparent in the course of the analyses of these patients were accompanied by some diminution in the extent of the disturbances of reality testing in each patient, a fact which we believe tends to support our view that their conflicts, from whichever stage and of whatever dynamic constituents, had produced substantial impairment of potentially available ego resources. We could not, however, consistently identify in our material specific conflicts related to any single developmental stage as central to the understanding and alteration of the disturbed reality testing.

Many manifestations of the problem with reality were in the context of sexual wishes and their attendant complications, both within the transference and without. This too is a long-familiar observation, explained by Freud, Ferenczi, and their contemporaries as a consequence of the special conditions which apply to sexual wishes in the mental life of man. Our present-day viewpoint would put the matter somewhat differently. We are all familiar with the tremendous amount of anxiety invariably associated with the child's observation of the anatomical difference between the sexes, and of the primal scene. Similar degrees of anxiety attend the child's theories of sex and childbirth as well as the elaboration of sexual wishes of all sorts throughout each stage of early development. It is precisely in connection with these experiences and the thoughts and memories derived from them that we encounter this increased frequency of perceptual distortion, the persistence of irrational beliefs in consciousness, and alterations of memory. Again, this cannot be offered as a specific explanation for the generation of severe deficits in reality testing since these factors are more or less ubiquitous. Some analysts believe, in fact, that more disturbed preoedipal development predisposes individuals to more serious reactions to these sexual concerns, and to disruptive consequences for subsequent reality testing. Certainly the dissection of such complex interrelationships is difficult, if not impossible, when viewed from the perspective of adult analytic data. We wish to emphasize the important contributory role played by the later instinctual conflicts implied above. It was unmistakably prominent in all of our cases.

For Case III, for example, a dramatic incident occurred following the first experience of coitus which had afforded her some satisfaction. In its immediate aftermath she thought she heard her telephone ring and was thrust into a panic, convinced beyond doubt that her parents were calling to berate her. She did not answer it, rushing instead to the window. Outside she saw the figure of a man looking at her apartment building and thought she recognized her father. Her terror lasted for some time, although it was not possible to reconstruct its duration precisely. Eventually she calmed down and then realized that

the sound of the telephone bell had been from the next apartment. Upon checking the street below, she still saw the figure
she had taken to be her father standing in front of the entrance,
but now she was able to recognize that it was merely the usual
doorman. On another occasion, during an analytic hour when
she was reporting some heavily guilt-laden sexual material, she
hallucinated the sound of the buzzer which usually announced
the arrival of the next patient and was so convinced it had really
sounded that she prepared to leave. She also had many hypochondriacal symptoms of such intensity that she went time
and again for medical consultations despite persistent interpretation from the analyst of the origin of her complaints in
unconscious sexual fantasies. These latter were invariably masochistic, punitive versions of sexual activity, childbirth, or both,
leading to genital and bodily destruction.

Case II suffered from a conviction that his mother had sexual
designs on him, a conviction of such fixity that it almost bordered on the delusional. He refused ever to change his clothing
in her apartment, even if it would have been most convenient
to have done so. He also had a persistent conscious conviction
that all other women sought to ensnare and control him. This
was a consequence in part of his own projected wishes to do
the same to them, and in part a reflection of his fantasy that
they would love him more if he were a girl. This was later
understood as a consequence of his fantasy of replacing his
dead sister in order to relieve his mother's profound depression.
The origin of these powerful, to him very persuasive, beliefs
reflected his own wishes, and his massive use of projection was
fundamental to his way of dealing with them. These factors
were only very gradually made clear to him by sustained and
patient analytic work.

Case I was convinced of the accuracy of many distorted ideas
regarding her body's size and strength, ideas which stemmed
from the unconscious wish that she had been born masculine.
Her sexual beliefs led her to constantly misinterpret and misjudge both her sexual partners and her experiences with them.
Confusion as to size and configuration of her organs and theirs,
stubborn beliefs as to why one or another sexual position or

practice was more or less satisfactory, and the inability to detect gross personal pathology in men with whom she was intimate, were all manifestations of conflict centering around a number of gender issues and gender confusion. She also believed unquestioningly that the analyst bore a striking physical resemblance to her long-lost father, even after this conviction was shown to rest only on a distant memory of a photograph of him in his youth.

The power of libidinal wishes to influence reality testing was also demonstrated in Case IV. The patient on one occasion telephoned her analyst at home and was enraged when a woman answered. During the next session she insisted she had thought herself to be the only woman in his life, and she sulked and fumed for several days. At other times she gave and demanded gifts, and once brought wine to the session, insisting that her analyst share it with her.

It is not our intention to point only to the influence of sexual fantasies and conflicts upon reality testing. The part played by aggressive conflicts was clearly demonstrated in our material as well. The two instinctual forces are of course never seen entirely in isolation. In some material the admixture of the two drives is particularly strong and obvious, as in the highly charged sadomasochistic transference situation in Case III, in which the patient's conviction that the analyst was a crazy, sadistic brute persisted through years of steady work. Similar though less dominant transference distortions occurred in the three other cases as well.

Though intense sibling rivalry has a hidden aim which is libidinal, i.e., a more unhindered claim on parental love, its immediate expression is often predominantly aggressive. In Case I intense competitive feelings derived from this source were dealt with by projection. As a result this patient regularly misinterpreted social and professional situations, was convinced of the hostility of individuals or groups toward her, personalized comments, exaggerated moods and minor events, and ascribed motives to acts and statements in conformity with her distorted views. Another instance of aggressive conflict, apparently dissociated from obvious libidinal admixture, affecting reality testing occurred in Case III, when the patient hallucinated a mocking laugh from her analyst during one of the early hours. Subsequent analysis revealed the hallucination to represent an anticipation that her mother's persistently critical and unsympathetic attitude would be re-encountered in the analyst.

As mentioned above, instances representative of the other causes of faulty reality testing noted in the literature also appeared in our clinical material. Hartmann's (1956) observation that adaptive pressure forces children to accept pathological views of reality held by disturbed parents was most vividly documented in Cases I and III. In the former, the facts behind the father's abandonments, and of the questionable activities with which his departures were probably connected, were surrounded by shame, denial, and secrecy. It was never entirely clear to the patient what the truth was, although in the course of the analysis it became increasingly evident that he had been a shady character. It was also unclear how much the mother knew but concealed, and how much she herself denied and distorted. Certainly the mother demanded of the children that they lie to others about circumstances surrounding his absences and buttressed these demands with explanations which must also have been untrue. These patterns of thought were incorporated into the patient's personality, contributing to her difficulty in assessing the character of men she met, and to her tendency to inappropriate secrecy regarding her background, as well as to the main character resistances of withholding and passive aggression in the analysis. In Case III the near-psychotic parent of the patient influenced the development of her own bizarre and unrealistic ideas and behavior in countless ways, most obviously in her beliefs about health and hypochondriacal preoccupations.

We also observed that powerful wishes to find a concretely gratifying, nurturing, and protective parent were very much in evidence in all these cases. As mentioned, Case IV, besides demanding advice, continuously sought gratifying interactions with her analyst. In Case I the analyst's comments were often distorted as intended to provide advice and guidance, and the patient seriously suggested that the analyst should find her an appropriate mate since he knew her needs so well. She also frequently brought such idealized and unrealistic expectations to her interactions with employers, landlords, and lovers as well.

In summary, we emphasize again that reality testing is a complex ego function, and the relation to reality of which it is part is more complex yet. Whatever role the early development of the mind, and of self-object differentiation, plays in establishing the substratum of reliable or unreliable reality testing—and it must indeed play an important part—is, in our experience, very difficult to demonstrate from analytic data obtained from adults. What one can see clearly are the influence of the childhood milieu in respect to reality, that is, the social reality of the patient's childhood, and the impact of conflict over libidinal and aggressive wishes on the ego functions which subserve reality testing. Furthermore, deficient reality testing is quite variable in our clinical experience. In one of our cases it was most prominent in the transference; in another it was by and large confined, both within and without the transference, to specific sexual wishes and their consequences; in a third it appeared in various aspects of the patient's life and functioning, as well as in different contexts in the analytic situation; and in the fourth, diffusely and profoundly disturbed reality testing characterized the patient's life and her analysis in a pervasive fashion, almost alarming in its tenacity and intensity, for a period of years.

This characteristic of variability was also true within the confines of each case, since functioning in certain areas might not show much evidence of the problem, whereas, as noted, in other aspects of life it could be a major problem, at least at times. The analytic work in each case was of course addressed to understanding the specific components and determinants of the situations in which faulty reality testing appeared, and the role played by the deficiency in these situations. In other words, the defective reality testing had to be analyzed not as an independent symptom or problem in its own right, but as one component of a pathological reaction, in whatever context(s) it appeared. It is noteworthy that the tendency to distort reality in all cases seemed to diminish in the course of each of the analyses. This supports our view that alteration of the pathogenic influence of conflict can lead to improvement of impaired ego functioning even in so fundamental an area as the testing of reality.

6.

Defenses

In this chapter we will take up several tasks. We intend to describe in some detail the defenses we observed in our study cases, with an eye toward demonstrating the complexity encountered when analytic material is dissected in this fashion. In spite of this complexity, we will nevertheless attempt to show which defensive operations seemed most prominent in these cases. This will lead us to address the more general questions in respect to the defenses of borderline patients enumerated on pages 32–33, which had to do with the possibility of differentiating borderline patients from others according to certain characteristics of their defense structures. In doing so we will pay particular attention to two relevant theoretical problems: (1) the applicability of the concept of a hierarchy of defenses from primitive to higher-level ones, and (2) an evaluation of Kernberg's theory of special defenses limited to, and pathognomonic of, the borderline conditions. In conclusion, we will summarize our own views on these matters, including an outlining of the conceptual approach to the question of defensive functioning in borderline patients which we have gradually come to prefer. In order to introduce these discussions, we must briefly review some stages in the evolution of the defense concept in psychoanalytic theory.

At the beginning of his psychoanalytic investigations Freud tried to understand different psychopathological entities by relating them to preferred defenses. In "The Neuropsychoses of Defence" (1894) he classified the clinical conditions hysteria, obsessional neurosis, and hallucinatory confusion according to the defense mechanisms most prominently employed in each. His emphasis soon shifted to repression, which came to occupy the central place in his theory of neurosogenesis, at least until the revision of anxiety theory in 1926. Thus repression was thought of as more or less synonymous with defense during that period, although such familiar terms as displacement, undoing, reaction formation, and projection continued to appear in connection with descriptions of specific symptoms, character traits, or both. With the publication of *Inhibitions, Symptoms and Anxiety* (1926) Freud reintroduced the idea that a number of methods of defense are employed in mental life, often in combination with repression, and perhaps with each other as well.

Defenses subsequently assumed a far more important place in the theory and practice of psychoanalytic technique than had been true previously, when they were merely regarded as obstacles to be overcome in the effort to uncover and understand the unconscious wishes they warded off or disguised. This monumental change in approach was presented in A. Freud's landmark book, *The Ego and the Mechanisms of Defense* (1936), in which a variety of so-called mechanisms of defense, both simple and complex, were enumerated.[1] It was made explicit that these defenses were to be regarded as specific unconscious mechanisms of the ego, and her contribution, along with Fenichel's (1935) book on technique, emphasized that defenses must be subjected to analytic scrutiny, just as were instinctual derivatives. Waelder, as quoted in Wallerstein (1969), later characterized the nature of this theoretical and technical shift by stating that *Inhibitions, Symptoms and Anxiety* required analysts to ask what it is that patients are afraid of, whereas *The Ego and The Mechanisms of Defense* elaborated this question into the more complex form, "when the patient is afraid, how does he behave." This change, according to Waelder, had elevated defenses to a place of importance in clinical psychoanalysis. Miss Freud also indicated, when she introduced the concepts of identification with the aggressor and altruistic surrender, that such more

---

[1] As listed, the basic defense mechanisms were "regression, repression, reaction-formation, isolation, undoing, projection, introjection, turning against the self, and reversal" (p. 47). To these were added identification with the aggressor and altruistic surrender (*ibid.*, pp. 117,132).

complex defensive behavior might consist of combinations of the fundamental mechanisms operating in concert. She furthermore suggested that there might exist a developmental hierarchy of defense mechanisms, although she acknowledged that one could not be specified at that time.

The intense investigation to which defenses, and indeed ego operations in general, were subsequently subjected gradually resulted in still further refinements and modifications in the concept of defense mechanisms. At the same time, the increased attention which analysts were beginning to pay to problems of normal adaptation, beginning with Hartmann's monograph, *Ego Psychology and the Problem of Adaptation* (1939) led in time to still more clarification of the role of defensive functioning in mental life.

A host of contributors, of whom Brenner was perhaps the first, and certainly the most systematic and far reaching, (1955, 1974, 1975, 1976, 1979) produced over the years a profound change in analytic understanding both of the nature and the role of defenses in psychic activity. The evolution of these ideas may be traced through a series of panels devoted to the role of defenses in theory and technique, the reports of which (Zetzel, 1954; Wallerstein, 1967; Pumpian-Mindlin, 1967; Krent, 1970) provide in condensed form a history of analysts' increasing comprehension of the issues involved. Abend (1981) reviewed these subsequent steps in summary fashion, noting that analytic experience had made it apparent that defense mechanisms were not really so simple, nor even for that matter really mechanisms, but appeared instead more like complex structures which serve purposes other than defensive ones. They have content and meaning (Schafer, 1968), serve to provide gratification of needs (Brenner, Greenson), and aid adaptation, as well as contributing to symptom formation and both normal and pathological character traits.

In some forms, defenses themselves seem to be the product of compromise formation among wish, defense, and superego components. It gradually became clear that all behavior may be said to include in its composition some manifestations of defense. To continue to think of defenses as automatic unconscious mechanisms thus becomes a kind of concretization which supports the admittedly widely held view that defenses are properly to be thought of as *specific* mental entities or structures. It now seems more in accord with the clinical facts to say instead that any aspect of ego functioning can be used for purposes of defense, as well as for the facilitation of gratification.

Analysts are certainly, however, likely to continue to speak and write about "defenses" and "defense mechanisms" as a kind of convenient shorthand. Indeed, we shall do so ourselves in this chapter, because we would otherwise be forced to employ awkward and artificial circumlocutions to avoid the use of the more familiar terminology. Thus, in spite of the gradual clarifications of defense theory which have been summarized above, we will follow conventional practice and describe as defense mechanisms, or more complex defenses, those aspects of mental functioning aimed at eliminating or reducing unpleasure.

Defenses do not only operate directly against the unpleasurable affects themselves. They may be seen to work to modify or oppose the instinctual drive derivatives which lead to unpleasure, or the superego threats, punishments, and derivatives dictated by remorse; they may work against perceptions and memories of the external world, or may modify other aspects of ego functioning such as reality testing. Defenses may also be said to act against any combination of these elements, or even against all of them at once. Some defenses may be described as defending against still other complex mental contents, such as unconscious fantasies, which themselves fulfill defensive functions. The balance between such alignments of mental contents probably varies according to where the greatest unpleasure is concentrated at any given moment in the life of the individual or in the course of his or her analysis.

It becomes easy to see why analysts have long since grown accustomed to describing certain complex behaviors as defensive on an empirical basis derived from clinical experience, despite the status of defense theory. Some have even stretched things to the point of speaking of some symptoms as defending against yet other mental consequences, while at the same time they continue to utilize the familiar list of defense mechanisms set down by A. Freud in 1936 in their clinical descriptions and summaries.

When we turned to the discussion of our case material we soon learned that it is surprisingly difficult for a group of analysts to agree upon which particular defense mechanisms are demonstrable in any given sample of clinical material. At first we did not realize that this is in part a reflection of some of the ambiguities and complexities of the theory of defenses which have been described above. Certain simpler "mechanisms" are so specifically descriptive of a particular behavior, or associated with particular symptoms or character traits, that there would be easy agreement among our participants as to its presence. Examples of reaction formation, undoing, or obvious displacements fell into this category, usually in connection with obsessional or phobic features of these patients. When the defensive behavior described was more complex, efforts to account for this by invoking combinations of basic defense mechanisms, as A. Freud had attempted, were less satisfactory. Different observers saw different combinations of defense mechanisms, and opinions varied widely as to which mechanisms were displayed most prominently. What is more, as we dissected the cases in more depth, we saw that the list of defense mechanisms employed by each patient became longer and longer. Some aspects of the defensive functioning of these patients, such as the tendency to action, narcissistic withdrawal, and the like, did not seem to lend themselves at all to further breakdown into component mechanisms. Thus we agreed among ourselves to do as other analysts have done and speak of "defense mechanisms" when they were clear, and of more complex "defensive behaviors" when that mode of description was more useful.

The Defenses Utilized by our Patients

The examination of our four cases showed without question that borderline patients use all types of defenses, both simple and complex. Although we will take up in detail in this chapter the problem of a hierarchy of defenses and the conception of higher-level versus primitive defenses which is derived from it, we can state at the outset that our patients all clearly demonstrated the use of so-called higher-level defenses such as repression, reaction formation, and identification from the beginning of their treatment. We also found that they used defenses customarily thought of by many analysts as more primitive, of which projection and denial are typical examples. In addition, each employed many more complex behaviors for defensive purposes, of which the aforementioned tendency toward action and narcissistic withdrawal represent commonly occurring instances.

In our proceedings we asked each participant to review the written material of each case and to enumerate all of the defenses identifiable in the analytic data. We then discussed each case in detail, making use of the respective treating analyst's vastly greater familiarity with his or her own patients, as well as the lists of observed defenses compiled by the other members. We attempted to come to agreement on which defenses were present and which were most prominent in each case. The enormous and surprising complexity that this examination revealed can be illustrated by a summary of our findings.

For example, in Case I we concluded that the patient demonstrated many of the simpler mechanisms of defense including repression, denial, projection, isolation, reaction formation, disavowal, avoidance, turning against the self, and displacement. She also showed more complex defensive behaviors as well. Identification with the aggressor was prominent. She acted like her abandoning father in fleeing from the anticipated pain of object loss. She criticized others as her mother had done and analytically scrutinized her boyfriends as she felt her analyst did to her. In all of these respects she shifted from a position of helplessness, vulnerability, and pain, to one of relative power, superiority, and certitude. Similarly, in her silent behavior she was acting like her father, punishing and rendering helpless the analyst, who she felt was depriving and abandoning her. Silence also represented a defensive identification with her mother, who dealt with shame and grief in that fashion and had encouraged the children to do so as well.

Disturbances of the ego functions of perception, memory, and integration contributed to her learning difficulties in life that were repeated in the analysis. The bewilderment and confusion which resulted represented many things; among them it repeated earlier mental states which were in part defensive against the painful knowledge of the disturbing events of her life, as well as against disturbing thoughts and impulses from within herself. Her narcissistic withdrawal was a protection against painful affects associated with separation, but it also followed any interpretation which she found damaging to her self-esteem. Silence and narcissistic withdrawal also served to express, and at the same time to defend against, more explicit expressions of her rage, which she feared would have still more devastating consequences of retaliation and abandonment.

Her tendency toward action was, in the service of gratification as well as of defense. For example in seeking to rent an apartment in her analyst's building, and in not discussing the wishes involved, she sought unconsciously to keep out of awareness many marginal consequences of her wishes to see, to be close to, and to be specially preferred by her analyst. The transference regression into a sadomasochistic mode also served in part to replace and disguise anxiety and guilt-laden aspects of her positive and negative oedipal constellations. Objects were idealized and degraded, in large measure to attempt to deal with painful consequences of her own envy and vulnerability. A list of the many defensive aspects of her behavior could easily be extended further, but the point to be illustrated has, we think, already been made abundantly clear. Defensive functioning is to be found in many aspects of the clinical material of an analysis, and any attempt at a comprehensive compilation of a given patient's defenses is likely to demonstrate this fact to analysts, as it did to our group.

It seems redundant to present similarly extensive lists of the observed defense mechanisms and other behaviors which we interpreted as representing more complex defenses for each of our cases. Instead we will merely try to indicate those defensive mechanisms, stances, and maneuvers which seemed most important in each of the other study cases, before attempting to assess the degree to which they can be regarded as similar to one another.

Projection was the most outstanding single aspect of defense in Case II. Both libidinal and aggressive impulses, as well as superego attitudes, were dealt with in that way. The patient's unconscious libidinal attachment to his mother was projected onto her and he was consequently convinced of her wish to seduce him. His unconscious wish for gratification, as a function of imagining himself turned into a little girl, was also projected, both onto the women in his masturbatory fantasies and later onto the analyst as well. Many years of analysis were required before he gained some acceptance of the fact that his own wishes were involved in these psychic elaborations.

Aggressive wishes and impulses also led to projections, so that he was convinced that all men, including his analyst, were competitive with him and out to defeat and humiliate him as well. Isolation, withholding, and reaction formation served to further bolster his defenses against his own sadistic wishes and some of the masochistic consequences as well, particularly in the transference.

Yet another complex defense was his unconscious identification with his dead sister, which, along with other aspects of his feminine wishes, aided in dealing with the castration anxiety connected with positive oedipal wishes toward his mother. Typically, however, they also led to castration anxiety, which had to be further defended against by isolation, withdrawal, repression, and disavowal.

Case III demonstrated more clearly than any of our other patients the marked oscillations in transference attitudes which Kernberg and others believe signify the presence of splitting mechanisms. At one moment she saw the analyst as omnipotent and benevolent, at another as equally powerful but sadistic. She might then turn on him and attack him as weak, degraded, stupid, and helpless before her own omnipotent, sadistic, and magically destructive self-image. Although these contradictory fantasies alternated, she remained conscious of this inconsistency and did not become anxious if the analyst brought them to her attention at the same time. These shifting transference features were understood and interpreted as manifestations of projection and of identification with the aggressor, chiefly her seductive and sadistic father. The paternal transference, combined with the projection of her sadistic impulses, made her feel as if the analyst was her torturer much of the time; in fact the analyst was almost constantly under attack from the patient.

Another prominent defense she displayed was the use of one drive derivative to defend against another. For example when sexually aroused she would become extremely aggressive, concentrating her attention on her feelings of frustration at the hands of her analyst rather than on her libidinal impulses. Conversely, when she was liable to feel overwhelmingly destructive toward the analyst her loving feelings would supervene. As these defenses were interpreted to her in the context of the transference she slowly became more aware of both her loving and her hostile impulses. This increased self-knowledge gradually helped to modify still other behavior which in part fulfilled defensive needs, such as her moral masochism, her oral sadistic binge eating, and her near-delusional hypochondriacal states.

Her tendency toward action[2] within and outside of the transference was another activity which was frequently employed for defensive purposes. To cite but a few representative examples, there were numerous phone calls to the analyst, recurrent crises, shouting or pouting in sessions, binge eating, displaced aggressive acts with friends or relatives, medical "emergencies," walking out of sessions, and threats to terminate treatment. All of these behaviors served, of course, to gratify libidinal and aggressive needs as well as to promote defensive aims. It should also be mentioned that a deeply hidden unconscious identification with her mother was also projected and transferred onto

---

[2] We were not satisfied with the commonly used term "acting out" to describe our patients' tendencies toward action. Neither were we in complete agreement with the narrow definition of "acting out in the transference," favored by Moore and Fine (1968), serving as a "resistance" to treatment and to the recovery of memory. "Acting out" clearly describes behavior which is not only a defensive maneuver but also a compromise formation serving multiple functions, of which defense is but one. We do, however, agree with them that to extend the term in a pejorative way to any aggressive or antisocial act is not helpful. Any other term we might wish to substitute for "acting out" to avoid these imprecise associations had equivalent limitations, not least among them was that of introducing yet another new and unnecessary term into the literature.

the analyst, although it was masked throughout much of her treatment by the more obvious identification with her father. The maternal identification manifested itself chiefly in the form of a quiet, smug, cooly hostile, critical, and contemptuous attitude, which she either attributed to the analyst or displayed toward him herself.

To complete the survey, Case IV illustrated the prominent use of displacement and of identification with the aggressor. Like her cruel image of her father, she treated the analyst, who represented to her unconscious mind her ineffectual mother, in a sadistic, condemnatory, and seductive fashion. Outside the analysis she enacted the other aspect of this sadomasochistic relationship by slavishly devoting herself to young men who seemed narcissistic and exploitative of her. Her pregnancy wishes, connected in her oedipal constellation to her reactions to the births of her two younger siblings, were altered because of guilt and anxiety, by reaction formation, conversion, and somatization into hypochondriacal preoccupations and recurrent fears of being or becoming pregnant. Her rage at men, which was expressed in her sadomasochistic orientation, illustrated the use of aggressive drive derivatives to defend against more manifest expressions of libidinal longings, and dread of abandonment, which she associated with the latter type of drive expression. At the conclusion of her analysis she also enacted her identification with her father by "abandoning" the analyst.

Although we have observed that our patients utilized a very broad range of simple and complex defensive modes, it does seem to us that the group as a whole tended to display certain defensive maneuvers with notable prominence. These included, in particular, projection and denial, enactment, identification with the aggressor, and the use of one drive derivative to defend against another. Regression of libidinal level to sadomasochistic organization was also notable. All of these were present so pervasively in their lives and in their behavior in the analytic situation that they were extremely disruptive in both of these environments. These defenses were most difficult to modify by interpretation, and they contributed to the not infrequently chaotic appearance of all of these analyses. They persisted relatively unchanged for an unusually long time, which played a part in the unusually slow and perhaps only intermittently evident analytic improvement of these patients.

The Concept of Primitive Defenses

In this section we will examine the concepts of primitive defenses and the developmental hierarchy of defense mechanisms. It is important for us to do so because many authors have stated that borderline patients use primitive defenses *lc* rather than higher-level ones. Kernberg, in particular, believes that the presence of certain primitive defenses is pathognomonic for the diagnosis of borderline personality disorder. The defenses he cited are splitting, projective indentification, primitive idealization, denial, and omnipotence and devaluation. The major primitive defense among them is splitting, and Kernberg contrasted the use of this defense in borderlines with the use of the higher-level defense of repression in neurotic patients. Other higher-level defenses thought to be used by healthier patients are the familiar ones of reaction formation,undoing, displacement, isolation, sublimation, and intellectualization.

As we mentioned, Anna Freud (1936) proposed that it might be possible to develop a chronological classification of defense mechanisms. She wrote ". . . possibly each defense mechanism is first evolved in order to master some specific instinctual urge and so is associated with a particular phase of infantile development" (p. 55). She went on to say that repression and sublimation could not be employed until relatively late in development, whereas such processes as regression, reversal, or turning around against the self were probably among the earliest defense mechanisms used by the ego. In contrast to the generally accepted view today, she stated that projection and introjection were, like repression, used later in development since they depended upon the differentiation of the ego from the outside world.

Actually Freud had already made two comments about the use of early defenses. One appeared in 1915, when he referred to certain vicissitudes of the instincts such as turning around against the self and reversal into its opposite as early modes of defense against the instincts themselves. The second is to be found in the Appendix to *Inhibitions, Symptoms and Anxiety,* where he stated, "It may well be that before its sharp cleavage into an ego and id, and before the formation of a superego, the mental apparatus makes use of different methods of defense from those which it employs after it has reached these stages of organization" (1926, p. 164).

But it remained for Anna Freud to elaborate on that concept, and she did so in her classic monograph. The idea was not only that some defenses are used earlier than others but that in more disturbed children these defenses may be resorted to once again, or even that the early defenses may persist throughout childhood and adult life if the ego does not develop properly. She felt that denial was an example of a primitive defense and speculated that it corresponded "to the defense against primarily painful stimuli which impinge upon the ego from the outside world" (p. 67).

Fenichel (1945) indicated that denial, projection, and introjection were more primitive defenses. Early in his writings Brenner (1955) stated that projection was one of those defense mechanisms which normally plays its greatest role early in life. Bak (1954, 1971) added regression to primary narcissism or dedifferentiation of the ego as an important primitive defense, and Hartmann (1953) added detachment of the libido to the list of primitive defenses already enumerated by Freud. Mahler and her co-workers (1968, 1975) cited denial, splitting, deanimation, and autistic withdrawal as early defenses.

The work of Melanie Klein (1946) and Fairbairn (1954) brought a new and important emphasis to the concept of primitive defenses, in addition to introducing new terms for certain of these defenses. These analysts introduced a concept of splitting which was different from Freud's use of the term. Splitting was seen to be one of the primary defenses of severely disturbed patients. Klein's list of primitive defenses specified splitting of the object and the impulses, splitting of the ego, denial of inner and outer reality, stifling of emotions, projection, introjection, omnipotence, and projective identification.

In addition to introducing some new terms, Klein was most explicit in stating that it is possible to reconstruct the presence of the operation of such defenses during the first few months of life from their appearance in disturbed adults. She believed that these defenses came into operation during the first three months of life as part of the paranoid-schizoid position. She felt that failure to overcome their use would not only interfere with the child's reaching the depressive position at six months but would result in these same defenses being used throughout life.

More recently Frosch (1970) differentiated primitive and mature defenses on the basis of the type of danger which called them into operation. He described neurotic defenses of repression, displacement, reaction formation, and conversion which are called into operation against the anxieties of separation, castration, and superego punishment, In order to ward off anxieties over the more profound dangers of preservation and survival of self and object and loss of identity, sicker patients resort to regressive dedifferentiation, introjective-projective techniques, projective identification, fragmentation, splitting, massive denial, and somatization.

The most comprehensive account of the primitive defenses used by borderline patients comes from Kernberg (1975, 1976), as noted above. We will return to an examination of the defenses he cited below. At this point we wish to emphasize that Kernberg feels that these defenses are used in contrast to repression and the other higher-level defenses which are used by healthier patients. He also believes that in borderline patients these primitive defenses persist because of ego weakness and in turn contribute to further ego weakness.

In general, the most frequently mentioned primitive defenses are denial and projection. More recently splitting and projective identification, along with projective-introjective techniques, are often included under this heading. In contrast, repression, displacement, reaction formation, isolation, conversion, intellectualization, and sublimation are thought of as higher-level defenses.

There are actually two ways in which the term "primitive

defenses" is currently used. In one, the term refers to those defenses employed by the ego very early in life—primarily before the age of two or three. But it also refers to those defenses used by psychotic or borderline patients. There is, in addition, a formulation about the development of psychopathology which links together the two uses of the term. This formulation proposes that sicker patients continue to use the primitive defenses of very early childhood and that the presence of such defenses in an adult is indicative of early pathology and trauma.

As we reviewed our work, we became dissatisfied with the concept of primitive defenses as it is currently applied to clinical phenomena and theoretical formulations. We have already mentioned that it is not accurate to think of defenses as simple mechanisms. Rather, they are very complex behaviors involving gratifications as well as defensive motives. The idea that we can specifically designate some defenses as primitive and others as more mature or of higher level seemed to us to create serious conceptual as well as clinical difficulties. The term "primitive," when applied to defenses, carries with it assumptions which, we felt, interfere with our clinical work and theoretical understanding.

One assumption is that a so-called primitive defense used by adults is the *same* as a defense used by a young child. Another is that the use of such primitive defenses means that the patient's pathology can be traced back to an early period of childhood when that defensive operation is presumed to be predominant. A third is that the presence of such a defense is indicative of serious psychopathology.

We felt that defenses should not be designated as primitive or mature without an evaluation of the total ego organization. What appears to be the operation of a primitive defense in an adult depends not merely on the type of defense which is employed but on the nature of the ego involved. The sicker a patient is, the more we see poor ego integration, poor ego organization, and breakdown of ego functions. The defensive processes called into service in such patients appear primitive primarily because of the low level of ego functioning.

Our findings indicated, as we have shown, that borderline

patients used all the defense mechanisms—whether designated as primitive or mature. We certainly saw the operation of repression in borderline patients, an observation which is contrary to the often expressed view that the ego of such patients is not strong enough to develop the countercathexis needed for the use of repression. This view is based on the theoretical formulation that repression requires a large quantity of countercathexis and therefore, that this defense does not operate successfully until neutralized energy is available to the ego at the time of the resolution of the Oedipus complex, when important identification takes place and the superego is formed. It is argued, in contrast, that the infant or toddler, not having this countercathectic energy at its disposal, cannot use repression and must resort to other defenses such as splitting and early forms of denial and projection.

Our own experience leads us to conclude that borderlines, as well as schizophrenic patients, use a good deal of repression, even though in acute regressive states formerly repressed instinctual drive derivatives may emerge. We found repression operating along with other defenses in our patients. We also observed that defenses like denial and projection were often so pervasive and rigidly utilized that one must imagine that they, too, require a great expenditure of the energy of the ego. It seemed to us, therefore, that the idea that we can differentiate primitive and mature defenses on the basis of the degree of countercathectic energy available is not in accord with clinical experience.

Another of our conclusions about primitive defenses had to do with the danger involved in reconstructing the presence of very early defenses from the complicated regressive behaviors and symptoms of adult patients. We were aware of the dangers of the "genetic fallacy" and were doubtful that a defense used by an adult, even in a regressed state, is the *same* as a similarly appearing defense used by a child.

Our findings also showed that the most commonly cited primitive defenses—projection and denial—are used by neurotics as well. It was not so much the presence of these defenses which should alert us to the possibility of more serious pathology but an evaluation of the total functioning of the patient who is using one or another defense predominantly.

Perhaps it would be helpful to restate our propositions with the aid of clinical examples. For example, how might different people manage the typical conflicts around hatred or rivalry toward a sibling? One person might resolve the conflict by developing character traits of altruism and overpoliteness, thereby demonstrating the use of reaction formation as the major defense mechanism. Another would react to every mildly aggressive action on his or her part with a subsequent act of helpfulness and charity. Here, "undoing" is the prominent defense mechanism. A third person might feel idealization and love toward siblings and sibling surrogates, but these feelings might be followed very rapidly by villification and hatred of these same individuals, or the reverse might be true. Is this last clinical picture a variant of the concept of a "primitive" or "special" defense, or might it be understood in a different way: the use of one drive derivative to defend against the other, in a patient whose ego functions and object relations are much more infantile in nature?

In the same manner, what might we observe if we examine a typical conflict over sexual impulses in a psychotic, an hysteric, or an obsessional patient? Reaction formation may be used by all three, but the psychotic patient may show asceticism and religious delusions, whereas the hysterical patient might show nausea and disgust, and the obsessional patient ritual cleanliness after sexual activity. It is clear that the same defense, reaction formation, is basic to all of those responses, but the clinical picture is very different. As stated above, we believe that we must look further than the defensive mechanisms and maneuvers alone and try to examine simultaneously the other crucial variables, particularly the general integration of the ego, reality testing, and the quality of object relationships, in order to explain the extensive psychopathology displayed by these patients.

One of the questions we raised on page 31 was whether it would be useful to assume gradations of primitivity within each defense mechanism. That is to say, would it be useful to say that some forms of each defense are more mature whereas other forms of the same defense are more primitive? We would then be describing earlier and later forms of projection, denial, and reaction formation. Kernberg made this kind of distinction when he calls projective identification an earlier form of projection. He does the same with denial. According to him, the primitive form of denial is "exemplified by 'mutual denial' of two emotionally independent areas of consciousness" (1975, p. 31). He considers it therefore to be intimately associated with splitting. He states, "Denial, then, is a broad group of defensive operations and probably related at its higher level to the mechanisms of isolation and other higher level defenses against affects (detachments, denial in fantasy, denial in 'word and act') and at its lower level to splitting" (pp. 32-33). He also included negation as a higher level of denial.

We felt that Kernberg's view emphasizes the complexity involved in assessing defense organization. However, we preferred to describe various defenses in relation to the level of ego integration and the intactness of ego functions rather than to label some forms of defense as more primitive and other forms of the same defense as more mature. We hope also that this would avoid such confusing designations as "psychotic denial" and "neurotic denial."

We are not proposing to do away with the concept of a developmental hierarchy of defenses or defense organization in childhood. A genetic frame of reference must be applied to defenses as well as psychosexual phases, object relations, and ego maturation. We understand that the capacity to use various ego functions for defensive purposes must change with development. It is obvious that a one-and-a-half year old toddler cannot have the same defensive capacities available to him as an adult. Rationalization and intellectualization, to take some obvious examples, cannot be used very early in life.

However, we felt that we cannot easily reconstruct a rigid chronological timetable for defenses from the regressive behavior and symptomatology of disturbed patients. Furthermore, we began to question whether the use of any particular defense, whether it be projection, denial, or splitting, can be traced back to a specific time in infancy when it is presumed that psychopathology develops.

Now that we have discussed some general propositions about defenses and the concept of primitive defenses, we will turn to an appraisal of Kernberg's contributions about defenses in borderline patients.

An Examination of Kernberg's Contribution on Defenses

Kernberg put forward the idea that borderline patients characteristically display "special primitive defenses," whose presence may be pathognomonic for the condition, or, at least, has strong diagnostic significance. In fact, this thesis derives from the concept of a developmental hierarchy of defenses, and the idea that sicker patients retain the primitive defenses utilized during infancy. We undertook to evaluate Kernberg's observations and propositions as fully and carefully as we could.

From clinical data similar to our own, Kernberg constructed a number of hypotheses about the conflicts underlying the observed behavior and the developmental phases from which they are derived. He believes that extreme, vacillating, ambivalent behavior, particularly in the transference, provides evidence for the existence of contradictory and polarized "ego states." According to Kernberg, these "ego states" are made up of "nonmetabolized" units of affect, object-representations, and self-representations. These "ego states" can rapidly shift as the affect associated with them changes from "all-good" to "all-bad." He believes that this organization around good and bad affect linkages takes place normally in earliest mental development because of the immaturity of the mental apparatus. However, an "essential task" of the "development and integration of the ego" is the synthesis of these polarized, affectively opposite, self and object images. A normal division may continue *pathologically beyond the first year of life*[3] as a result of the pathological defense of "splitting," which presents the "generalization of anxiety"

---

[3] In more recent publications, Kernberg moved his chronological timetable forward to coincide more with the "rapprochement" subphase of separation-individuation as described by Mahler. However, he still feels that "splitting" mechanisms are most prominent in the first year of life (1976, p. 37).

and "protects the ego core." Pathological "splitting" is, therefore, a central concept in his theory of "internalized object relations." It is a consequence of the weakness of the ego in certain instances, since in such cases there will be a preference for "splitting" over "higher level" defense mechanisms, because the former requires the expenditure of less countercathectic energy (1975, pp. 25-30).[4] At the same time, it creates ego weakness as it prevents crucial ego integration from proceeding.

Early in his writings Kernberg (1966) felt that such "splitting" was probably the result of the excessive development of, or excessive endowment with, aggression, constitutionally determined lack of anxiety tolerance, and excessive oral frustration. In his later works, he moved more toward an emphasis on faulty mothering and away from the overendowment with aggressive drive as the causative factor. Throughout his writings to date, he contrasted "splitting" with "higher level" defenses. He believes the latter are used only later in development, by a more mature ego in the oedipal phase. Thus, according to his theory, primitive defenses are used predominantly or exclusively during the preoedipal years (six months to three years, but mainly in the first year), whereas higher-level defenses mainly come to be important only when the oedipal phase has been reached. Kernberg believes that it is the pathological persistence of the "special primitive" defenses which contributes to the formation of a clearly defined entity, the "borderline personality organization."[5]

Splitting

A brief review of the use of the term "splitting" in the literature quickly demonstrated that different authors use the term in very different ways, and, although Kernberg attempts to define it clearly, his view is only one among many.

---

[4] The rationale behind this idea is that less countercathexis is needed for "splitting" because no "repression" occurs and both contradictory "ego states" can exist in consciousness.

[5] Noting that this conceptualization must hold true for psychotic as well as borderline patients, Kernberg offered a distinction between the two groups based on the belief that psychotic patients may have further constitutional impairments which lead to a degree of fusion of self- and object-representation not seen in borderline patients.

Freud (1938b) wrote about "splitting" in the course of his discussion of fetishism. If the child has a powerful instinctual demand, such as masturbation, and sees "an almost intolerable real danger [i.e., the threat of castration, he can either decide to] renounce the instinctual satisfaction, or to disavow reality and make itself believe that there is no reason for fear. . . . But in fact, the child takes neither course, or rather he takes both simultaneously. . . . On the one hand . . . he rejects reality and refuses to accept any prohibition; on the other hand . . . he recognizes the danger of reality, takes over the fear of that danger as a pathological symptom and tries subsequently to divest himself of the fear. . . . The two contrary reactions to the conflict persist as the centre-point of a *splitting* [emphasis added] of the ego" (pp. 275-76). Freud means that the child continues to masturbate, but denies the existence of castration, by the use of the fetish, thus creating a "split" in the ego. In a similar fashion, in the "Outline of Psycho-Analysis" (1938a), he speaks of the split between instincts and reality in psychosis, "Two psychical attitudes have been formed instead of a single one—one, the normal one, which takes account of reality, and another which under the influence of the instincts detaches the ego from reality" (p. 202). In these two papers the *split* in the ego relates to the disruption of reality testing in the face of pressure from the drives, both in the fetishist and in the psychotic patient.

In the work of Melanie Klein and her followers, we see the term used in an altogether different way. Segal (1964) wrote,

> When faced with the anxiety produced by the death instinct, the ego deflects it. . . . The ego *splits* [emphasis added] itself and projects that part of itself which contains the death instinct outwards onto the original external object—the breast. . . . As with the death instinct, so with the libido . . . the ego projects part of it outwards, and the remainder is used to establish a libidinal relationship to this ideal object. Thus, quite early, the ego has a relationship to two objects: the primary object, the breast, being at this stage *split* [emphasis added] into two parts, the ideal breast and the persecutory one [p. 256].

This theoretical presentation makes "splitting" one of the central mechanisms of the early infantile paranoid-schizoid "position." A "position," as Segal has written, "implies a specific configuration of object relations, anxiety, and defenses which persist throughout life" (p. 18). As far as we can see, this view bears little relation to Freud's use of the term "splitting." It involves the postulation of instincts connected to formed conscious fantasies in the first months of life, a doubtful conclusion which has been criticized by numerous authors in the literature.

In a more recent publication, Green (1977) wrote,

> The child's *splitting* [emphasis added] is a basic reaction to the object's attitude, which can be twofold: 1) a lack of fusion on the part of the mother, to the effect that even in the actual experience of encounter, the child meets a blank breast; 2) an excess of fusion, the mother being unable to renounce for the sake of her child's growth the paradisiac bliss regained through the experience of pregnancy [p. 34].

Whereas this idiosyncratic view is not widely held, it illustrates how the use of this term continues to be expanded in an inevitably confusing fashion.

Kernberg, as we have seen, attempted to redefine "splitting." He used some of Klein's ideas, while at the same time trying to integrate them with those of Jacobson and Mahler. He specifically repudiated Klein's ideas about the linkage between drive and conscious fantasy in earliest mental life. He also played down the role of the death instinct, seeing it as an unprovable biological theory. He retained from her work, however, the idea that all-good and all-bad "nonmetabolized" self and object images are split off from one another in earliest mental life. According to Kernberg, the all-bad ones are projected outward, "to protect the ego-core" and "to prevent the generalization of anxiety" (1975, p. 25). Although he stated that "splitting" is not the result of the "death instinct," it is clearly linked to excessive aggression, strong oral frustration in earliest infancy, and generalized ego weakness. It would appear that much of his work rests on hypotheses about intrapsychic development in the first year of life. As Meissner (1978) pointed out,

> . . . Kernberg's argument concerns itself very little with
> object relations as such, but rather with the 'internalized
> object relationships.' They seem to come much closer to
> what had been described in other contexts as
> 'introjects' . . . rather than being a theory of object rep-
> resentations, addressing itself to the vicissitudes and me-
> tabolism of such internalized objects with little attention
> to the relationships with objects as such [p. 588].

In elaboration of Meissner's point, it appears to us that Kernberg does not give sufficient weight in his discussions to the
real experiences of the child in relation to the real objects in
his early life, that is to say, his parents and siblings and their
surrogates. Instead, Kernberg focuses on the infantile "primitive," "fantastic" images of mixed self and object introjects in
their earliest and most primitive form. Thus, when he speaks
of the conflict which necessitates "splitting" as a defense, he
writes that "splitting" is useful in "preventing the anxiety arising
at the foci of negative introjections from being generalized
throughout the ego and protects the integration of positive
introjections into a primitive ego core" (1976, p. 36). Although
we understand that Kernberg believes that these early introjects
are derived from the object relationships in the infant's life, he
hypothesizes that the critical conflicts which dominate the growing child's psychic development continue to be between these
polarized "internalized objects," rather than between the child's
changing self-representations and the ever-changing mental
representations of the objects in his environment. Hypotheses
such as the "protection of the ego core" or the protection of
"positive introjects" focus too exclusively on very early psychic
development and must be considered highly speculative at this
point in our understanding of early mental life.

Kernberg also derives his hypotheses from Jacobson's theoretical work (1964), in particular, her proposals about earliest
identity formation. However, there are many points of disagreement as well as points of agreement between these two
authors. Although she did not use the term "splitting," she did
write, "Simultaneously, there is a tendency to cathect one such
composite image unit with libido only, while all the aggression

is directed to another one until ambivalence can be tolerated" (p. 44). She also speculated about the development of the sense of self in the first year of life, but, in contrast to Klein and Kernberg, she saw psychological development during this time as extraordinarily fluid rather than fixed into "positions" or rigidified defensive maneuvers. Her time frame was not clearly spelled out, but she wrote that these processes are at work up to three years and beyond, and therefore are not limited to the first year of life. Furthermore, she emphasized that the danger to further development of the ego rests on the persistent wish for "fusion" with the mother, whereas Klein and Kernberg saw "splitting" of self and object images as the major danger to further ego development.

Jacobson went on to focus on the interaction with the parents and the gradual relinquishment of fantasies of magical, symbiotic fusion in the preoedipal child (1964, pp. 33-70). During this time, she suggested, one can see the development of more selective internalization of partial identifications, so that the child gradually becomes more like the love object in some ways and different from the love object in other ways, with the frequent persistence of more infantile modes of behavior at the same time as advances are being made. This description of the child's development avoids the somewhat rigid, stepwise descriptions which Kernberg seems to imply. It is also very clear that Jacobson considered parental interaction with the child of crucial importance rather than those conflicts which go on between "primitive introjects," and she observed the benefits and the problems which are created by both libidinal and aggressive conflicts. In these chapters she emphasized the danger of prolonging the symbiotic phase of development, and its concomitant danger of continuing fusion of self-representations and object-representations. Jacobson maintained that fusion with the mother during the preoedipal and oedipal years is an intermittent regressive state, whereas according to Kernberg polarization of good and bad introjects mainly during the first year of life causes the failure of healthy ego development. Jacobson postulated regression and progression during a time of fluid ego development, whereas Kernberg pictured a time of fixed, split self- and object-representations.

Jacobson's picture of the child moving toward and away from the mother is consistent with the major work of Mahler and her colleagues (1971, 1975), which describes, in the language of child observation, the gradual emergence of the child from his symbiotic state. Mahler noted the extreme ambivalence of the toddler, but she, like Jacobson, did not believe it to be a fixed defensive position which persists immutably throughout later development. She wrote,

> This phenomenon of "confident expectation," as well as its opposite—more than optimal stranger anxiety and 'basic mistrust'—*contributes and relates* to later attitudes in life even though *intervening drive and defense vicissitudes will, of course, greatly influence and may even change the patterns* [p. 406; emphasis added].

Mahler then went on to speak of "splitting" descriptively. "This may be in some cases a reflection of the fact that the child has split the object world more permanently than is optimal into 'good' and 'bad.' By means of this 'splitting,' the 'good' object is defended against the derivatives of the aggressive drive" (p. 413). We understand this to mean that the so-called "splitting" refers to the displacement of the aggression from one object-representation onto another or onto the self-representation. The purpose of this defensive displacement is to avoid the anxiety engendered by the typical danger situations described by Freud—i.e., loss of the object or loss of the object's love. We believe that this mechanism derives from, or is in the service of, insuring the preservation of the gratifying object by protecting it against the fantasy danger of annihilation which results from the child's destructive wishes. For Kernberg, the aim which is specified is to avoid the "destruction of certain positive introjects" or the "destruction of the ego-core." Once again it appears to us that Kernberg's emphasis utilizes abstractions concerning very early mental life which are far removed from the derivatives of conflict which we see in adult mental life.

To summarize our views on "splitting," we believe that many analysts use the term to describe similar, related clinical events. However, we believe that "splitting" is simply a phenomenological description which has different implications for different authors. It suffers from this fact, and many authors, using diverse developmental and etiological schemata, use the term to support their own quite variable theoretical positions. We agree that the toddler may "split" the mental representation of the mother into all-good and all-bad and may displace the latter feelings onto another or onto the self, in order to preserve the relationship with the mother. However, we believe that it is insufficient and potentially misleading to place such great emphasis on the hypothesis that"splitting" protects the "ego core" (a term which is not easy to define) or protects the "positive introjects." Finally, we also believe that such "splitting" does not represent an immutable fixation which persists unchanged into adult mental life.

Projective Identification

We also discovered that the term "projective identification" has been used by different authors in different ways. The literature does not provide any clear clinical description which would help in the understanding of what various authors mean by the term. Only in Kernberg's papers does one find a consistent usage and definition. Kernberg stated that patients with "borderline personality organization" have strong "projective needs" in order to externalize "the all bad aggressive self and object images so as to protect the 'ego core,' which is made up of good, libidinally charged images." This "projective need" plus "generalized ego weakness" "weakens their ego boundaries particularly in the area of projection of aggression." Therefore, although differentiation between self-representations and object-representations has occurred, thus distinguishing these patients from psychotic ones, they still "identify" with the object onto whom the aggression has been projected. Their "empathy" with the aggressive object increases their fear, so they must attack and control the object who is perceived as sadistic (1975, pp. 30-31). As we understand this description, the fundamental mechanism underlying projective identification is still the pathological "splitting" of all-good and all-bad self- and object-representations, the all bad ones being projected.

When we compare Kernberg's clinical descriptions of his patients to our descriptions of our own patients, we, too, see that our patients project their impulses, both aggressive and libidinal, and then react as if they are about to be attacked or seduced, and in turn, defend themselves. However, we question whether this behavior should be considered to be the result of a "special primitive" defense. How does this defense mechanism differ from ordinary projection? If this is a primitive form of projection, why is it that more severely disturbed psychotics "project" and may not have any "empathy" with the objects of their projected impulse? What is described clinically is apt and accurate, and we frequently see such behavior, particularly with disturbed patients. However, we usually call this maneuver "projection" or, if it can be related to past parental attitudes, we may add the term "identification with the aggressor."

Let us take the example of Case III. She saw the analyst as a sadist who was literally crazy and torturing her. This was in part a projection of her own sadism. She continued to have awareness of feelings that she was abusing him, while, at the same time, she was trying to control him as she feared he would make her his victim. We believe we are observing projection and identification in a patient whose ego boundaries are more fluid than are those of neurotic patients, and whose reality testing is more impaired. We think this is a less cumbersome explanation than postulating a very early "special primitive defense" mechanism.

In effect, we are connecting the observed clinical picture, not to a highly specific, "special primitive defense," but to a greater degree of poor self-object differentiation than that which is seen in most neurotic patients. Furthermore, this characteristic itself is quite variable. In some areas of object relations, such patients may preserve the distinction between the mental representations of themselves and others, while in other areas there may be a failure of such distinctions. Such vicissitudes may depend on frustrations, disappointments, the necessity of using such confusions as a defense, and the pressures of the drives.

Perhaps this is what Kernberg suggested when he conceived of "projective identification" as being related to the "weakening of ego boundaries." However, we were dissatisfied by his limitation of this use of projection to conflicts over aggression, since, as we have stated, all conflicts as well as defensive needs, may produce a weakening of self boundaries and a relative failure of self-object differentiation. Finally, we must add that our clinical experience makes it clear that such failures are not limited to more disturbed patients alone and are present in many neurotic patients as well, particularly in the areas of their most intense conflicts.

In the end, we concluded that "projective identification" was another poorly defined term with more potential for confusing clinical issues than for clarifying them. The actual behavior which it attempts to describe is commonplace and can be understood well enough without postulating this "special defense." In addition, we concluded that such clinical behavior can be observed in patients from all diagnostic categories, although we would agree that it is more frequently to be found in sicker patients, whose self-object differentiations are less stable and whose reality testing is more seriously impaired.

Other Special Primitive Defenses

The other three special defenses postulated by Kernberg as pathognomonic for borderline patients are "primitive idealization," "denial," and "omnipotence and devaluation." By Kernberg's definition, "primitive idealization," as distinct from "idealization," does not involve aggression toward an object with the consequent formation of guilt. According to Kernberg it is based on "splitting" of "all-good" and "all-bad" self- and object-representations, before superego formation and the capacity for internalized guilt have fully developed. "Denial," too, in his terms, refers to the disavowal of one or the other of the polarized ego states and is therefore based on "splitting." "Omnipotence and devaluation," as well, are derived from the same "all-good"/"all-bad" "splitting" which he hypothesizes (1975, pp.

30-34). It is our impression that these three "defenses" are in fact clinical descriptions of isolated, highly organized unconscious fantasies. For example, consistent with Arlow's (1969a, 1969b) beliefs, we think one should not, upon hearing a patient's description of the ideal or devalued analyst, conclude quickly that it represents a transference reaction based on a primitive defense of early life. The initial presentation would have to be elaborated upon and given more detail before one could reconstruct what the underlying unconscious fantasy might be.

From our expressed reservations about Kernberg's postulates regarding "splitting" as a defense mechanism, it follows that we did not find these three derivative "primitive defenses" to be useful concepts. We would prefer to view the presence of extreme idealization, denial of extreme ambivalent feelings, and alternation of omnipotent and devalued feelings toward oneself or others as being quite complex derivatives of unconscious fantasies. Although they certainly may serve defensive purposes as one of their functions, they may be expressions of libidinal, aggressive, narcissistic, and superego needs as well. As to the form which these expressions may take, we would consider the clinical manifestations to be the resultant of the strengths and deficiencies of many ego functions which are simultaneously operating. Therefore, we would consider the "primitivity" to be a reflection of disturbances of many ego functions and not created by the presence of a "special primitive defense."

Kernberg's Views on Repression

In addition to our doubts regarding the absolute applicability of these "special primitive defenses" to borderline patients, we also found ourselves in disagreement with Kernberg's contention that repression is not a major defense in borderline patients. He reached this conclusion by observing the extremes of ambivalence in the transference, which he believes are representative of polarized "ego states." Since he believes that both "all-good" and "all-bad" self- and object-representations are present in consciousness, he concluded that repression is not being used as a defense in these patients. Furthermore, he postulated that this clinical picture is the result of conflict which begins so early that it antedates repression, which he considers a "higher level," i.e., more mature, defense mechanism.

Our clinical observations about the use of repression were strikingly different and support a very different point of view. When we observed the manifestations of extreme ambivalence in the transference, we understood that what was consciously available to the patient at the start of treatment was only a very small portion of the complexly intertwined *unconscious* fantasies, which were only gradually revealed. In this sense, the transference reactions in these patients are no different from the transference behavior of neurotic patients. What is apparent in their behavior from the start is only, metaphorically, the "tip of the iceberg." The complex underpinnings are unconscious. Let us take, for example, Kernberg's patient who idealized and overvalued the analyst and only gradually became aware of his struggle not to devalue him (1975, p. 97). We would certainly be impressed by the intensity of the ambivalence and the suddenness of the shift in the patient's feelings toward the analyst. However, we would wonder what fantasies lay behind the idealization. If it was a defense, what was it a defense against? Was it the projection of an omnipotent, narcissistic image of the self or an object? What made it change? What was the painful affect that led to the change? In our experience, many of the answers to these questions have been repressed, and it requires much analytic scrutiny to expose and clarify them. Therefore, with these patients, as with all others, repression is a central defense mechanism, and only a very small portion of their central dynamic conflicts are present in consciousness during the early phases of treatment.

Summary

We undertook to examine the defense mechanisms and defensive maneuvers displayed by our four analyzed cases. When we did so, we found that we had to review the concept of defense functioning in general. We realized that the ego makes use of any and all of its functions for the purposes of warding off unpleasurable affects, unacceptable mental contents, or both. Some defenses appeared to be more simple in their operation whereas others were more complex, consisting of combinations of fundamental mechanisms. These complex defenses frequently served to express libidinal and aggressive drives, have content and meaning, and aid adaptation, as well as contributing to symptom formation and both normal and pathological character traits.

We felt, however, that analysts would continue to speak and write about "defense mechanisms" because of the generally accepted use of the terms designating specific defensive operations. When we then examined the defenses of our four borderline cases we found that they used all of the different defense mechanisms, both simple and complex. This group of sicker patients did use certain defenses preferentially and more pervasively than do less sick psychoneurotics. Projection, denial, "acting out," identification with the aggressor, and the use of one drive derivative to defend against the other were the preferred defenses we observed. Sadomasochistic libidinal regression should also be included, if regression is considered to be a defense.

Since many authors have concluded that borderlines use more primitive defenses while neurotics use more mature or higher-level ones, we addressed ourselves to the concepts of primitive defenses and the developmental hierarchy of defense mechanisms. We believe that certain assumptions about primitive defenses interfere with our clinical work and theoretical understanding. One assumption is that a so-called primitive defense used by an adult is the *same* as a defense used by a young child. Another is that the use of such primitive defenses means that the patient's pathology can be traced back to an early period of childhood when that defensive operation is presumed to be predominant. A third is that the presence of such a defense is indicative of serious psychopathology.

We felt that defenses should not be designated as primitive

or mature without an evaluation of the total ego organization. What appears to be the operation of a primitive defense depends not merely on the type of defense which is employed but on the nature of the ego involved. The sicker a patient is, the more we see poor ego integration, poor ego organization, and breakdown of ego functions. The defensive processes called into service in such patients appear primitive primarily because of the low level of ego functioning.

We also concluded that we cannot reconstruct a rigid chronological timetable for defenses from the regressive behavior and symptomatology of disturbed patients. We question whether the use of any particular defense, whether it be projection, denial, or splitting, can be traced back to a specific time in infancy when it is theorized that psychopathology may develop.

We studied Kernberg's writings extensively to try to evaluate his hypothesis that "special primitive" defenses are pathognomonic for the clinical entity he calls "borderline personality organization." He suggested that these defenses are not seen in neurotic patients, who use exclusively "higher-level" defenses. In contrast to his beliefs, our cases could not be distinguished from neurotic patients by the defense mechanisms which were present.

Furthermore, a careful evaluation of the term "splitting" led us to conclude that although many authors use the term to describe related clinical phenomena, the term seems to mean different things to different analysts. In our opinion the "split" images observed clinically may well relate to the ambivalence of the anal phase, where the nurturing maternal object is spared from the toddler's fantasy of annihilating her by the latter's displacement of aggression onto an alternate object or onto the self. In this view, there is less need to postulate a fixation point during the first eighteen months of life in order to support hypothetical constructs such as the "ego core" or the "positive introjects." The proposition that "splitting" is based on very early object relationships and the development of fixed, pathological "internalized object relations" is difficult to substantiate from analytic data alone. For these reasons, we feel it is of questionable value to base a specific diagnostic entity, "borderline personality organization," or a therapeutic model on speculations of this order.

An extensive examination of the term "projective identification" revealed that it, too, was ill-defined and confusing. The clinical behavior described is commonly observed and reveals an excessive use of projection, which results in a greater than usual degree of confusion between self-representations and object-representations. This confusion is seen more commonly in sicker patients, who therefore demonstrate a fluidity of ego boundaries and a greater degree of impairment in their reality testing. However, it is not clear that this disturbance is the result of very early disturbances of object relations such as has been suggested by Kernberg. It may well be that throughout childhood, and certainly until some reasonable measure of object constancy has been achieved, there will continue to be an unusually prevalent use of projection as a psychological mechanism, and that it is too restrictive conceptually to limit its use to the first eighteen months of life.

These same considerations would apply to the postulated defenses of "primitive idealization," "denial," and "omnipotence and devaluation." Kernberg related them all to "splitting" mechanisms, a concept about which we have already expressed our reservations. However, we believe that these so-called "primitive defenses" are in themselves highly complex derivatives of unconscious fantasies, each of which must be analyzed for its specific content and must be understood in terms of the total organization of the ego.

We also evaluated the place of repression as a defense in our borderline patients and concluded that it is central in these cases, as it is in all other patients. We observed that the initial "all-good" and "all-bad" polarizations in the transference gradually gave way to reveal more clearly the derivatives of the repressed, unconscious fantasies behind the surface behavior. Analytic treatment indicated that repression was at work against many elements of these underlying fantasies, and it could only gradually be undone. Our observations, therefore, did not support Kernberg's hypothesis that since these extreme polarizations represent "split," conscious "ego states" these patients do not utilize repression as a defense mechanism.

Finally, we wish to comment once again on our changing views of the nature of defenses and defensive structures which are used by all patients. We no longer consider defenses to be rigid or simple mechanisms. We view all psychological behavior as having the capacity to be used for defensive purposes. Furthermore, defensive behavior cannot be viewed as only pathological—i.e., leading to symptom formation or to resistance during treatment. Defensive behavior is a product of compromise formation and serves purposes of drive discharge, superego pressures, and adaptation to reality. As Brenner has written (1976), "Indeed the same ego functions that serve as executants of the drives, the same ones that promote instinctual gratification under one set of circumstances are used defensively at other times, or, for that matter, simultaneously" (p. 77).

7.

Transference and Technique

In the preceding sections, we have attempted to compare our clinical observations concerning borderline patients with the descriptions of the pathology offered by other authors and with the theoretical conclusions they have proposed. Two additional sets of clinical phenomena remain to be considered. These are the special way in which these patients behave in treatment, particularly their transference reactions, and the variations in technical approach which have been proposed for dealing with such patients. Both of these issues have been discussed repeatedly over the past forty years by many authors. We will limit our discussion to just a few of the relevant papers before examining our own clinical findings.

Transference

Stern (1938), one of the earliest writers on this subject, offered both a comprehensive clinical description and a thorough attempt at dynamic understanding of these patients. He described their transference behavior as follows:

> Those patients who come into the analysis with an overt neurosis of which anxiety is the main symptom develop at the very outset of the treatment a violent, clamoring, grasping at the analyst in their great need for protection and assurance. They almost literally attach themselves by every childhood organ or sense of prehension. . . . Those patients who do not develop any acute anxiety present a stolid, at times solid immobile exterior . . . [p. 486].

It is noteworthy that in this early description of these patients Stern included the frozen patient, i.e., that patient whose demeanor is immobile rather than dramatic, a variant of borderline pathology overlooked by a number of other writers who focused exclusively on the more dramatic presentations.

Fifteen years later Stone (1954) presented another comprehensive and thorough description. He suggested that some of these sicker patients could be analyzed, although with more than the usual difficulty. In these analyses, he found "atypical reactions in the early phases of treatment (immediate primitive transference reactions, extreme rigidity, early archaic material, euphoric rapid improvement, terror of the analytic situation, and many other subtle considerations)" (p. 582). Or,

> . . . insatiable demands may appear; or the need to control or tyrannize over the therapist; or failing that, the polar alternative—to be completely submissive, passive, obedient . . . or the transference may be literally narcissistic, i.e., the therapist is confused with the self, or is like the self in all respects . . . or the therapist may be omnipotent, omniscient, God-like . . . [pp. 584-585].

Kernberg (1975) described the transference within the framework of object relations theory. In these patients there is

> premature activation of the transference of very early conflict-laden object relationships in the context of ego states that are dissociated from each other. It is as if each of these ego states represents a full-fledged transference paradigm, a highly developed regressive transference reaction within which a specific internalized object relationship is activated in the transference [p. 77].

Further, he stated that the conflicts which emerge "with the reactivation of these early internalized object relations may be characterized as a particular pathological condensation of pregenital and genital aims under the overlying influence of pregenital aggression" (p. 78). The projection of oral aggression, in particular, creates a paranoid distortion of the early parental images, particularly the mother. Within the transference, after an initially chaotic picture, predominantly "negative transference paradigms" appear. Speaking of "projective identification" (see Chapter 6), he concluded that it is this mechanism which leads to the "intense distrust and fear of the therapist who is experienced as attacking the patient while the patient tries to control the therapist in a sadistic overpowering way" (p. 80).

Keeping the descriptions of these authors in mind, let us go on to examine the transference patterns observed in our own cases.

Immediacy of the Transference Reactions and Distortion of Reality Around the Person of the Analyst

In our cases, the transference was intense from the beginning of treatment, as had been described by the other authors. A tendency toward action was noticed from the start. In addition, there was an inability to accept the "as if" quality of the transference, with an insistence upon literal gratification from the analyst, the "soup, with dumplings" attitude described by Freud (1915a). Although the "as if" quality of the transference feelings is often lost during the most intense periods of the transference neurosis in less sick patients, in our cases the distortions in the sense of reality around the person of the analyst began earlier, lasted longer, and were more blatant throughout most of the treatment despite thorough and careful analytic attention to them. This is quantitatively different from the transference picture found in most neurotic cases and agrees with the findings of the other authors, particularly Kernberg.

A detailed examination of the records of our four cases also revealed that in Cases I, III, and IV there was an important additional feature in that the analyst was unconsciously seen as a literal replacement for the father.

In Case I, for example, the patient maintained that the analyst looked like her father from the first time she saw him, even though it turned out later that the imagined similarity was based on a dim recollection of a photograph of her father. She could not tolerate the frustration involved in his not answering her questions and his not giving her advice. She tried to rent an apartment near him in order to be close to him, and even toward the end of her lengthy analysis, she felt that he should find her a husband since he knew her so well. This was not presented as a wish which could be investigated analytically but as "common sense" to be acted upon directly.

From early on, she consciously tried to make a favorable impression on her analyst/father while unconsciously withholding from him, punishing him, and trying to cause the abandonment by him which she so much feared. Only after she had reached the point of apparent failure and possible termination of her analysis could she modify this behavior so that substantial analytic progress could be made.

In Case III the sadomasochistic paternal transference dominated the analysis from the beginning of treatment. The analyst was believed to be highly critical and easily enrageable. In addition, he was omnipotent and full of knowledge which would prevent all the innumerable dangers of life which surrounded her, particularly medical and psychological dangers. She had to be passive and obedient. However, when she was enraged, he seemed weak, pitiful, and overblown in his presentation of himself, whereas she was now powerful and omniscient. Even at these times, she feared his violent temper and believed she had to back down quickly or he might physically attack her.

Case IV felt that the analyst was not interested in her from the beginning. She believed that he did not care about her possible pregnancies, her medical preoccupations, and her weight problem. Her fear that he would abandon her, which she felt both mother and father had done, led her to constantly provoke him, to both torture him and test him. Her sadomasochistic sexual teasing was a repetition of the exciting tooth extractions and tutoring sessions with her father during her latency years. Late in her treatment she dressed up as a prostitute and brought champagne to her New Year's Eve session to excite, tease, and castrate her analyst and to provoke the rejection she both feared and wished as a punishment. In addition, near the end of her treatment after her father had died, she believed that her analyst would cancel his summer vacation in order to be with her, and she moved to an apartment near his office because he was the "center of my life." At another time when she called his apartment and a woman answered, she was devastated and said, "I thought I was the only one in your life."

Case II deserves special attention because its features depict an important variant of the transference situation which is often seen in borderline patients, as has been indicated by both Stern (1938) and Stone (1954). This patient's transference was also intense and profound from the outset but was silent and hidden from view. Such an absence of expressed transference thoughts and feelings often indicates the unusual intensity of the concealed transference reactions, and it proved to be so in this case. This young man vowed never to have, nor to show, feelings toward his analyst. Such demonstrations of feeling would have represented to him a sign of weakness and of humiliation signifying that he had submitted to his analyst, who would thus experience a triumph over him. His own wishes to humiliate the analyst were hidden behind these feelings. Behind all of these concerns lay his unconscious passive longings to be loved and taken care of by his analyst, which made him fear and wish that he would be changed into a little girl, as in his masturbatory fantasy.

Issues of Separation and Loss

In each of our four cases, issues of separation and loss assumed major proportions although characteristically Case II warded off such feelings for most of his treatment. In our other cases, outbursts of rage and the need to control the analyst were often triggered by separation conflicts. Our patients' sensitivity to these issues was exquisite and extreme. Not only could these feelings be provoked by a weekend separation, the analyst's illness, or a vacation, but even by the end of an hour, or the interruption of the hour by the ringing of an unanswered telephone, or by the next patient ringing the doorbell. Some analysts regularly assume that such sensitivity to loss is always indicative of problems stemming from early maternal deprivation or from a childhood marked by maternal insensitivity.

However, in all of our patients there were significant histories of later object loss and abandonment which had a profound effect on their psychopathology.

In Case I, the father left for the first time in her second year, again at 4 1/2, and permanently during her latency years. She became very attached to her mother and became anxious when she was separated from her. In the transference, she stopped talking before and after interruptions in the treatment, often consoling herself with sweets. "Leaving first" was a method of retaliation. Before the first summer separation she became withdrawn and silent, and before the second summer separation she began planning to move to another city.

Although Case II denied his feelings as much as possible, he came forty-five minutes late to his first session after the analyst's summer vacation during which time he had had the "unacceptable" thought that he would "miss" his analyst. Later in treatment, when his analyst brought up the issue of a consultation, he began to talk about his feelings of loss and his fear of separation from his mother. Her depression and withdrawal after the stillbirth of his sister when he was four were a crucial determinant of this sensitivity. His dreams of being in a cavity, his fantasy of being "tied down" to a woman, and his wish never to be separated from his mother were highly defended against and emerged very slowly in the transference.

Case III had memories from the age of twenty-eight months of her mother being in the hospital to give birth to the patient's sister. She always felt tearful when she recalled the tender reunion after mother returned home. The move from her grandparents' house when she was four years old was upsetting to her and led the analyst to speculate about the importance of the previous separation from her grandparents around the time of her sister's birth as well. Being in her grandmother's bed gave her a sensation of fullness and warmth, whereas summer separations from the analyst led to a feeling of being "dry and dusty inside." The analytic hour was seen "like a hamburger"—one bite and there is less left. Obviously these symbolic presentations had many unconscious meanings, but they dramatized her intense feelings about separation. Her usual overt response was withdrawal or rage.

Separation was one of the two major themes in Case IV. The separation at the time of her mother's splenectomy and her turning toward her father at that time were crucial determinants of her psychopathology. Father's going into the army, the repetitive telephoning, and the fear that he would be sent overseas were coupled with the birth of her brother, which added to her vulnerability in this area. In response to longings for her analyst, she moved close to his office to be near him and she refused to believe that he would leave her for his summer vacation. Outside of the office, she clung to her boyfriends over the telephone in part because of her separation fears as well as her rage and her sadomasochistic involvement with them.

The working through of these repetitive object losses during the patients' early years was of critical importance for their capacity to change. Although we assume, as do other authors, that very early problems between mother and infant may very well have been present in these cases; since there were so many failures of parenting throughout childhood, we could not assign to these early conflicts the exclusive or high priority for the understanding of these patients' sensitivity to separation which many other authors have suggested.

Narcissistic Features

Another facet of the transference relationship encountered in borderline patients, which many authors have described, is its narcissistic character. However, the use of the term "narcissism" involves different conceptual schemata for different authors. Thus for Stern (1938) narcissism meant "frank tendencies in the direction of the psychotic . . . the 'narcissistic neuroses' " (p. 469); and he speculated that the roots of such narcissistic disturbances were in the chronic tension between mother and child. Stone (1954), as quoted above, said "literally narcissistic, i.e., the therapist is confused with the self, or is like the self in all respects. . . ." Followers of Klein might well see the use of the analyst as a "part object," often the all-giving good breast to be loved or envied or the all-bad breast to be defended against, as a similar phenomenon.[1] Kernberg (1975) presented a thorough overview of narcissistic character pathology in all of its clinical aspects. In his view varying levels of conflict may create narcissistic pathology, but in the severe cases he refers to as having "borderline personality organization," the idealization of the analyst is the result of the analyst being seen as an extension of the patient, "a primitive fusion of the self with the ego ideal, and concomitant processes of devaluation of external objects and object images . . . in order to protect the self against primitive oral conflicts and frustration" (p. 241). There is a striking similarity between Kernberg's idea and that of Stern (1938), who wrote: ". . . the patient never identifies himself with the analyst but with his conception of him—through a process of projection of his own ego ideal as embodied in the gigantic size of the analyst (imago)" (p. 484). Kohut (1971), although he used different terminology and did not include the narcissistic character in the borderline category, wrote about similar phenomena. He felt that the analyst represents a "self-object," a structure which represents either the "grandiose self" or the "idealized parent imago." Kohut believed that these structures persist in these patients because they have experienced a failure in parenting during their development which leads to a deficiency in their capacity to regulate self-esteem. He then believes that the analyst, as seen in the transference, will become a compensatory "self-object" for these patients, so that more mature narcissistic structures may develop via "transmuting internalizations." Only then will the more primitive narcissistic structures disappear.

Each of these authors emphasized that the narcissistic pathology seen in these patients gives evidence of the partial failure of separation between self-representations and object-representations, and many authors agree that such pathology involves self-esteem–regulating forces, either related to the ego ideal or its postulated precursors. Kernberg, in particular, following Jacobson, emphasized, however, that such a refusion of self and object may represent a regressive defense against var-

[1] Although Klein does not define this as "narcissistic," it would fit under this category for our purposes.

ious conflicts over aggression, particularly oral aggression, rather than a developmental failure.

Clinically, our four cases evidenced narcissistic pathology similar to that described by all of the authors mentioned above. There were significant failures of empathy by these patients within the analytic situation and in social situations as well. These patients were extremely sensitive to any slight, real or imagined, and would often experience interpretations, no matter how tactfully presented, as assaults on them and as a cause for mental anguish. At the same time, their preoccupation with their own discomfort made them unusually insensitive to the discomfort they tended to arouse in others, including the analyst. Their view of themselves as well as their view of the analyst was unrealistically aggrandized or degraded, and there were frequent shifts between the one of these positions and the other.

Case I had an idealized, romantic fantasy about the analyst and his wife as well as about her sister and her husband. They were all bright and happy and very much in love, in contrast to her own misery and relative isolation. Her analyst was thought to be wise and knowledgeable on all topics and was expected to give her advice on how to live her life. She even believed that he should select a husband for her. All competitive and hostile feelings toward him were denied.

Case II avoided closeness with anyone to avoid being hurt or humiliated. He felt that the only one he ever loved was his dog. His analyst was seen as competitive with him and out to humiliate him. He was also seen as trying to ensnare him. To protect himself he had to remain isolated and aloof, using defensive withdrawal to ward off libidinal and aggressive impulses, which were then projected. His projection was so extensive that the distinction between himself and his analyst often seemed to be blurred.

Case III was preoccupied with herself to such a degree that she placed herself at the center of everyone's thinking and behavior, including her analyst's. All interpretations were felt as slights and accusations, and she felt the analyst should be totally preoccupied with her. Her self-esteem underwent wide swings. Sometimes she saw herself as aggrandized and omniscient, but more commonly her analyst was idealized while she was devalued and worthless. Frequently she could not believe that her analyst was not having exactly the same thoughts or feelings as she was, and equally often she imagined that he had the same expectations of her as she had of him.

Case IV was often obtuse to the feelings and needs of others. She drew her friends into her conflicts over her separation fears and pregnancy fears. She insisted that her boyfriends and her analyst share her panics and concerns. She dangled her diet pills in front of her analyst to prove his lack of interest in her while demanding that he rescue her from the "quack" doctors. Often the men in her life were seen as ideal, contrasting with the often degraded view of the analyst, who himself might be idealized at other times. There were many instances where she not only assumed that her analyst felt the same way that she did but tried to induce him to enact her fantasies with her. For example, she brought champagne to her New Year's Eve session to dramatically act out her oedipal fantasy.

We understood these narcissistic features in our patients to be derived from instinctual conflicts, sexual as well as aggressive, rather than to be the result of developmental failure. Narcissistic isolation or withdrawal could defend against aggression, or it could convey it, or both. It could be intended to produce guilt in others. It could represent a retreat from libidinal desires which created painful affects of anxiety or guilt. It could prevent shame or "narcissistic mortification"; or it could be an identification with the narcissistic position of the hated/needed parent. Our findings confirmed the observations of other authors who stated that there was an underlying wish to fuse with the analyst as an idealized figure or as a part of the self, or that there was a wish for the analyst to function as a supportive and esteem-regulating parent to make up for past parental deficiencies. Often these wishes were expressed with the additional desire that the analyst/parent/lover magically know the patient's thoughts and feelings without their having to be expressed. However, such wishes served at the same time to help avoid and defend against the expression of forbidden sexual and aggressive wishes which might lead to unpleasurable affects such as anxiety, guilt, and shame.

We noted that in our patients these wishes masked profound sadomasochistic conflicts. In cases I, III, and IV, the wish to fuse and to be understood by the ideal, supportive, and nurturing analyst as an idealized parent or as an extenstion of the self would rapidly be supplanted by rage at the analyst when disappointment supervened. The analyst was then seen as the insensitive torturer, abusing and humiliating the vulnerable patient. At the same time, the analyst would feel attacked and abused by the patient, who viewed his own rage as secondary protection against the sadistic analyst. As discussed in the section on defenses, there are different ways to understand this clinical behavior. As we understood these relationships and attitudes, the analyst was a repository of the patient's projected sadism, which itself often had been stimulated via the mechanism of identification with the aggressor in childhood. The narcissistic withdrawal and fantasies of fusion in our patients gradually diminished with the elucidation and understanding of these sadomasochistic conflicts.

In summary, then, we could not subscribe to the position that narcissistic fixation in our patients resulted exclusively from specific developmental failures, specific developmental conflicts, or specific aggressive conflicts alone. We felt instead that the narcissistic position was a defensive one which was developed and maintained to control and express both sexual and aggressive drives in order to avoid the typical danger situations as outlined by Freud and to prevent the development of painful affects.

Shifting Transference Images

Another clinical finding of some interest is that in these cases the transference shifted unusually rapidly, with the analyst representing father, mother, and projected self, as well as other important figures from the patients' lives. Whereas many neurotic patients may stay fixed in a particular transference posture for weeks or months or may manifest certain transference attitudes related to an important figure from their past, these patients would often, within the same or adjacent hours, have transference reactions derived from different past experiences. This shifting imagery increased the difficulty of consistent interpretation and contributed to the chaotic and staccato quality of the treatment.

In Case I, the analyst was seen primarily as the longed-for father who would not abandon her and would guide her life. In the midst of talking about a man she had met, she remembered crying for her father at the window. Suddenly the analyst was seen as her interfering and disapproving mother. In addition, the analyst could never separate her positive oedipal longings from her negative oedipal ones so that interpretation of one often was given while the patient had shifted to the other.

This was certainly true in Case III as well. Associations to her analyst as critic and torturer were derived from both her father and her mother, and although father dominated the sadomasochistic associations, others seemed derived equally from both parents. In addition, as in Case I, whenever she longed for her analyst or had loving feelings toward him as a positive or negative oedipal partner, he also was seen as the disapproving and interfering rival parent of the opposite sex. Such double imagery made transference interpretation exceedingly difficult.

Case IV's problems with separation and abandonment were clearly tied historically to both her parents, as were her pregnancy wishes and fears. Even late in her analysis, associations would shift from one parental figure to the other. In this case, as in Cases I and III, the analyst was viewed simultaneously as the longed-for parent as well as the intruder in the triangular relationship.

In Case II, however, the analyst was seen first as the competitive father and projected sadistic self-image who was trying to break the patient down and was gloating at his defeat. Later it seemed clear that behind that image lay that of the seducing woman who wanted to change him into a little girl. However, in this case the images were layered in a much more consistent way, similar to those of neurotic cases with which we are more familiar.

Our understanding of this transference behavior agrees in

part with Kernberg's suggestion that such shifts may derive from the fused parental images of the preoedipal years. However, we also think it likely that this behavior serves defensive purposes as well, by the employment of one drive derivative to defend against the other as well as projection, displacement, and regression. Furthermore, it seems evident from our material that any triangular love relationship is intensely laden with guilt, anxiety, or both so that the punishing rival is always present in the transference picture. This may account in part for the double image of the analyst which we have reported. All of these factors contribute to the confusing clinical picture one encounters with these patients.

Countertransference

As a final note on our clinical experience with these patients, we observed that the intense, repetitive transference patterns, along with the use of "acting out," projection, identification with the aggressor, and the use of one drive derivative to defend against the other, elicited intense countertransference feelings in the broad sense of the term.[2] Most prominent were feelings of being attacked, confusion, frustration, guilt, and counter-aggression on the part of the analyst. Because of the analyst's conflicts over such feelings, he tended to become silent or inactive, inhibit his interpretative efforts, or withdraw emotionally, any of which might increase the patient's anxiety and guilt. Each patient was sensitive to the analyst's reaction formation and withdrawal, and the resultant feelings often intensified the patient's fear of his own sadism and destructiveness.

A number of comments from our case reports are relevant here. In Case I the analyst described his "pessimism" and "frustration," and he questioned the "viability of treatment" because of her "surface withholding and her apparent inability to respond and behave like more typically cooperative analysands." Later, in the third year, he described "hopelessness," "guilt,"

---

[2] We use "countertransference" here not as limited to those personal neurotic conflicts evoked in the analyst, but rather, to designate all of the feelings produced in the analyst by the patient.

and a sense of "analytic inadequacy." He tried to keep these feelings from showing, but they obviously contributed to his thoughts about "stalemate" and "termination."

Case II tried to elicit in the analyst feelings of "helplessness," "defeat," and "humiliation." The whole treatment was conducted with the pervasive question "Can this patient be analyzed?" in the background.

In Case III, the analyst felt chronically tortured and bullied. He felt confused and irritated and desired to punish or abandon the patient, or to do both. Guilt feelings and rescue fantasies, often with unrealistic personal countertransference elements, were often reactive to his own more sadistic impulses or pessimistic moods. Similar feelings were created in the analyst in Case IV. Her endless provocativeness and belittling of the analyst stimulated his sadistic and abandoning impulses, which led to reactive feelings on his part.

We believe that these countertransference feelings, once understood, were most useful in the treatment of these patients. As with psychotic patients, and to a lesser extent with neurotics, these patients frequently seemed able to create in the analyst those specific feelings that the patients themselves experienced *vis-à-vis* their parents in childhood. The growing awareness that the mechanism involved was identification with the aggressor helped us to understand these important unconscious conflicts. As many other authors have emphasized, we found that awareness of "countertransference reactions" in the broad sense is a crucial tool for understanding these sicker patients.

Summary

In summary, our major findings concerning borderline patients agreed with the clinical picture various authors have drawn to describe them. We would characterize them in the following way: (1) These patients demonstrated a notable immediacy, intensity, and fixity of transference reactions whether they were dramatically revealed or rigidly blocked; (2) they showed a persistent defect in the capacity to test reality concerning the person of the analyst along with the wish for literal gratification from

him; (3) there was exquisite sensitivity to separation and loss;
(4) there was a pronounced narcissistic transference attitude;
(5) there were prominent unconscious sadomasochistic conflicts; (6) these patients demonstrated shifting or fused transference imagery; (7) intense countertransference reactions were
regularly stimulated in the analyst by their behavior.

The reader will note that these prominent transference features closely resemble our characterization of the object relations outlined in Chapter 4. Upon reflection, this is not
surprising, and it would be remarkable if it were otherwise since
our best understanding of the object relations of all patients is
gained through the analysis of the transference.

Technique

In describing the clinical picture of the borderline patient, we
emphasized transference and countertransference reactions.
We will now consider the technical recommendations these features imply for the treatment of such patients. We have already
expressed our reservations as to the usefulness of "borderline"
as a diagnostic category or even as a term to denote a cohesive
group of patients with special problems in common with one
another. We prefer to view "borderline" as only a broad classification of illness containing within it widely different specific
symptom configurations with a considerable range of variation
in the degree of psychopathological disability involved. As a
result, we do not subscribe to the idea that there is one specific
treatment approach which is optimal in all cases. Instead, we
believe that there are a variety of technical approaches which
may be applicable to patients who fall within this category. Some
would require hospital treatment, others pharmacotherapy, still
others various forms of psychotherapy, including family, group,
and analytically oriented psychotherapy. However, our experience leads us to conclude that there are some, such as our
four cases, who can be treated by the psychoanalytic method.
It is to the treatment of this group that we wish to address
ourselves.

Assessment

In attempting to determine whether psychoanalysis is likely to be the optimal treatment for one of these cases, our assessment techniques are not any different from those used with other prospective analysands. We conduct relatively unstructured interviews, not for diagnostic purposes alone, but also to determine the analyzability of the patient. With this as our frame of reference certain issues are always kept in mind. What is the individual's capacity to work within the psychoanalytic framework and profit from it? Which are the major conflicts discernible? How stable and how flexible is the patient's defensive structure? How extensive is the use of projection and denial? What is the quality of the patient's object relations? What do we estimate to be the degree of ego strength? How likely are impulsive activity, severe self-destructive behavior, or both to be a serious problem? What is the motivation for treatment? Can the patient sustain the controlled regression necessary for analysis?

These are difficult questions to answer in regard to any patient. Every experienced analyst is aware that accurate prediction of analytic success at the time of the initial evaluation is problematic even with less sick patients. As a rule, only after an analysis is well under way does one form a more reliable impression about how well the work will proceed, and even at later stages in the treatment, experience has taught us that surprises in either direction may well occur. However, in these "borderline" cases, because of the greater degree of illness present, early assessment is likely to be more than usually difficult and the conclusions drawn must be even more tentative than with a healthier group of patients. In our own group of four cases, each analyst came to regard the patient as borderline, and the Kris Study Group concurred (see Chapter 2), but not all were so diagnosed at the time of initial evaluation. In any event an analysis of unusual difficulty was anticipated in each case based upon the data of the initial assessment.

Kernberg's approach to diagnosis and assessment in these cases contrasts in some ways with what we have described. He recommends conducting what he calls a "structural" diagnostic assessment. In these interviews he investigates issues similar to those evaluated in our interviews, such as object relations, anxiety tolerance, subliminatory capacity, and the nature of the defensive structure. However, he puts special emphasis on the need to search for the presence of "splitting" mechanisms since he believes they are of crucial diagnostic significance and will influence the type of therapy to be prescribed. Therefore, in his diagnostic interviews he recommends the active confrontation of any contradictions which the patient may present within what he calls "a framework of technical neutrality." He feels that this approach will highlight the pathology which may be present. According to Kernberg, if the patient is psychotic, such confrontations will produce further regression and decompensation. In the cases he calls "borderline personality organization," the patient will become markedly anxious or will temporarily disorganize, but not to as severe a degree as would psychotic patients. In his early papers, Kernberg believed that either response would contraindicate the recommendation of psychoanalysis as the treatment of choice and would lead him to prescribe instead "expressive psychotherapy." This latter recommendation might often include adjunctive therapies, including pharmacotherapy, hospitalization, and the use of cotherapists to direct the patients in their everyday lives. More recently, however, Kernberg modified his views and came to believe that some borderline patients can undergo the psychoanalytic method of treatment (1976).

Our group's combined clinical experience did not confirm Kernberg's contention that confronting patients with conscious contradictions during the evaluative sessions would necessarily yield the type of useful data he believes will be forthcoming. In order to illustrate and clarify this issue, we decided to select examples of the contradictions which we believe Kernberg might have chosen from these data to illustrate his ideas. Our selections are based on our understanding of his published work as well as the conceptualizations of his technique that we gained from his discussions with the study group.

Let us examine Case II with this in mind. The patient came to treatment, in part, because he had been fighting with his mother and felt that she had babied him excessively. When his father separated from his mother and left the parental home, the patient became increasingly argumentative and angry with his mother, without any realization that he was frightened by the increased closeness to her. Yet, when his mother urged him to enter treatment, he accepted a referral from his mother's former analyst. Our discussion with Kernberg led us to believe that he would say that this represented a major contradiction in the patient's mental life, and that this paradoxical situation should have been presented to him during the evaluation interviews. If the patient was so distrustful of his mother and her wishes to seduce and baby him, how could he accept her recommendation for an analyst? Another apparent contradiction was the discrepancy between his conscious fear of being humiliated by the analyst and his conscious desire to continue to come to treatment. By confronting such contradictory attitudes, Kernberg believes that one increases the patient's anxiety, since the presence of "splitting mechanisms" requires that contradictory and polarized "all-good" or "all-bad" images, in this case of mother or father and analyst, be kept apart.

We did not understand the patient's contradictory attitudes as a consequence of "splitting" mechanisms. Instead, we felt that these attitudes were derived from complex sets of interrelated fantasies, many components of which were unconscious, and that the affects associated with these multiple fantasies were contradictory to one another, but appropriate to their unconscious roots. He trusted his mother and took her recommendation for an analyst, but at the same time he distrusted her in other ways. He loved her but also wished to seduce her, which frightened him and made him fear her. He also wished to reject and punish her and then wished to escape from her because of the guilt stimulated by his hostile fantasies toward her. Therefore, though he feared and distrusted her, these feelings and fantasies would not necessarily be incompatible with his taking her recommendation for an analyst since there were also strong loving ties between the two of them.

In a similar fashion, we saw nothing unusual in the ambivalent fantasies about his analyst/father. He could admire, revere, and passively submit to him, while at the same time he had to be extremely wary of him and express as little feeling as possible toward him since he was sure that he would be humiliated or attacked by him. These competing sets of feelings would be surface derivatives of complex interrelated unconscious fantasies, whose full elaborations we would expect to emerge more clearly during the course of analysis.

In Case III the analyst did comment on her contradictory feelings about herself, although not in the initial interviews. On the one hand she saw herself as a degraded object, a worthless "piece of shit," while simultaneously she believed herself to be omnipotent and special. When confronted with these contradictions, no increase of anxiety or disorganization was observed. These feelings continued to be present in consciousness throughout much of the treatment, often existing simultaneously, and she would refer to them as images of herself, both of which were felt intensely. In this case, as in Case II, our findings did not support the thesis that these different images represented early polarized "ego states." Only as a result of her long and difficult treatment were the analyst and the patient eventually able to understand the complicated, unconscious roots of these feelings about herself. Among the numerous unconscious determinants of her degraded, dirty image of herself was an enormous sense of guilt over sexual impulses and feelings, many of which had sadistic overtones. There was a fusion in her mind of the representation of her vagina and her anus, resulting in the belief that these were smelly and dirty organs used for bad purposes, i.e., masturbation, sex, and elimination. Derivatives of her phallic fantasies, on the other hand, contributed to her feeling clean, powerful, and competent. In many associations the images of herself as a phallic woman were extensions of the earlier "queen" fantasies derived from her early life with her grandparents, the all-good parents of her family romance. Degraded and omnipotent feelings also represented the two sides of her sadomasochistic conflicts: the victim, helpless and worthless, on the one hand and the Nazi/jailer/sadist with the powerful phallus on the other.

When we understood our patients' feelings and fantasies in

this way, we concluded that it is not the existence of differing and polarized self and object images that is of crucial importance in our clinical assessment of these patients. In fact, the concept of polarized "ego states" may in some way detract from the analyst's attention to, and understanding of, the unconscious fantasies which always lie behind these ambivalent images. The extremely ambivalent attitudes toward self and others in our patients, when fully analyzed, were understood in terms of ubiquitous instinctual conflicts similar to those found in our less sick patients. In the case of these patients, as with all others, the conflicts had to be understood in relation to drive, defense, ego strength, unconscious fantasy, and historical events. The degree of ambivalence presented by our patients in our assessment interviews gave us insufficient information by itself to decide for or against analysis. Our decision rested on a multitude of other factors, as we have indicated.

Finally, we could not confirm Kernberg's technical postulate that the bringing together of the polarized images produces anxiety and disorganization which indicates the degree of psychopathology present, since such responses were absent in our patients. In fact, it did not seem reasonable to us that all borderline patients would respond in any single characteristic way to confrontation or any other stress.

Technical Recommendations

Thus far, we have focused on the questions of diagnostic and prognostic assessment. In our discussion of the technical approach to the analytic treatment of these patients, we will find it instructive once again to compare our ideas with those of Kernberg and of Rinsley and Masterson, who have written extensively on this subject.

Consistent with his theoretical ideas about polarized and split ego states and the maturational failure which results from the persistence of these pathological defense mechanisms, Kernberg offered some definite recommendations about the technical sequence he believes is essential for treating these patients. Since he believes that the first task of treatment must be to bring about the progressive fusion of these "split" polarized images and the gradual tolerance of ambivalence, he recommends consistent and persistent confrontation of the contradictions within the patients' productions in order to make the patients increasingly aware of their need to maintain the "split" states. For example, he might point out to a patient that for weeks he or she had had only idealizing and loving feelings toward him whereas now he or she feels only hostile and belittling feelings toward him. He would not add any clarifying genetic or historical material, nor would he interpret that one group of feelings may have given way to the other in the face of anxiety, guilt, or other painful affects. He believes such interpretations are premature during the early stages of treatment and do not help the patient deal with the primary problem, which, in his opinion, is pathological "splitting" and the other related primitive defenses which are present. In essence, he does not recommend attempting to get the patient to wonder why the split images of self and object are in focus at this point in the treatment but contents himself with bringing the split images together. He would not interpret, as we might, that the idealizing and loving feelings which the patient had must have made him or her anxious or guilty or vulnerable and may well have been connected to fantasies which made him or her so uncomfortable that he or she shifted to the other side of the ambivalence in order to reduce the tension. Kernberg made it clear to us that he believes such approaches or the addition of genetic connections do not help these patients in these early stages of treatment until the "splitting" mechanisms have been significantly modified.

Our experience leads us to different conclusions. We found it to be therapeutically helpful and useful to the patients to interpret why their feelings had shifted so rapidly and suddenly from one attitude to its opposite. It was helpful also to connect such shifting attitudes to their past experiences with others if sufficient information was available to believe that the connections were reasonably valid. We are well aware that premature genetic and dynamic interpretations may at times lead to intellectualized responses, increased rigidity of defensive patterns, or both, but we did not observe that our approach had these negative effects. From the beginning of the treatment of these cases an understanding of the past, viewed through the transference and in relation to outside figures in the patients' present lives, offered a framework and a structure to their views about themselves which allowed the patients to begin to undo their confusion and defensiveness, even though, as has been noted, these patients made very slow analytic progress.

In Case I the negative atmosphere of the treatment was slowly understood by her to relate mainly to her complex relationship to her father. Her need to fail, to do analysis badly, to provoke rejection, and to avoid abandonment were all placed in a genetic framework. This allowed her to gain some perspective on her difficulties despite the intense resistances which have been described.

Case II entered treatment with "respect and admiration" for his father. He readily submitted to his father's will and to what evolved as an "often insensitive, mocking, impatient, and sarcastic" attitude on his father's part. Gradually he became aware of his fear that his own anger would end their relationship. As he became more aware of his own anger, he became less dependent on his father and did better in his studies. All of this took place early in his treatment.

Early in her treatment Case III began to see, albeit with difficulty, how her sexual inhibitions, her binge eating, her poor self-esteem, and her hypochondriasis were related to the intense sadomasochistic relationship with her father. Both the libidinal and the aggressive conflicts which were reactivated in the transference gave her some beginning perspective on her symptomatology and her character pathology.

Case IV was quite similar. Like Case III, she found it difficult to believe that her pregnancy fears and her hypochondriasis had other meanings, but she slowly developed some insight into the relationship between these problems and past events in her life. A symptom, pointing her finger to her temple, abated quite early in the treatment.

Another technical recommendation made by Kernberg and many other authors is that certain transference interpretations, particularly those focusing on negative transference feelings, are of critical importance early in the treatment of these cases. Kernberg believes strongly that one must pursue the negative transference within a framework of "technical neutrality" (1976, pp. 161-165). However, we believe that selective emphasis upon the pursuit of negative transference or the persistent confrontation of contradictions may have an impact on the analytic process which distorts analytic neutrality. It is, to be sure, "neutral" in the sense that the analyst does not interfere in the patient's life nor is he moralistic or judgmental. However, we believe such predetermined selectivity produces an artificial interruption of free association and constitutes a preplanned approach which attempts to organize the treatment in a way which we believe is less analytically "neutral" than to deal with the material as the patient presents it, including, of course, his response to the analyst and the analytic situation.

Furthermore, we believe it is too restrictive to consider that negative transference feelings are caused solely by aggressive conflicts. Although these patients have profound difficulties dealing with their aggressive impulses, they have equal difficulty in dealing with libidinal impulses and closeness in general. In fact, one of the most striking features of all four cases was their need to regressively distort and defend against the profound libidinally exciting material which had been stimulated in the transference. Case I denied her conscious masturbatory excitement until the analysis itself was jeopardized. Case II withheld his fantasy of wanting to be changed into a little girl. In Case III the transference was dominated by flooding of regressive material, but little was said about her romantic and sexual wishes because of the degree of anxiety and guilt they engendered. One has only to think of the dream at the end of her second analytic year. "She was riding in a bus with a man but preferred the man behind her. She lifted her skirt and farted in his face." Case IV also revealed many of her sado-masochistic wishes during the early phases of treatment, but the intensity of her libidinal and romantic feelings toward the analyst were usually acted out with young men outside of the treatment.

As one can see, the presence of negative transference feelings should not be exclusively related to agressive conflicts. Equal attention must be paid to libidinal and aggressive impulses and to the defenses against both.

It should also be noted that during the very earliest times in the treatment of all four cases, superego interpretations were made. Despite the presence of all sorts of impulsive behavior, interpretation of guilt, both conscious and unconscious, was an important aspect of their treatment.

As may be seen from these comments, we could not agree with the idea of a specific treatment program for these patients in which the analyst focuses first on "split ego states" or "primitive transference paradigms" or negative transference and works them through before going on to deal with intersystemic structural conflicts, particularly libidinal ones, and "higher-level" defenses such as repression. In the treatment of our patients, sexual and aggressive conflicts, anamnestic material lifted from repression, superego conflicts, and prominent defenses were all dealt with as they were evident in the material from the beginning of the treatment, subject to the analyst's judgment of what the patients could begin to understand about themselves. Therefore, our actual work concentrated more on conflictual elements when they were most prominent, rather than on a preconceived order of treatment which was based on the diagnosis of borderline. Although Kernberg suggested that his approach may shorten the length of the analytic work, evidence to support such a claim is difficult to document in any convincing manner at this time.

Rinsley (1977) and Masterson and Rinsley (1975) also wrote extensively about borderline patients and recommended a specific interpretative focus and special treatment technique for dealing with such cases. These authors believe that the mother of the borderline patient has created with her infant/child the following mental representations: a "rewarding part unit" for clinging, regressive behavior and a "withdrawing part unit" for any attempt by the infant/child at separation and individuation. They believe that from the beginning of treatment the therapist must confront this regressive alliance between the "pleasure ego" and the "rewarding part unit." He must also confront the patient's expectation of withdrawal by the therapist/mother for attempts to individuate. Gradually then, the patient can make an alliance between the "therapist's healthy ego and the patient's embattled reality ego." This creates for the patient "a new object relations unit: the therapist as a positive (libidinal) object representation who approves of separation-individuation + a self representation as a capable, developing person + a 'good' feeling (affect) which ensues from the exercise of constructive coping and mastery rather than regressive behaviour" (*ibid.,* p. 172). They believe that gradually the patient can become aware of both good and bad self-representations and good and bad object-representations which have been clearly separated from one another. Finally, the integration of good and bad self- and object-representations as described by Kernberg takes place.

Again we found that the conceptualization of a single phase-specific determinant for the pathology of these patients and a therapeutic approach geared to such a hypothesis were at variance with our views of the complexity and individuality of our patients. Although the authors use terminology different from ours, consistent with their "object relations" theoretical approach, there is no doubt that their observations about the frequent reinforcement of passive behavior by the mothers of these patients were not uncommon clinical findings. However, it is not an exclusive finding in sicker patients alone, nor was it always observed in our sicker patients. Even when treating patients whose parents supported passive and dependent behavior and created guilt for independent strivings and freedom from control, we could not agree with the thesis that such behavior is always primarily or exclusively derived from conflicts around the "depressive position" in infancy or the rapprochement subphase of the separation-individuation process. In fact, we were impressed by how much the material reflected concerns related to anal and phallic phase conflicts. Most typical of the anal phase conflicts were excessive compliance, rebelliousness, or both, and constant concerns over control and power. The phallic level conflicts, usually centered around issues of how much sexual freedom was allowed versus how much sexual constriction had to be displayed to the parent in order to maintain parental love. Since we have found that the issue of reinforcement of passivity may be derived from any or all developmental phases, we are skeptical of the value of a pre-patterned technical approach confined to a single set of developmental issues such as these authors have suggested.

Some clinical examples from our cases illustrate the over-determination and complexity of the unconscious determinants of patients' behavior and will further demonstrate the basis for our differing viewpoint. Case II provides a particularly suitable example because passivity, so strongly emphasized by these authors, was a central conflict for this patient. We understood his passivity to result from the influence of a series of interrelated unconscious fantasies and important historical events which had to be gradually unraveled and reconstructed. These included his identification with his dead sister, his fear of castration by his father in response to his oedipal wishes toward his mother, and his desire to be trapped by a woman which in turn defended him against his wish to control her so that she would never leave him. These fears and wishes were reinforced by the family myth built around the story of his father's efforts to rescue the dying sister. In his unconscious he believed that his father had killed the sister and feared his father might also kill him. He also felt guilty about his own death wishes toward the baby. His passivity was reinforced by the injections administered by both parents for his recurrent ear infections. These experiences intensified his passive phallic wishes to be penetrated by both parents. All of his passive wishes to be controlled and held were reinforced, as well, by his sensitivity to object loss. His mother's preference for his brother and her depression following the death of his sister made his need to hold onto objects, as well as his defenses against that need, particularly important to him. By recognizing the importance of these fantasies and conflicts, we could explain his passivity in a more thorough and meaningful way than if we viewed it primarily as the result of conflicts between a rewarding or punishing image of his mother as part-object based on separation-individuation conflicts.

In Case III as well, the patient demonstrated excessive passivity toward authority figures, her parents, and the analyst. Her behavior can largely be understood as the result of her belief that her father and the analyst were omnipotent sadists who were to be feared. Because of her fear and her guilt, she projected her own sadism and remained passive in order to keep her violent impulses under control. When she was four years old, her father's presence in the operating room when an acute strangulated hernia was repaired by the local surgeon increased her fear of him, as did her witnessing of parental intercourse when she was between two-and-a-half and three years old. Her family's anti-Semitism also heightened her identifications with Nazi and Jew, and the fantasies associated with both images reinforced her guilt and fear. Passivity as a behavioral manifestation or character trait should be understood as a resultant of many conflict-induced compromise formations, of which those centering around separation-individuation issues are only one variety. To focus exclusively or even primarily on those conflicts would risk neglecting many of the determinants which seemed crucial in our series of cases.

Our work with these patients confirmed our opinion that no special techniques need be recommended for the analysis of borderline patients. Defenses of all types, transference reactions, superego pressures, genetic material, and anamnestic data from all stages of development were interpreted, worked through, and understood as significant material emerged from repression with sufficient clarity. As the patient's and the analyst's understanding broadened, it was very clear that the initial transference behavior, rather than representing an infantile "ego state," could better be considered the proverbial "tip of the iceberg." Underlying this highly condensed behavior, there could be found the usual set of complex and intertwined intersystemic conflicts from all developmental stages, including the later ones of latency and adolescence.

However, we must emphasize once again that our cases represented a group of analyzable borderline patients, although analyzable with difficulty. Many severe borderline cases are probably not suitable for traditional analytic treatment. Some of the patients discussed by the Kris Study Group fell into this latter category. Often they had been treated more supportively with psychotherapy, and, in consequence, less was understood about their conflicts. In those cases there seemed to be even more extensive failures of reality testing and more pervasive uses of projection, "acting out," and drive discharge than in our four reported analyzed cases. However, even in this small group of cases, no set format of therapy can be recommended because they do not comprise a homogeneous group of patients.

Between the advocacy of specific alterations of analytic technique for borderlines and our own recommendation of adherence to traditional analytic principles and technique, there exists a grey area. Some analysts recommend, for certain sicker patients at least, what might be called minor modifications of technique. Stone (1954), for example, suggested that making occasional supportive remarks, answering more questions, giving some personal information, or dealing more directly with some life crises may be helpful in these more disturbed cases. His views come close to what Loewenstein (personal communication) described as maintaining an "optimal level of frustration," i.e., that amount of frustration which the patient can tolerate so as to enable the analysis to proceed, as contrasted with a degree of frustration which for that patient would lead to an unnecessary disruption of the analytic work.

For many analysts an effort to "titrate" the patient's ability to accept frustration in such ways as Stone describes would not constitute any modification at all. Instead, it would be taken as a matter of course that such modulation of technique naturally follows from one's clinical judgment of the patient's capacities, and this would apply to analyzing less sick patients as well. Others would look askance at even the slightest calculated departure from the application of strict analytic principles. They would consider such modification as an impediment to achieving optimal analytic results in the long run even if they appear to achieve some immediate therapeutic gains. Obviously it is difficult to categorize or evaluate absolutely recommendations of this kind, and the authors of this report do not always agree among themselves on these matters. However, we all do feel that these variations often reflect differences in the temperament and style of the analyst as well as that of the patient. Differences of this sort in the treatment ambiance are at times colloquially referred to as problems of "fit," and we believe it is likely that such factors are particularly important in determining the success of the analytic treatment of borderlines, especially those at the more difficult end of the spectrum of analyzability. In our view, the major principle of technique with borderlines is the need to maintain, insofar as possible, an analytic relationship with the patient in each case, and not to substitute for it an exhortatory, educational, or managerial one.

To return to our own group of analyzable cases, we do not mean to imply that the treatment was not different from our treatment of our usual neurotic cases. Although no special techniques were used, certain special features were evident. There was a need to interpret and reinterpret projection mechanisms with care and tact, combined with the necessity of paying constant attention to the partial failure of the reality function. Sadomasochistic conflicts required painstaking working through, as did the analysis of "acting out" and the unusual pervasiveness of the transference distortions. All of this took place in an atmosphere of discouragement and doubt, accompanied by unusually strong anxiety, shame, and guilt; any change resulting from the interpretations took place slowly and intermittently. To quote one group member: "It was like conducting an analysis in molasses." Furthermore, in all of the cases, the degree of discouragement and the difficulty of the treatment led the analysts to suggest consultation or termination, and in one case the patient was allowed to sit up for the final few years of treatment.

In contrast to those authors who believe that they can clearly see conflicts of the earliest time of life from the beginning of the treatment, we found the opening phases of treatment extremely chaotic, puzzling, and obscure. Although some conflicts were interpretable quite early, it was only much later in the treatment that both the analyst and the patient were able to develop a clearer picture of the interplay of psychological forces which underlay the patient's problems despite the fact that overt manifestations of these problems had been present from the beginning of the analysis. These observations made it difficult for us to understand how other authors were able to see "primitive transference paradigms" or infantile "positions" deriving from early in life so clearly in the very early months of treatment.

In the face of the slow progress and the feeling of futility and impotence often aroused in the analyst, attention to countertransference attitudes seemed even more critical in these cases than in our neurotic cases, where such issues tended to be more circumscribed. In these cases, which were analyzable only with difficulty, there was a constant temptation to modify or abandon the treatment approach. As has been mentioned above, it was our conclusion, well documented by many other authors, that such countertransference feelings of impotence, discouragement, and confusion are often important parts of a communication made by the patient to the analyst as to how the patient may have felt when dealing with his or her own parents throughout childhood.

Summary

We do not believe that borderline is a specific diagnostic category, nor is it a cohesive group of patients with special conflicts in common with one another. Rather, we believe the term represents a broad classification of mental illness with a wide and varied range of symptomatology and psychopathology. As a result, we do not subscribe to the idea that there is one specific treatment approach which is optimal in all cases.

We limited our attention to our four cases, which we considered to be analyzable. Special attention was given to the process of assessment or analyzability, particularly the recommendations made by Kernberg. Based on our understanding of his writings and our all-day conference with him, we examined some of the contradictions which two of our patients presented in their early sessions in order to see if such confrontations of what he calls "split," polarized ego states would aid in our diagnostic and predictive capacities. When we did so, we found that the extremely ambivalent attitudes toward self and others

which these patients demonstrated were based on the ubiquitous instinctual conflicts similar to those found in our less sick
patients. We could not see any predictive value in trying to
confront these contradictions, and we further believe that the
concept of split ego states may detract from the analyst's attention to, and understanding of, the unconscious fantasies underlying these superficial contradictions. In addition, we could
not confirm Kernberg's technical postulate that the bringing
together of the polarized images would produce anxiety and
disorganization. In fact, such results did not occur in our patients, and we felt that it was not reasonable to assume that any
group of patients would respond so uniformly to a particular
stress.

We then reviewed our cases to evaluate the technical recommendations made for the treatment of these patients by
Kernberg and by Rinsley and Masterson. Kernberg suggested
that the first task of treatment is to bring about the progressive
fusion of the "split," polarized images of self and object. This
may be accomplished, in his view, by persistent confrontation
of such contradictions without the addition of clarifying genetic
material. We could not confirm his recommendations. In our
cases we found it helpful from the beginning of treatment to
show the patient why his or her attitude shifted from one po-
larity to another and, whenever possible, to link such shifts to
pertinent genetic material. Although analytic progress was quite
slow with these patients, we believe that such interventions were
gradually helpful in undoing the patient's confusion and defensiveness. Kernberg also recommended focusing primarily
on negative transference and aggressive conflicts within a
framework of "technical neutrality." We do not believe that it
is analytically neutral to use such predetermined selectivity.
Furthermore, we believe that it is incorrect to relate negative
transference attitudes to aggressive conflicts alone since our
cases demonstrated such negative transference attitudes just as
frequently in response to libidinal conflicts.

We also examined the thesis of Rinsley and Masterson that
borderline pathology is derived from the mother of the in-
fant/child rewarding clinging and regressive behavior and with-

drawing in the face of independent strivings. We believe these views to be overly simplistic and could not agree that there is a phase-specific determinant of borderline pathology centered on the "depressive position" of infancy or the "rapprochement crisis" of the separation-individuation process such as these authors suggest. In our patients, the tendency to passivity was a complex character trait reflecting conflicts from all phases of development. Since we could not agree with the phase-specific hypothesis, we could not subscribe to a therapeutic approach geared to a single conflict. Such a suggestion is at variance with our belief in the complexity and individuality of all psychopathology and treatment. Consistent with these ideas, we could not offer any special technique for the analyses of these patients. Defenses of all types, transference reactions, superego conflicts, genetic material, and anamnestic data from all stages of development were interpreted and worked through as they emerged with sufficient clarity in the treatment.

However, we should emphasize that ours was a group of analyzable borderline patients, albeit analyzable with difficulty. Many other such patients would be too disturbed for an analysis and would have to be treated by various forms of psychotherapy. Furthermore, these patients may need minor modifications of technique and a particularly good "fit" between analyst and patient because of the degree of psychopathology present. Even in our cases, progress was extremely slow, reinterpretation of conflicts and defenses went on for many years, and countertransference feelings of doubt and discouragement were part of the atmosphere of the treatment.

8.

Etiology

Before we summarize our conclusions about etiology, we must emphasize that this topic can only be approached in a most tentative way because of the uncertainties and complexities which still exist in this area. We cannot reasonably expect to achieve greater clarity or precision about the etiology of the borderline conditions than we can about that of other types of mental illness. As a matter of fact, the very diversity and heterogeneity of the borderline group of disturbances suggested to us that in all likelihood there must be many important etiological determinants rather than any single crucial factor to produce such a wide array of clinical phenomena.

Nevertheless, thorough and prolonged study and discussion of the histories and analyses of our four cases did permit us to reach certain tentative conclusions about the major factors which could be said to be central to the development of our patients' pathology. We were impressed with the fact that the parents of our patients often seemed to have been severely disturbed themselves. Our patients had fathers who were sadistic or overly seductive or frequently absent, and mothers who were periodically depressed and unavailable or overprotective. These parents apparently failed to meet their children's needs for understanding, for reasonable need gratification, and for the imposition of useful limits and controls. They often worked at cross-purposes, subjected their offspring to severe tests of loyalty, and overstimulated them or failed to protect them from overwhelming stimulation, or both. In addition, these parents appear to have provided very poor models for identification, something which in itself had a profoundly detrimental effect on the development of character structure in our patients.

The current psychoanalytic literature on the borderline patient places particular etiological emphasis on the disturbed relationship between the child and his caretaking person during the first eighteen months of life. This early developmental phase is often considered crucial to the development of borderline conditions. Our own data, derived from the long analyses of our cases, indicated that the parents' pathological behavior and attitudes contributed to difficulties during *every phase of psychosexual and ego development.* There was, in fact, quite significant trauma during and after the oedipal phase itself. Every one of our patients showed marked failures in resolving oedipal conflicts, with resulting inhibitions, disturbances in superego functioning, and difficulties in control of their drives. We would also like to emphasize that there were a number of abandonments or experiences of object loss which took place during different phases of childhood, some of these of a recurrent nature.

This is not to suggest that our patients did not show significant preoedipal conflict. Derivatives of the oral and anal libidinal and aggressive drives were constantly in focus during the analyses, along with the defenses used in relation to them, as well as the disturbances of object relations which seemed to be derived from these conflicts. We were aware and made note of the influence of preoedipal conflicts on the development of the ego and on the intensity, configuration, and outcome of the resolution of the oedipal phase. We tried to address ourselves to the issue of whether profound early disturbances in the mother-child relationship—during the oral or early anal phase—led to developmental arrests or ego deviations which were never fully overcome but only compensated for. Such early disturbances would naturally be expected to affect object relations as well as the unfolding of drive expression and ego development and would therefore inevitably exert influences on oedipal phase development as well and would increase the likelihood of later serious pathology. However, after extensive study of our four cases we were unable to conclude that very

early preoedipal conflicts were more important than later conflicts of childhood in contributing to the subsequent borderline
pathology. Indeed, both stages of development were important
and interrelated.

The Nature of Evidence

Before we detail our findings concerning the traumas and experiences which we found to be of major etiological importance
in our analyzed cases, it might prove useful to discuss briefly
the nature of the evidence which psychoanalysts use to reach
conclusions about etiological factors in mental illness. What kind
of data do we utilize, and how do we determine what is of most
significance?

There are two major etiological issues we can try to investi-
gate. One would be that of the possible contributory role of
genetic endowment or constitution. The other would be the
question of crucial experiential factors, i.e., whether profound
difficulties during some specific developmental phase of childhood lead to the borderline condition. Of course, we would also
consider that these two major issues could occur together, as
Freud emphasized so often, even for the etiology of the neuroses.

In regard to the issue of constitutional factors, Kernberg
(1975) postulated that there may be a greater amount of innate
aggression present in the borderline patient. He also speculated
that an inborn disturbance in frustration tolerance might exist.
A recent study by Wender (1977) utilizing adoption data likewise implicates hereditary factors in the etiology of what he calls
"borderline schizophrenias." However, we were unable to conclude from our data that there was a greater amount of innate
aggression present in our patients or a constitutional disturbance in the modulation of aggressive drive discharge. None of
our patients reported early histories which would support this
conclusion. It was certainly true that our patients struggled
more than is usual with aggressive drive impulses. However, we
felt that this could be adequately explained by the nature of

their experiences and development. It is probably correct to say that the determination of excessive innate aggression cannot be made on the basis of analytic data alone.

As far as hereditary factors were concerned, we were impressed with the fact that one or both parents were severely disturbed themselves. However, none of the relatives of our four cases had been hospitalized or had been diagnosed as schizophrenic, or as having a major affective disorder.

The issue of innate poor frustration tolerance is one that should be grouped together with other kinds of constitutional impairments which are difficult to document. We refer here to findings such as severe hyperactivity, mild neurological impairment, indications of physiological imbalances in eating or sleeping, and profound lags in the development of the usual maturational sequences. We did not hear from our patients of the presence of any such possibility, or presumptively, constitutional difficulties, and none of them reported being told of such deficiencies during the first year of life. As a matter of fact, one of the patients, Case III, was told that she was a particularly happy, easy baby during her first year.

We are aware that children born with such difficulties as poor frustration tolerance or various physiological or mild neurological impairments might very well experience more problems as they develop, especially if their parents have a particularly difficult adjustment to the abnormality. There is, however, no reason to believe that the presence of inborn deficiencies will lead to borderline pathology in particular, although they certainly play an important role in ego development. As noted, our patients gave no evidence of such deficiencies, whereas they have been reported often enough to be present in other, neurotic, i.e., less seriously ill patients. Such findings speak against the hypothesis that constitutional factors play an unusully prominent role in the development of borderline problems.

Let us now turn to the important question of whether we could implicate difficulties during a particular developmental stage as crucial to the etiology of borderline disorders. Specifically, did we find evidence that major trauma or difficulties in the mother-child relationship occur during the first year of life of borderline patients, or that the most important period for the development of borderline pathology is the second year of life during the separation-individuation phase (an idea put forward by Masterson and Rinsley [1975] based on their understanding of Mahler's work), or is there any justification for the notion that the preoedipal years in these patients are no more traumatic than they are for others, but that oedipal phase conflicts of an extreme nature can produce severe abnormalities —severe enough to distinguish these patients from neurotic ones?

Before answering, we must ask, as we did above: What would be the nature of the evidence to support the view that difficulties during a *particular* developmental phase are crucial to the etiology of borderline conditions? How do we as analysts proceed to collect such evidence? What kind of data would be helpful to us to answer these questions?

One type of useful data would be derived from reports from the parents of our patients about certain specific phases of childhood. For example, if we were interested in accurately documenting severe difficulties during the first year of life we would be listening for signs and symptoms of severe disturbances during that time. A patient's mother may have told her child about being unable to soothe or quiet him. Severe feeding difficulties might be reported: the child refusing food, vomiting, or stubbornly refusing to open its mouth. Parents may have told the patient of extreme stranger anxiety, separation anxiety, or sleep disturbances lasting throughout the first year. We could hear of the child having severe temper tantrums, turning blue from holding its breath, or head-banging and rocking. We would also be interested in those physiological disturbances of infancy which may indicate emotional sensitivity manifesting itself primarily in psychosomatic forms. In addition, the patient may have been told of disturbing events in his or her life which we know would have an important effect. We would pay particular attention to indications that mother became depressed or emotionally unavailable, and we would attach importance to a history of prolonged illness or hospitalizations of the child or the caretaking person.

The presence of any one of these disturbances may not specifically suggest severe trauma or guarantee failure of ego development from an early age, but if many of the problems just cited had been present, we could conclude that significant difficulties were already in evidence before the age of twelve months. Once again, we must not automatically assume that such early disturbances are found only in borderline patients, since *some* of these problems are seen in the childhood of patients we regard as more typically neurotic. Nevertheless, such data would tend to strengthen the hypothesis that early difficulties were present and etiologically significant, although they would not be sufficient to prove its correctness.

Anamnestic data could also be used to demonstrate that conflicts during the second year of life were significant and crucial. Patients might reveal that they were told that it was during this period that they developed severe ambivalence, struggles over autonomy, speech disturbances, and major difficulties with toilet training. Their parents may have recalled that they showed severe separation reactions or terror of bodily damage. Early phobias may have been seen at this time. They may even have been told of rapid mood swings or the first indications of depressive moods. Difficulty in controlling their rage might have appeared at this time, and we also would again be interested in prolonged separations, illness, or hospitalizations.

We would have to add the cautionary note at this point that such disturbances during the second year would already rest on more subtle or unnoticed difficulties during the first year. This would be in keeping with the view put forward by Mahler that the child's reaction to the rapprochement phase is already influenced by the earlier relationship with the mother, as well as the observations of Galenson and Roiphe (1971) that little girls who demonstrate the most pronounced castration anxiety between eighteen and twenty-four months are those who have already shown problems with the mothering figure beforehand.

Studies such as those just cited which concern themselves with longitudinal child observational research offer to us another way to collect data about early phases of child development. However, to be certain of the effect of early childhood trauma on the developing ego, we would need long term follow-up studies to be able to specify the type of adult psychopathology that would follow from early disturbances.

At present, it seems fair to say that convincing correlations between specific early trauma and precisely defined constellations of adult pathology are not available. Indeed, the variability of human mental life and the multiplicity of etiologic factors involved in adult psychopathology seem to suggest that simple linear correlations are probably not likely to be demonstrated.

It is also possible to utilize the data derived from child analysis or psychotherapy. Children with severe ego disturbances and multiple symptoms have been treated and studied extensively, and many child analysts have been impressed by the lasting influence of difficulties occurring during the first two years of life. We ourselves did not have such data available to us from the analysis of child cases although some of the members of the study group were child analysts. It is clear that those children who already show marked ego impairments, symptoms, and problems in their early object relations enter the oedipal phase already especially burdened by conflict. The phallic-oedipal conflicts which ensue seem more difficult to resolve under those circumstances, a fact which leads to more profound pathology in adult life. It should also be stressed, however, that the difficulties brought on by parental neglect or insensitivity and by overstimulation or inconsistency, as well as by severe ego disturbances in the parents themselves, continue to affect the child after the age of one or two. We were impressed with the cumulative effects of the parents' pathology in our cases, as mentioned above, and we tried to trace our patients' disturbances to every phase of childhood psychosexual and object relations development involved.

Another avenue of approach to the question of whether there is a specific period of development which is most crucial in respect to the etiology of borderline disturbance in adult life might be by means of a statistical study of the accumulated data reported by many analysts. If a large number of borderline patients who had been studied in the course of treatment could be shown to have had major significant trauma clustering primarily at some specific period of life, we could feel more certain that the difficulties during this period were crucial to the development of this disorder. We cannot say that at present we have such concrete evidence from a large number of cases so studied.

Most of the propositions about the crucial etiological determinants for borderline pathology come, at present, from inferences drawn from the long-term treatment of these patients. These provisional conclusions are gathered and integrated as the analysis unfolds and often cannot be verified by specific historical data alone. In the course of analytic work we also utilize reconstructions based on the understanding of the patient's pathology and transference reactions. Appropriate conclusions can only be reached after a thorough analysis of the patients' character structure, symptom formation, and defenses, as well as through an appreciation of the quality of the patient's ego functions and the nature of the superego. Perhaps of greatest importance is the study of the nature of the transference which occurs throughout the analysis, since it provides the analyst with the most convincing insight into the nature of the patient's object relations and conflicts. In addition, we must try to identify, if possible, those areas of interpretations which prove to be most mutative, i.e., the insights which lead to changes in the patient's functioning.

However, it is precisely in this endeavor to draw conclusions about etiology from the unfolding of the analytic process that most of the disagreement occurs. Analysts listening to a continuous case seminar, with detailed reports on a number of sessions, often come to different conclusions about the significance of what they are hearing. This was even true when the members of our study group reviewed the extensive written accounts of our four cases as well as listened to the verbal presentation by the analyst involved in the treatment. We spent many hours discussing the relative weight of preoedipal and oedipal factors in determining the severity of our patients' illness, the nature of their object relations, and the development of their respective egos.

We gradually came to the conclusion that it is extremely difficult to separate the effects of preoedipal from oedipal trauma when one is conducting an analysis of an adult. It was certainly clear that our patients showed marked oedipal conflict, with pronounced castration anxiety, sexual inhibitions, and preoccupation with familiar triangular issues of jealousy and rivalry. That there was ample confirmation of severe difficulties and traumas during the oedipal phase itself can be seen from the case histories. We were also aware, however, that disturbances from earlier periods of development were very important as well in determining the nature of the object relations, the development of ego functions, and the vicissitudes of the instinctual drives. Regression and fixation seemed to be part of every manifestation of the diffuse psychopathology.

We were more cautious than other analysts who seem to trace patients' adult symptomatology directly to specific developmental periods. Our patients showed conflicts caused by intense ambivalence which led them to a tendency to view objects as all-good or all-bad, but we were not persuaded that such outcomes were specifically derived from experiences during the first year of life alone, merely because it is hypothesized that this is a period of time during which the infant is likely to be unable to integrate loving and hating feelings toward the same person. We know that such ambivalence is pronounced during the second year of life and continues to be a serious problem during the phallic-oedipal phase as well as the later years of childhood. It does not seem plausible to claim that such ambivalence is derived primarily from experiences during the first year of life. Similarly, although we noted the pervasive use of projection as an important mechanism of defense in the borderline patient, we were hesitant to conclude that this is an indication that crucial disturbances which promoted the preferential use of this defense occurred mainly in the first two years of life.

Kernberg, noting the prominent ambivalence (which he calls splitting), as well as projection occurring along with a fluidity of ego boundaries (which he calls projective identification), drew the conclusion that this pathology can be specifically traced to the first eighteen months or two years of life. He stressed that the etiological factors leading to these defenses and to a particular kind of fixation of object relations are most probably the existence of a greater than normal amount of innate aggression, or constitutionally poor frustration tolerance, or the inordinate arousal of aggression in the infant due to conflicts with the mother during this early phase of development. Kernberg and others are not necessarily mistaken in the specific conclusions they draw, but we questioned whether the evidence to support these conclusions with certainty is available to us at the present time.

One of the features of our day-long discussion with Kernberg was the agreement that the clinical material we had studied so carefully corresponded to that which led him to many of his own findings and conclusions. Yet we were hard pressed to reconstruct from our own clinical data, even when it corresponded to that of Kernberg, such a specific early time of life in which a group of special defensive operations as well as pathological object relations is solidified. We were more inclined to view the disturbance in object relations, as well as the predominant use of projection as a defense, as having developed gradually during the course of child development. We must also leave room for another possibility—that certain profound traumas during the oedipal phase and later in development might be significant enough to cause a severe regression without the pre-existence of overwhelming preoedipal pathology. The clinical picture following such a regression might be severe enough to lead to a borderline disturbance. It is by no means obvious how one can with certainty distinguish this possibility from the others on the basis of adult analyses.

A Case Example

Perhaps we can use the clinical data from Case II to illustrate some of these considerations. The patient and his older brother lived with his mother and maternal grandparents from the time he was born until he was three. He did not see his father until he was three years old when his father returned from military service and the reunited family moved to their own apartment.

Sometime between the age of four and five his mother gave birth to a little girl who died a few hours after delivery. During the course of the analysis a reconstruction of his mother's depression and withdrawal was confirmed when the patient questioned his mother about the effect of this event on her and the family.

This patient had revealed that he could not reach orgasm unless he imagined that a woman was enticing him to change into a little girl and only if he did would she caress him and give him pleasure. Although the reasons for his fantasy were overdetermined, one important aspect (the understanding of which actually led to the reconstruction that the mother had become depressed after she lost the baby girl) was that he wanted to replace this child and make his mother happy again.

This patient had profound fears that women would entrap him and force him to give up his independence and freedom. He also had the belief that his mother might actually want to seduce him into sexual activity. He expressed the fantasy that if he drew too close to a woman he "would be sucked up into her as if she were a vacuum cleaner."

During our discussions of this material some members felt that the patient had strong wishes to merge with and fears of merging with the object and had poor ego boundaries. They wondered about the kinds of experiences with his mother prior to the age of three which might have led to the disturbances noted as well as to his pervasive use of projection. Although the patient was in analysis for ten years, little information was gathered or revealed about these very early years. An unusual opportunity presented itself at one point for the treating analyst to discuss this case with the senior colleague who had analyzed the patient's mother. The mother's analyst could not recall from his work with his patient that significant early mothering problems had been evident. He contributed the observation that the maternal grandfather, who must have been a surrogate father for the patient, was a domineering, harsh, insensitive man, much like the patient's father. He also recalled that the mother was more preoccupied with the older brother than with the patient.

In view of these facts we could not be certain in this case of profound early disturbances. The indications that the traumas of the oedipal phase and afterward were themselves quite crucial to his regression and disturbed object relations were quite compelling.

We recognized the inappropriateness of drawing conclusions about the maturity of the patient's object relations or the degree of regression involved on the basis of a particular fantasy alone, e.g., needing to be changed into a little girl or fearing that he would be "sucked up by the woman as if she were a vacuum cleaner." Every such fantasy has to be evaluated not in terms of its manifest content but rather by its unconscious meaning. In addition, the presence of a particular fantasy alone does not tell us enough about the functioning of the ego, the level of maturity of the object relations, or the degree of differentiation of self- and object-representations. Fantasies may be remnants of archaic feelings or experiences but are not therefore necessarily indicative of severe ego regression.

Fantasies, wishes, and fears from early phases of development are always intertwined with those of later phases. In every analysis we encounter significant oral or anal fantasies and impulses as well as the defenses against their expression. In this patient, analysis revealed the profound longings to be close to and even inside of his mother so that he would never have to separate from her. Analysis of his dreams, fears, symptoms, and character seemed to demonstrate his profound feelings of jealousy when she was pregnant and feelings of loss when she became depressed after the death of the infant sibling. His feelings of entrapment were the consequence of the projection of his wishes to tie his mother down and never let her leave him. They also represented fears of retaliation related to his death wishes toward the fantasied new rival in his mother's womb. Some time later, when he was six, he had sexual fantasies of women tying *him* down, with the added detail that they were playing with him sexually. These fantasies were also stimulated by a new determinant, the fact that at this time his parents held him down while giving him injections of penicillin for chronic ear infections. The patient also had intense phallic sexual fantasies toward his mother which frightened him and made him feel guilty. The wishes were projected and he feared castration and entrapment of his penis. In addition, his own wishes to suck on and control women were projected onto them.

He suspected that his mother wanted to have sex with him but he also imagined that all women were trying to "tie him down" in an emotional sense. When his mother called him by an affectionate, demonstrative name he would become outraged that she was trying to keep him as her baby. When a woman with whom he was having intercourse suggested he need not use a condom because she was in the "safe period" of her cycle, he immediately became anxious and decided she wanted to get pregnant so that he would have to marry her and thereby give up his "freedom."

It should be borne in mind that all of these childhood "experiences" were taking place in an atmosphere in which his parents' behavior was continually affecting his growth and development in a negative way. His father was a coarse and harsh man, derisive and critical to his son and often insensitive to his feelings. His mother was more involved with his older brother and although seemingly empathic with the patient, often placed more conditions than we think of as usual on her love.

Accordingly, the patient had profound difficulties in his relations with others, and the same patterns were re-enacted in the transference. He was often convinced that his analyst desired to humiliate, abuse, and infantilize him. Only long and patient work on his projections, fears, and guilt feelings, together with a reconstruction of his childhood development, led to the understanding which made his gradual but steady improvement possible.

Thus, to determine the etiology of his disturbance, each and every phase of his development had to be examined. In general, we felt that the greater the degree of early conflict, the more would successive phases of ego development be affected. However, we were impressed with the difficulty of adequately separating the effect of early trauma from those of later phases. Similarly, we found that in any given symptom complex, the various sources and types of anxiety involved will be combined and intertwined. This was recently emphasized by Brenner (1979), who pointed out that fears of loss of the object, loss of love of the object, castration anxiety, and superego anxiety may all be present in any one symptom complex. Fears of loss of the love of the object, while they may be experienced very early in life, are still very prominent during the height of the oedipal phase as well.

We are aware that the presence of such a severe oedipal conflict in this patient with marked castration anxiety, ambivalence toward both men and women, as well as a profound belief in his mother's wish to seduce him might be due to more subtle difficulties in his first three years which were not learned of or reconstructed during his long analysis. This might be similar, for example, to a woman's dependent clinging attachment to a male oedipal figure having its roots in a strong preoedipal attachment to her mother. Kernberg postulated that there is a "premature oedipalization" in the borderline patient which is an attempt to master the fixations caused by splitting and the preponderance of pathological internalized object relations.

What we have attempted to do by using this case as an example is to show how difficult it is to reach conclusions about these propositions. When the members of the study group reviewed the material, we did pay attention to those aspects of the patient's object relations and conflicts which presumably related to his experiences during the first three years of his life. Special emphasis was given to the fact that his father was away from home during this time. However, it seemed to most of us that this patient's particularly traumatic experiences during the oedipal phase and latency were crucial to the development of his symptoms, character traits, ego structure, and object relations.

Other Considerations

There is another important point which deserves emphasis in regard to inferences about etiology which are drawn from our analytic work. An analyst never learns "everything" about a patient's conflicts and development, no matter how well the analysis proceeds and how much change occurs. Even when there is profound change and recovery, one cannot be absolutely certain precisely which insights from which interpretations, reconstructions, recovery of memories, and convictions gained through the understanding of powerful transference emotions and fantasies produced the beneficial effect. Nevertheless, since it is the fact that precisely because of such analytic work that progress is made, it is pertinent to address the question: "What kinds of interpretations and reconstructions led to further insight and change?" Many analysts writing about the borderline patient seem to concentrate primarily on dyadic issues apparently related to conflicts aroused during the first two years of life. Less attention is paid to triangular conflicts, phallic oedipal issues, and superego analysis. In addition, these same analysts stress conflicts derived from the aggressive drive over and above those of the libidinal drive.

Our own work with these four cases, as well as with other cases presented in the Kris Study Group, indicated that our interpretative efforts dealt with both dyadic and triangular conflicts, with oral and anal phase conflicts and their derivatives as well as phallic oedipal ones. Analysis of the superego, whether it was manifested in an internalized way or by fears of punishment, abandonment, or sadistic torturing was an important part of our work. We also felt that the analysis of libidinal wishes and fears as well as those of narcissistic needs and their frustration could not really be separated from analysis of conflicts derived from the aggressive drive. Indeed, in every conflict, in every object relationship, in every phase of ego development the derivatives of the aggressive and libidinal drives as well as the narcissistic injuries which accompany them are intertwined and inseparable. We could not therefore conclude that our analytic experience supported the idea that it is useful to single out one drive as opposed to the other in the etiology of the borderline patients.

Since we did note change of a significant degree in all of our patients who were analyzed in the manner described, we concluded that many factors operating in conjunction with one another were responsible for the development of borderline pathology. Therefore, we feel that one should not concentrate on issues derived from a particular childhood phase of development but rather analyze, as best as one can with any given patient, all of the major conflicts and sources of anxiety and disturbed object relations.

9.

Summary and Conclusions

A detailed collaborative examination of analytic case material has provided the primary basis for our understanding of these patients, as well as for our disagreement with certain observations and theoretical propositions regarding borderlines which have appeared in the literature. On the whole, we have been led to adopt a far more skeptical attitude toward the validity of constructs based largely upon theories of early psychic development than have many other analysts. We believe that much of what they propose is based on a speculative interpretation of necessarily sketchy data. However plausible such constructions may be, they are difficult if not impossible to substantiate with analytic data gathered from clinical work with adults. Some of the hypothetical formulations of mental development propounded may not greatly affect the way analysts actually work with patients. In other instances, however, we believe that subscribing to certain speculative theories of this sort may lead to unsatisfactory ways of viewing clinical data, and to the implementation of technical recommendations which we think are disadvantageous.

As we have noted, we decided early in our work to concentrate our efforts on what could be learned from analyses of borderline adult patients. We began our deliberations by asking each member to explain what he understood the meaning of the term borderline to be. It became apparent quite quickly that there were many differences of opinion and certainly differences in emphasis. Our review of the literature revealed the existence of the same divergence, but we compiled a composite from various authors which described many aspects of the clinical picture. Each analyst was then asked to write up and discuss patients who had been treated over a long period of time by psychoanalysis. We felt that by choosing to study patients whose analyses had been completed we would derive the maximum benefit from the clinical material. Each analyst who submitted a detailed case report felt that his patient fit the clinical criteria for the borderline category we had agreed to adopt.

All of the patients therefore had already undergone psychoanalysis and although not all had achieved an optimal analytic result, they had each benefited greatly from their treatment. In all of the cases, the analyses had been conducted with few modifications of technique. Since none of these patients had undergone severe regression approaching a psychotic state, our sample of cases differed from many of those reported in the literature who could not tolerate or benefit from classical analysis. Many of our members reported briefly on other cases they believed to be borderline whom they had elected to treat, not with analysis but with some other form of psychotherapy instead.

The chief advantage of looking at completed analyses in retrospect is obvious: It affords the maximum degree of understanding of the origin, structure, and meaning of a given patient's symptomatology which it is possible for the analyst to achieve. What may have been puzzling and incomprehensible at the outset of treatment, or even for many years, often seemed convincingly and clearly explained at the end of the analysis. Furthermore, the best assessment of the modifiability of specific personality qualities and behaviors is only available at the conclusion of treatment, as is whatever support and validation of the analyst's understanding of the case the fact of clinical improvement has to offer.

There are corresponding disadvantages to this approach to a clinical survey. For one thing, not even the most comprehensive summary can hope to do more than suggest what the day-to-day analytic experience with the patient was like. For another, alternate explanations of specific detailed material, which could conceivably be of great interest and importance, are simply not possible to evaluate retroactively. Testing of such alternatives is also eliminated. Only continuous case studies could provide such opportunities and of course they also have their practical limitations. Finally, retrospective condensation also tends to increase the impression that dynamic material unfolds in complex but intertwined and interrelated patterns. Conflicts from all stages of libidinal development may appear as a thematic syncytium, with shifts and modifications seen as serving purposes of defense as well as reflecting the variety of genetic sources of each patient's difficulties. At the same time, a post-treatment summary imposes on the analytic data a certain integrated, orderly comprehensibility which is inevitably somewhat selective in its focus, depending on the analyst's final understanding of the case. Perhaps the total effect lends a false clarity or unwarranted synthetic integrity to the whole case.

Furthermore, we cannot claim that detailed inspection of analytic material provides assurance that analysts' theoretical and conceptual biases have been eliminated. Past controversies and current debates in our field make it abundantly clear that analysts of different persuasions hear the same material differently, and each finds "confirmations" of fundamental assumptions in the raw data of his work, and perhaps in the work of others as well. Our best available safeguard against this problem lies in group endeavor, though this is far from perfect. There is some assurance that highly idiosyncratic views are likely to be exposed, and major oversights detected, by means of communal discussion. While the members of our group, on the whole, had similar training, there were significant variations among us in experience, interest, and point of view, in regard to both theoretical and technical approaches. The dominant position, it must be apparent, was an ego psychological approach within the framework of classical Freudian structural theory. This description best applies to the general orientation of the authors as well and inevitably lends its stamp to the material we present. Those colleagues who have adopted a different point of view will no doubt keep this firmly in mind when reviewing our findings.

Diagnostic Considerations

It has long been apparent that the traditional concept of mental disorders as being divided into neuroses and psychoses is too crude and oversimplified to account satisfactorily for the enormous variety of clinical observations that confront us. In addition, for many years analysts have realized that they encounter many patients who, while not conforming to the diagnostic patterns associated with the various recognized psychoses, nevertheless exhibit such severe psychopathology that either they cannot successfully be treated at all with the usual psychoanalytic technique or that such analyses present unusual difficulties. As observations on these patients accumulated, the literature began to include efforts to conceptualize the pathology of this group. The term "borderline," first used by Stern, reflects the prevailing opinion that they fall into an intermediate category, which, in respect to severity of illness, lies between the more familiar neuroses and milder character problems, on the one hand, and psychotic disturbances, on the other.

Many analysts have expressed dissatisfaction with the term "borderline" as a diagnosis on the grounds that it is too diffuse, that it covers a broad group of disturbances which vary widely one from another, and that it has been difficult to identify features common to all these cases which might serve as reliable diagnostic criteria. This problem in clinical definition led us to extract from the literature a composite clinical description based upon phenomenology to serve as a guideline for choosing cases to study. Our review revealed that there is actually substantial agreement among the various descriptions of these borderline cases, and we did not experience much difficulty in finding cases which seemed to match this broad template rather well. However, we usually do not group patients into rigid classifications based on phenomenology alone, especially where there is such variability in respect to specific individual characteristics as is displayed by the group of borderlines. One of our colleagues, Dr. David Beres, felt that the term "borderline" is so general as to become a catch-all diagnosis, serving no useful purpose. He believed it would be preferable to discard it and simply use the concept of severe character pathology to account for the phenomena exhibited. Conclusions about the degree of pathology should rest on a detailed examination of the ego functions and object relations, according to his recommendation. Kernberg also recognized that many different types of cases belong in the category he proposes we call Borderline Personality Organization. He includes among them: Chronic Diffuse Anxiety States, Polysymptomatic Neuroses, Polymorphous Perverse Sexual Trends including some perversions, Paranoid, Schizoid, and Hypomanic Personalities, Impulse Disorders and Addictions, the "As-if" Personality, and the Infantile Personality, Narcissistic Personality, Depressive Masochistic Character Structure, and Depressive Character Structure. It should be noted that cases from these different diagnostic entities vary enormously from one another in their symptomatology and character structure. Even if we were to find certain developmental conflicts common to all of them, we would still have to explain the diversity of the clinical picture and to make some attempt to understand why some borderline patients develop a paranoid personality or an addiction, whereas others turn out to be narcissistic personalities or patients with a depressive masochistic character structure. Kernberg believes that patients of all these types do exhibit certain features in common, that is, a specific type of ego structure and a qualitatively different type of object relationship. These are organized, he says, by pathological internalized object relations and utilize pathognomonic primitive defenses derived from splitting. The members of our study group were interested to see if we could find these common features described by Kernberg in our clinical material or, if we could not confirm his observations, to see whether we could detect other common features which would justify grouping these patients together in a way that enhances our understanding of the development of their psychopathology.

As we have stated in some detail, a careful examination of our cases did not show these specific features which he described as present. However, we could identify certain common clinical findings emphasized in our composite description.

These findings are on the level of phenomenological general-izations, and at that they tend to emphasize differences of de-gree rather than of kind. We do not feel that these observations warrant a recommendation that the term "borderline" be re-garded as a formal diagnostic entity, and we prefer to use the diagnosis, in each case, appropriate to that case's specific struc-ture—Severe Sadomasochistic Character Disorder, for exam-ple. However, we all recognize that the term "borderline" has achieved a broad acceptance among analysts as well as other psychiatrists and therapists, and most of us felt that it can be of use *provided* it is understood to refer, in a rather nonspecific descriptive way, to a large and varied group of patients who show more severe and widespread pathology than do most neu-rotics and neurotic character disorders. Unlike Kernberg and others, we do not believe that the "borderline" designation should carry with it implications of specific developmental or structural problems common to the entire group of patients.

Object Relations

We have attempted to describe and delineate those special char-acteristics and qualities of object relations which are typical of, or prominent in, borderline patients. We tried to find *common features* which would differentiate this group from psychoneu-rotics, on the one hand, and from psychotics, on the other.

Our discussions led us to review certain theorists who have contributed to our understanding of the development of the child's object relations. Their concepts, theories, models, and developmental schemata have been specifically utilized by many in an attempt to understand the development of borderline pathology. The authors whom we reviewed, whose approaches were different from one another, were Mahler, Jacobson, Ko-hut, Klein, and Kernberg. In addition, we presented a brief review of Freud's theories which is important not only because, as we believe, they deal with the development of object relations but also because some of the conclusions we reached are related to his conceptualizations. We also addressed ourselves to the difficulty of reconstructing developmental phases by extrapolation from adult pathological phenomena. This cautious approach seems applicable especially to attempts to correlate specific early periods of childhood development with the disturbances observed in the object relations of borderline patients.

We found that a detailed study of four analyzed borderline cases showed that they suffered from a number of serious disturbances in their object relations:

1. All of our patients showed evidence of severe oedipal problems rather than primarily pregenital ones. There was a persistence of intense triangular conflicts with marked frustration, jealousy, and sadomasochistic reactions. Castration conflicts in both sexes were very prominent. These patients could not adequately resolve their oedipal conflicts without serious distortions in their object relations and marked disturbances in their ego and superego functioning. All of our patients experienced significant trauma during the oedipal phase itself, frequently related to object loss.

2. We found that all of our patients had made strong identifications with their very disturbed parents. These identifications frequently served a defensive function, as in identification with the aggressor, particularly as they involved taking on the sadistic aspects of their parents' behavior. The identifications formed, which affected their concepts of themselves and others, as well as their behavior, were not necessarily ones formed only very early in their childhood, but were also derived from later phases of development.

3. The object relations of our patients were characterized by marked sadomasochistic features. Their sexual lives and their relationships in general were permeated with aggression —directed outward, toward the self, or both. Projections of aggression made them fear objects and led to the need to control them. Oral, anal, and phallic phase issues were all involved in these sadomasochistic features. We did observe severe ambivalence, but we did not regularly encounter the dramatic and persistent division into "all-good" and "all-bad" self and object images which has been emphasized in the literature.

4. We did not observe the severe, gross psychotic distortions of self-object differentiation that one sees in schizophrenic regression. However, insofar as projection was a very prominent defense mechanism, these patients often distorted their perceptions about themselves and others. In addition to the projection of aggression, we found projection of envy, greed, homosexual impulses, heterosexual needs, impulses to control, enslave, and exploit others, and superego condemnations and punishments. The intensity, fixity, and pervasiveness of projection went along with, or were a corollary of, a failure to differentiate clearly between the self and the object. Despite our finding of poor self-object differentiation in *certain* areas of our patients' lives, we did not feel we could trace it to a specific fixation point of childhood development.

5. We were all struck by the profound degree of narcissism in our patients. They were more than usually concerned with gratifying their own needs rather than relating to other people in a more mutual give-and-take manner. They often expected that their needs would be gratified in a most concrete way. In their analyses, words and interpretations were clearly not sufficient—real gratification was demanded. They also used people for self-esteem regulation, and they would react with such disappointment to people failing to supply them with libidinal and narcissistic gratifications that withdrawal or outbursts of rage would ensue. We did not find it helpful to view narcissistic problems as necessarily caused by failures of parental empathy, or to consider narcissism as having a separate line of development from object-related libidinal and aggressive drive maturation. Often we found that narcissistic traits were *solutions* to conflicts and not unrelated to conflict.

6. Our patients demonstrated severe reactions to separation—both in their analyses and in their relations to people in general. Our case histories revealed a significant degree of actual object loss in childhood. However, it was clear to us that the day-to-day interactions between the child and his caretaker may be more important than actual separation experiences. Fears of loss of the object and loss of object love were found to be present during each phase of psychosexual development.

It was always important to analyze the specific, unique fantasies of the patients which provoked separation fears, in order to understand the meaning of these fears and to trace their developmental roots.

7. We found, in contrast to much of the present literature on borderline patients, that superego conflicts played an important role in their object relations. It was not easy to distinguish between more mature feelings of "internalized" guilt and those of fear of bodily damage or persecution. Considerable attention had to be given to the defenses used to ward off self-punitive condemnations and behavior. Often the analyst and others would be attacked to make him feel guilty, in order to defend against guilt over the patient's greedy, exploitative, and controlling wishes. Masochistic fantasies, depressive trends, self-punitive behavior, fears of being hurt or persecuted were all often the result of the compromises formed between sexual and aggressive impulses and the harsh demands of the superego.

In general, we found ourselves in agreement with many authors who have described the object relations of borderline patients. We were more cautious than many, however, in attributing the development of these disturbed object relations to a specific pregenital phase of development.

Reality Testing

Because reality testing is a compound and complex ego function involving perception, memory, and judgment, we regard efforts to characterize it as merely defective or intact as oversimplifications. We believe that whatever the role of early developmental processes may be in providing the substratum of reality testing, conflicts occurring at other developmental stages can produce marked interference with the capacity to test reality. All distortions of reality testing are indicative of the impact of unconscious mental activity on perception, memory, or judgment, or all three. We find such distortions to be ubiquitous among normals, milder neurotics, and the more severely ill, although almost certainly to be of greater degree, intensity, and persistence in the sicker patients. Furthermore, reality testing is a variable capacity in all individuals, fluctuating from day to day, and even from moment to moment, as close examination of analytic material will reveal. We did not encounter very marked disturbances of feelings of reality in our study population, contrary to expectation, and, in fact, seriously question whether such symptoms are fundamentally connected with the actual capacity to test reality. We used the concept of faulty reality testing to express the clinical judgment that our patients' views of the world, that is to say, of people and situations, were often quite unrealistic. All of our patients gave indication of a considerable amount of disturbance in this area, which led us to differ with the suggestion that borderlines were relatively free of this difficulty. Furthermore, it was not true that their difficulties were readily reversible.

We noted that Hartmann's observation about the powerful influence of a pathological environment on reality testing, i.e., the social reality which may oppose objective reality, was confirmed by the experiences of our patients. In our cases we observed that the alteration of reality testing capacity often seemed to be based on wishful and defensive aspects of conflicts over various sexual and aggressive impulses from all stages of development. Projection was a prominent mechanism in all our patients, and its relation to reality testing deficiency was noted, although we were not prepared to attribute a primary, crucial significance to this relationship. Faulty reality testing was studied in our cases as part of each clinical setting in which it appeared as a factor, not as a phenomenon in and of itself. We felt that the fact that all four patients demonstrated significant improvement in reality testing as their analyses progressed supported our view that its faulty operation is, in large measure, a consequence of the impact of conflicts on ego functioning, and hence reversible to some degree, even in borderline individuals.

Defenses

As we discussed the defenses used by our borderline patients, we felt we could identify many of the classical defense mechanisms in the analytic material of each case, and also observed that these individuals seemed to use more complex behaviors and psychological reactions for defensive purposes as well. We are aware that defense theory has progressed substantially in recent years, and that the term is no longer limited to describing certain stereotyped pathological mental operations which are involved in symptom formation, character distortions, and resistance. Gradually it has become recognized that they are ubiquitous phenomena in mental life which play a role in adaptation and normal development as well as in psychopathology. It has become apparent that all aspects of ego functioning may at times serve defensive purposes just as they may serve adaptive ones, and that defenses are in fact defined by the role they play in mental life rather than by their intrinsic structure. Nevertheless we have continued to use the familiar terminology of defense mechanisms, and also to speak of more complex defensive behavior and reactions, in the expectation that these descriptions would be readily understood by members of the study group, and by analytic colleagues who review our findings.

Examining our case material, we discovered that our four patients used many of the so-called "higher-level" defenses as well as those considered by some authors to be more "primitive." This finding was consistent with the variability in symptomatology and character traits demonstrated by this diverse group of patients. However, we found that there were certain defenses which were used more prominently by these patients. These defenses were disruptive both within the treatment situation and in their lives outside of treatment as well. Despite accurate and well-timed interpretations, these defensive maneuvers proved quite difficult to modify. The most prevalent ones were projection, denial, "acting out," identification with the aggressor, the use of one drive derivative to defend against another, and sadomasochistic libidinal regression.

From our observations, we concluded that we could not differentiate borderline patients from other patients on the basis of their defensive structure alone. Furthermore, we did not find it helpful to attempt to categorize defenses hierarchically, from most "primitive" to "higher level," as some authors have suggested. Nor did we think it quite accurate to conceptualize certain defenses as ranging in degree from more primitive to more normal. Instead, we felt that the most comprehensive way of viewing the clinical data was to conceive of the defenses as varying, depending on their interaction with other ego functions, such as reality testing, object relations, and the general integration of the ego.

We tried to evaluate Kernberg's hypothesis that there are a group of special primitive defenses whose presence he considers pathognomonic for "borderline personality organization." According to him, these patients use these defenses preferentially, in contrast to neurotic patients, and they do not use the so-called "higher-level" defenses, like repression, until treatment has produced some modifications. Our observations did not confirm this general hypothesis.

When we reviewed the concept of "splitting," we found that it is derived by various authors from diverse etiological and developmental schemata. We were not convinced that the clinical phenomena described as splitting are accounted for by conflict and failures in ego development which occur in the first eighteen months of life. We preferred to describe what was observed in more traditional terms, such as extreme ambivalence, identification with the aggressor, the use of one drive derivative to defend against another, idealization to defend against aggression, reaction formation, isolation, and displacement. All of these defenses are prominent in the second year of life, during the anal phase. We believe that what others call "splitting" is a result of the toddler's need to deal with its ambivalence by displacing aggression away from the nurturing maternal object onto an alternative object, or onto the self. This formulation does not require hypothetical constructs such as the "ego core" of "foci of positive introjects," which cannot be substantiated from analytic data alone.

Our group also discussed the meaning of the term "projective identification." We had great difficulty in defining it and noted that it is used differently by various authors, notably Klein and Kernberg. We also found a good deal of disagreement among ourselves when clinical data were offered as examples of the defense described as projective identification. We came to the conclusion that the term "projective identification," as used by Kernberg in particular, most accurately describes the familiar defense of projection used by those sicker patients who demonstrate poor self-object differentiation. We preferred, therefore, to view the integration of the egos of such patients as being impaired, rather than conceptualizing the specific defense mechanisms as being more primitive.

We found that the postulated defenses of "primitive idealization," "denial," and "omnipotence and devaluation" were also based on "splitting" as a pathologically persistent "primitive" defense. We believe that these so-called "primitive defenses" are in themselves highly complex derivatives of unconscious fantasies which must be analyzed for their specific content and understood in terms of the total organization of the ego.

We also evaluated the place of repression as a defense in borderline patients. In contrast to Kernberg, we found it to be an active and crucial part of the defensive structure of these patients, as it is in all other patients. The presenting clinical manifestations which to Kernberg represented polarized conscious "ego states" and the absence of repression were understood as a result of our clinical experience to represent only the proverbial "tip of the iceberg." Underneath lay a complex matrix of intertwined unconscious fantasies from which these surface phenomena were derived.

Accordingly, we could not agree with the suggestion that there are special defenses in borderline patients, nor could we agree that it is, at this time and at our current level of knowledge, possible to describe a hierarchy of defense mechanisms. We believe that the psychopathology of the borderline patients can best be understood not from the nature of their defenses alone but by considering their defensive maneuvers in conjunction with other complex ego functions, such as reality testing, the general integration of the ego, and object relations.

Transference and Technique

Our observations were in agreement with those of most other analysts in respect to the tendency of borderline patients to develop intense transference reactions almost from the beginning of the treatment. These patients also display an unusual propensity to express the wishes and fears mobilized by the transference in "acting out," both inside and outside of the analytic situation itself. We also found that the intense transference reactions of some patients could lead to a determined, persistent conscious and unconscious blockage of transference expression, with the result that a quite different manifest transference appears than would be expected.

We noted an increased use of projection in the relationship to the analyst, as is the case in other relationships. This was particularly important as a component of the sadomasochistic transferences which developed in all four of our patients. The highly erotized quality of these transferences was ultimately demonstrated in each case, but the exact nature of the sadomasochistic attitudes and fantasies was usually obscured by very rigidly maintained defenses for a long time.

These patients all impressed us with their relative inability to accept the "as-if" quality of their transference wishes and fears, and with their insistence on literal gratifications from their analysts. Whereas other analysts might prefer to discuss this behavior as a consequence of ego defects, of defective self-observation, or more generally as a limitation in their capacity to form a therapeutic alliance, we were of the opinion that these designations did not offer very much that was useful in the way of understanding their behavior. Instead, we viewed the persistence of this tendency as expressing a relative failure of reality testing. This pattern seemed to result from the complex interplay of defenses against anxiety, guilt, and other unpleasurable affects, combined with attempts to obtain direct gratification of libidinal and aggressive drive derivatives, according to the principle of multiple function. The results were severe conscious distortions of the image of the analyst, which differ from those of milder neurotic patients not so much in their quality as in their intensity, persistence, and relative imperviousness to interpretive attention on the part of the analyst.

We noted also that these patients had profound reactions to separation and loss. We did not consider that these responses

were caused primarily or exclusively by early maternal deprivation or insensitivity. We observed that our patients had repetitive losses throughout their childhoods, as well as pronounced
and persistent conflicts with both parents during all psychosexual phases of development. These factors, plus their intense
sadomasochistic conflicts, combined to make them more exquisitely sensitive to separation and loss than are most neurotic
patients.

We also observed the presence of narcissistic pathology in
these cases. We agree with most authors who believe that this
pathology may result from a partial failure of the separation
between self-representations and object-representations, or
from pathological self-esteem–regulating functions, with a persistence of unusually unrealistic, grandiose and idealized self
and object images in the ego ideal or its precursors, or from
both types of antecedents. However, when we observed our
patients' clinical behavior, including their extreme sensitivity to
real or imagined slights, their significant empathic failures in
social situations as well as in the transference, and their unrealistic views of themselves and others, we felt that the narcissistic position was primarily a defensive one. It served to mask
and also to express conflicts of both a libidinal and aggressive
nature, often sadomasochistic, in a manner designed to mini-
mize anxiety, shame, or guilt. Consequently, we did not view
this narcissistic stance as the result of specific developmental
conflicts or developmental failures, as others have suggested.

In three of the four cases, the transference was rapidly shifting, and images of the projected self, father, mother, siblings,
and surrogate objects could replace one another so quickly that
accurate interpretation was often difficult. We were unsure
whether to view this rapid shifting as evidence of a pregenital
fusion of self and object images, as Kernberg has suggested, or
as defensive in nature—in effect, displacements to ward off
painful affects. It was also clear that whenever these young
women expressed their erotic libidinal longings in the transference, the analyst was also seen as the forbidding and punitive
parent of the opposite sex, thus creating a confusing double
image of the analyst which could shift from moment to moment.

Countertransference problems were unusually intense while working with these patients. The fixity of their defensive patterns, the use of projection, denial, "acting out," identification with the aggressor, and one drive to defend against another, the partial failures in their reality function, and the immaturity of their object relations often created in the analyst feelings of being attacked, confusion, helplessness, and frustration, so that counteraggression often developed. Most often, in the face of these intense feelings, the analyst tended to become silent or inactive, both of which increased the patients' fear of their own destructiveness and vulnerability. Often the analyst was prone to hostile fantasies of ending the treatment, or, in reaction to those feelings, unusually intense rescue fantasies. We realized that these strong countertransference feelings were usable as aids to our understanding of the patients' reactions to their own parents during childhood. By identifying with the aggressors, they were making the analyst feel as they themselves had felt with their own parents.

In summary, then, all of the transference behavior which we observed could be understood as deriving from unconscious conflicts which expressed and defended against drive derivatives and painful affects. We did not believe that the transference behavior of our patients reflected early "ego states" or fixed "positions," nor did we believe that such behavior could easily be traced to specific early developmental deficiencies.

When we turned to the question of the technical approach which we might recommend for these patients, we were guided first by our view that the borderline diagnosis is no more than a broad, loose category of character pathology and not a clear diagnostic entity with specific conflicts, defenses, and developmental problems. Our initial technique of assessment reflected this conviction, and these patients were evaluated in a manner similar to that used with all our patients who are being considered for analytic treatment. Their general ego strength, their motivation for treatment, their capacity to work within the analytic method and profit from it, the degree to which projection is used, the pressure toward action, the flexibility of their defensive apparatus, the potential for suicidal or self-de-

structive activity, the degree of their narcissism, and the capacity
to form healthy object relations were some of the major areas
which we felt should be evaluated. We did realize, however,
that prediction of analytic success, which is always difficult, was
even more difficult in these cases. Nonetheless, we concluded
that some borderline patients are analyzable without major
technical modifications, as was true in our four cases.

We found that we could not agree with Kernberg's belief that
confronting the patient's contradictory positions during the
assessment interviews would necessarily yield the type of useful
data which he suggested would be forthcoming. We believe that
what he calls split "ego states" are merely surface contradictory
attitudes, derived from complex sets of interrelated fantasies,
many components of which are unconscious. In fact, we believe
that conceptualizing such contradictory behavior as evidence
of polarized "ego states" may detract from the eventual understanding of these unconscious fantasies. Furthermore, we
could not support Kernberg's observation that the bringing
together of such contradictory images always created anxiety.
Therefore, we concluded that extreme ambivalent attitudes
about oneself and others, including the analyst, can be understood in these patients, as in all others, in relation to drive,
defense, superego conflicts, unconscious fantasies, and historical events. The presence of such ambivalent and contradictory
attitudes was not pathognomonic of borderline patients.

In addition to special assessment techniques, some authors
have suggested specific technical approaches to these patients.
Again we could not agree with Kernberg's suggestion that one
should avoid genetic interpretations early in the treatment and
should pursue mainly the identification of, and work on, "splitting" mechanisms and the negative transference as a derivative
of the aggressive drive. On the contrary, we found that early
genetic interpretations, when possible, gave our patients an increased understanding about their lives, and this understanding
decreased their massive anxiety without increasing the defenses
of intellectualization and isolation. It helped the patients make
sense of their present in terms of their past right from the
beginning of the treatment. In addition, we did not feel that

it would be advisable to pursue one aspect of the transference or one drive and its derivatives to the relative exclusion of others. We believe that in these patients, as with all patients, material should be understood and interpreted as it is presented by the patient and not in any preplanned manner. In particular, we believe that libidinal conflicts are present from the beginning of the treatment and should be interpreted as soon as it is technically feasible and appropriate to do so.

We also considered the technical suggestions offered by Rinsley and Masterson, who believe that passive behavior in borderline patients represents a failure to successfully resolve the "depressive position" of infancy and the "rapprochement crisis" of the separation-individuation process. They believe that the mother of such a patient sets up a "rewarding part unit" for her child's regressive behavior and a "withdrawing part unit" for assertions of separateness and independence. The therapeutic effort which they recommend is geared to approaches which confront and reverse this process. Although we could agree that some, but by no means all, of our patients' mothers rewarded regressive and passive behavior in their children and interdicted expressions of autonomy and independence, we felt that the clinical picture which results was not simply a derivative of the conflicts which the authors emphasize. In fact, we were greatly impressed that much of the passive behavior which we observed in our patients was the result of conflict between the patients and their parents over anal, phallic, and sexual issues. Since we believe that the observed behavior was derived from all stages of psychosexual development, we could not recommend the prepatterned treatment approach suggested by these authors.

We do not suggest that all, or even most, borderline patients can be analyzed. Many must be treated by other modalities. Still others fall into a grey area where relatively minor modifications of technique may be necessary, consistent with the temperament and style of the analyst and the patient. However, some, such as our four cases, *can* be analyzed, albeit with a greater than usual amount of difficulty. Their problems with reality testing, their use of certain defenses, plus their infantile object relations, all made the transference particularly difficult to manage. Change as the result of treatment came with great difficulty. Nonetheless, we found that we did not need to deviate significantly from our usual analytic approach with these patients, and could not subscribe to the suggestion that special and specific treatment techniques are necessary for the analytic treatment of borderline patients in general.

Etiology

We believe that conclusions drawn about the etiology of borderline disturbances must at this time be uncertain and tentative. Each of our cases showed many different features which were felt to be crucial to the development of the pathology. Since the label "borderline" seems to apply to a wide variety of patients who often show marked differences in symptomatology, character structure, ego functioning, and object relations, we feel there must be a number of different etiological influences to produce such a varied picture. Therefore, we feel it is not possible to designate one specific etiological factor in the development of borderline pathology.

We were impressed with the fact that the parents of our patients were severely disturbed themselves and provided very poor models for identification, something which had a profoundly detrimental effect on the development of character structure. The patients had fathers who were sadistic or overly seductive or frequently absent. Their mothers were periodically depressed and unavailable or overprotective. There were a significant number of experiences of abandonment and object loss during childhood.

We could not, from our data derived from the long analyses of four cases, implicate special difficulties during a specific phase of development which would invariably lead to borderline disturbances. We were impressed with the fact that the parents' pathological behavior and attitudes created difficulties during every phase of psychosexual and ego development.

Although the current psychoanalytic literature on the borderline patient places great etiological emphasis on the disturbed relationship between the child and his caretaking person during the first two years of life, we found that our patients experienced significant trauma during the oedipal phase itself and frequently afterward as well. While we attempted to understand how significant preoedipal conflicts influenced their ego development and the nature of their object relations, we could not determine that these early conflicts were *more crucial* than later ones of childhood in producing borderline pathology.

Our own four cases did not demonstrate constitutional abnormalities or defects, as far as we could determine. We could find no evidence to support the idea that there is a greater amount of innate aggressive drive or innate difficulty in modulating aggressive drive discharge in borderline patients. We believe that there was significant arousal of aggression as a result of the nature of their childhood experiences. We also wish to stress that there were likewise marked disturbances in the nature of libidinal drive development which necessitated strong and pathological defenses just as disruptive as those needed to deal with conflicts over aggression. In addition, there were serious disturbances in the development of self-esteem regulation leading to an excessive range of narcissistic features in the clinical picture.

We believe, in general, that the greater the degree of early conflict the more would successive phases of ego development be affected. However, we were impressed with the difficulty of separating out the effects of early traumata from those of later phases. Our analytic work, which led to improvement in all four cases, dealt with conflicts derived from every phase of psychosexual and ego development. We also felt analysis of superego conflict was extremely important in leading to beneficial results.

Our conclusion that the term "borderline" does not refer to a specific diagnostic entity but to a diffuse and heterogeneous group of patients who are sicker than the more typical neurotic but not as severely disturbed as patients with psychosis is consistent with our view that there is no specific etiological determinant in the development of borderline pathology.

A Final Word

We have said a good deal about each one of the long list of specific questions about borderlines we set down in the introductory chapter. In retrospect, we became aware that we also had a more ambitious goal, although not one which was clearly articulated at any time during the course of our work. We had started out with the belief, shared by many of our analytic colleagues, that "borderline" was an important clinical concept which was still lacking a definitive, authoritative clarification, in spite of the efforts of many colleagues to provide one. Surely we nourished the hope that out of our endeavor would come forth the long-awaited solution to the puzzling questions: What exactly is a borderline case, how do they get that way, and what is to be done about them in therapy? How well have we succeeded?

Before very long we found it relatively easy to describe what borderline patients "look like" and how they act in analysis. By the end of our study we had concluded that a description does not constitute a definition. Nor a diagnosis. Far from supplying the hoped-for enduring definition and clear-cut diagnostic criteria, we were forced to say that "borderline" is not a diagnostic entity, or a discrete recognizable syndrome; it is at best a loose supra-classification. Our definition amounts to the statement that these cases are more disturbed than are most individuals we analyze, though less so than the sickest, psychotic persons we encounter.

Upon examining the suggested criteria for identification of borderline cases and the explanations of the origin and nature of their pathology which have been offered by others, we found ourselves less than satisfied. In each case we felt that either or both of the following were true: The issues were more complex or the theories less well substantiated than did the proponents of the various formulations we studied. Our own efforts to explain what we had observed certainly proved no more satisfactory as far as providing a convincing hypothesis regarding what was wrong with these patients and what had caused it. No central conflict, developmental defect, or crucial structural abnormality emerged as an organizing nucleus around which an orderly, precise clinical theory could be constructed. Instead, we realized that borderlines are a heterogeneous group and that they appeared to suffer in each case from a variety of conflicts caused by complex admixtures of pathogenic experiences and predilections from all stages of psychic development. Our attempt to study their ego functioning taught us that some aspects we had previously assumed we understood quite well turned out to be far more complicated, multifaceted, multi-determined, and variable than we had appreciated. Not even the broad assumption of the central role of preoedipal problems in these sicker patients proved easy to document. What we found was an inseparable intertwining of preoedipal and oedipal issues, conflicts, and fantasies in the material of all the analyses we studied. If that constitutes a clarification, it surely is of a different nature from what we had hoped to find when we commenced our investigation.

As for treatment, we concluded once more that generalizations are unwarranted because of the diversity of the borderline group. Our recommendation is therefore a most modest one. It consists of our finding that a certain number of these difficult, sicker patients can undergo successful analytic treatment if they are properly selected. What is of vital importance is careful analytic attention to the transference and countertransference distortions which can be so disruptive to the treatment situation, and a courageous preparedness for very slow progress. No more than the exercise of the conventional analytic skills and an understanding of familiar analytic concepts is called for, provided they are employed with unusual tact, patience, confidence, and persistence. In some favorable cases these will be enough to bring results which are ultimately rewarding both to analyst and analysand. Although this summation may be less than we had hoped for, it is nevertheless, in our opinion, far from negligible in value and significance.

References

Abend, S. M. (1974), Problems of identity: theoretical and clinical applications. *Psychoanal. Quart.*, 43:606-637.

――― (1981), Psychic conflict and the concept of defense. *Psychoanal. Quart.*, 50:67-76.

Arlow, J. A. (1966), Depersonalization and derealization. In: *Psychoanalysis—A General Psychology: Essays in Honor of Heinz Hartmann*, ed. R. Loewenstein, L. M. Newman, M. Schur, and A. J. Solnit. New York: International Universities Press.

――― (1969a), Unconscious fantasy and disturbances of conscious experience. *Psychoanal. Quart.*, 38:1-27.

――― (1969b), Fantasy, memory, and reality testing. *Psychoanal. Quart.*, 38:28-51.

Bak, R. C. (1954), The schizophrenic defense against aggression. Internat. J. Psycho-Anal., 35:1-6.

――― (1971), Object relations in schizophrenia and perversion. *Internat. J. Psycho-Anal.*, 52:235-242.

Beres, D. (1956), Ego deviation and the concept of schizophrenia. *The Psychoanalytic Study of the Child*, 11:164-235. New York: International Universities Press.

Bion, W. R. (1957), Differentiation of the psychotic from the non-psychotic personalities. *Internat. J. Psycho-Anal.*, 38:266-275.

Boyer, L. B., & Giovacchini, P. (1967), *Psychoanalytic Treatment of Characterological and Schizophrenic Disorders*. New York: Jason Aronson.

Brenner, C. (1955), *An Elementary Textbook of Psychoanalysis*. New York: International Universities Press.

――― (1974), On the nature and development of affects: A unified theory. *Psychoanal. Quart.*, 43:532-556.

――― (1975), Affects and psychic conflict. *Psychooanal. Quart.*, 44:5-28.

――― (1976), *Psychoanalytic Technique and Psychic Conflict*. New York: International Universities Press.

――― (1979), Depressive affect, anxiety and psychic conflict in the phallic-oedipal phase. *Psychoanal. Quart.*, 48:177-197.

Calef, V., & Weinshel, E. M. (1979), The new psychoanalysis and psychoanalytic revisionism. [Book review essay on *Borderline Conditions and Pathological Narcissism*.] *Psychoanal. Quart.*, 48:470-491.

Deutsch, H. (1942), Some forms of emotional disturbance and their relation to schizophrenia. *Psychoanal. Quart.*, 11:301-321.

Dickes, R. (1974), The concept of borderline states: An alternative proposal. *Internat. J. Psychoanal. Psychother.*, 3:1-27.

Fairbairn, W. R. D. (1954), *An Object Relations Theory of the Personality*. New York: Basic Books.

Federn, P. (1952), *Ego Psychology and the Psychoses*, ed. E. Weiss. New York: Basic Books.

Fenichel, O. (1935), *Problems of Psychoanalytic Technique*. Albany: Psychoanalytic Quarterly, Inc. (1941).

――― (1945), *The Psychoanalytic Theory of Neurosis*. New York: Norton.

Ferenczi, S. (1913), Stages in the development of the sense of reality. In: *Sex in Psychoanalysis*. Boston: The Gorham Press, pp. 213-239.

Freud, A. (1936), *The Ego and the Mechanisms of Defense*. New York: International Universities Press, 1946.

Freud, S. (1894), The neuro-psychoses of defence. *Standard Edition*, 3:43-61. London: Hogarth Press, 1962.

—— (1896), Further remarks on the neuro-psychoses of defence. *Standard Edition*, 3:159-185. London: Hogarth Press, 1962.

—— (1900), The Interpretation of Dreams. *Standard Edition*, 5:509-623. London: Hogarth Press, 1953.

—— (1905), Three essays on the theory of sexuality. *Standard Edition*, 7:165-243. London: Hogarth Press, 1953.

—— (1911a), Psychoanalytic notes on an autobiographical account of a case of paranoia (dementia paranoides). *Standard Edition*, 12:3-82. London: Hogarth Press, 1958.

—— (1911b), Formulations on the two principles of mental functioning. *Standard Edition*, 12:218-226. London: Hogarth Press, 1958.

—— (1914), On narcissism: An introduction. *Standard Edition*, 14:69-102. London: Hogarth Press, 1957.

—— (1915a), Observations on transference love. *Standard Edition*, 12:159-171. London: Hogarth Press, 1958.

—— (1915b), Instincts and their vicissitudes. *Standard Edition*, 14:117-140. London: Hogarth Press, 1957.

—— (1915c), The unconscious. *Standard Edition*, 14:161-215. London: Hogarth Press, 1957.

—— (1917a), A metapsychological supplement to the theory of dreams. *Standard Edition*, 14:222-235. London: Hogarth Press, 1957.

—— (1917b), Mourning and melancholia. *Standard Edition*, 14:243-258. London: Hogarth Press, 1957.

—— (1923), The ego and the id. *Standard Edition*, 19:3-66. London: Hogarth Press, 1961.

—— (1924), Neurosis and psychosis. *Standard Edition*, 19:147-153. London: Hogarth Press, 1961.

—— (1925), Negation. *Standard Edition*, 19:235-239. London: Hogarth Press, 1961.

—— (1926), Inhibitions, symptoms and anxiety. *Standard Edition*, 20:75-175. London: Hogarth Press, 1957.

—— (1927), Fetishism. *Standard Edition*, 21:149-157. London: Hogarth Press, 1961.

—— (1938a), An outline of psycho-analysis. *Standard Edition*, 23:141-207. London: Hogarth Press, 1964.

—— (1938b), Splitting of the ego in the process of defence. *Standard Edition*, 23:273-278. London: Hogarth Press, 1964.

Frosch, J. (1959), The psychotic character: psychoanalytic considerations. Presented at The American Psychoanalytic Association. Abstr. in: *J. Amer. Psychoanal. Assn.*, 8:544-548, 1960.

—— (1964), The psychotic character: clinical psychiatric considerations. *Psychiat. Quart.*, 38:81-96.

—— (1970), Psychoanalytic considerations of the psychotic character. *J. Amer. Psychoanal. Assn.*, 18:24-50.

Galenson, E., & Roiphe, H. (1971), The impact of early sexual discovery on mood, defensive organization and symbolization. *The Psychoanalytic Study of the Child*, 26:195-216. New York: Quadrangle.

Gitelson, M. (1958), On ego distortions. *Internat. J. Psycho-Anal.*, 39:243-257.

Green, A. (1977), The borderline concept. In: *Borderline Personality Disorders*, ed. P. Hartocollis. New York: International Universities Press.

Greenacre, P. (1971), *Emotional Growth*, Vols. 1 & 2. New York: International Universities Press.

Hartmann, H. (1939), *Ego Psychology and The Problem of Adaptation*. New York: International Universities Press, 1958.

———— (1953), Contribution to the metapsychology of schizophrenia. *The Psychoanalytic Study of the Child*, 8:177-198. New York: International Universities Press.

———— (1956), Notes on the reality principle. *The Psychoanalytic Study of the Child*, 11:149-155. New York: International Universities Press.

———— (1964), *Essays on Ego Psychology*, New York: International Universities Press.

Hoch, P., & Polatin, P. (1949), Pseudoneurotic forms of schizophrenia. *Psychiat. Quart.*, 23:248-276.

Jacobson, E. (1954), Contribution to the metapsychology of psychotic identifications. *J. Amer. Psychoanal. Assn.*, 2:239-267.

———— (1964), *The Self and the Object World*. New York: International Universities Press.

Kernberg, O. (1966), Structural derivatives of object relations. *Internat. J. Psycho-Anal.*, 47:236-253.

———— (1967), Borderline personality organization. *J. Amer. Psychoanal. Assn.*, 15:641-685.

———— (1975), *Borderline Conditions and Pathological Narcissism*. New York: Jason Aronson.

———— (1976), *Object Relations Theory and Clinical Psychoanalysis*. New York: Jason Aronson.

Klein, M. (1946), Some notes on schizoid mechanisms. *Internat. J. Psycho-Anal.*, 27:99-110.

———— (1948), *Contributions to Psycho-Analysis, 1921–1945*. London: Hogarth Press.

Knight, R. (1953), Borderline states. *Bull. Menninger Clinic*, 17:1-12.

Kohut, H. (1971), *The Analysis of the Self*. New York: International Universities Press.

Krent, J., reporter (1970), The fate of the defenses in the psychoanalytic process. *J. Amer. Psychoanal. Assn.*, 18:177-194.

Mahler, M. (1971), A study of the separation-individuation process: and its possible application to borderline phenomena in the psychoanalytic situation. *The Psychoanalytic Study of the Child*, 26:403-424. New York: Quadrangle.

————, & Furer, M. (1968), *On Human Symbiosis and the Vicissitudes of Individuation*. I. *Infantile Psychosis*. New York: International Universities Press.

————, Pine, F., & Bergman, A. (1975), *The Psychological Birth of the Human Infant*. New York: Basic Books.

Masterson, J. F. (1972), *Treatment of the Borderline Adolescent: A Developmental Approach*. New York: Wiley-Interscience.

————, & Rinsley, D. B. (1975), The borderline syndrome: The role of the mother in the genesis and psychic structure of the borderline personality. *Internat. J. Psycho-Anal.*, 56:163-177.

Meissner, W. (1978), Theoretical assumptions of concepts of the borderline personality. *J. Amer. Psychoanal. Assn.*, 26:557-595.

———— (1979), Internalization and object relations. *J. Amer. Psychoanal. Assn.*, 27:345-359.

Modell, A. H. (1968), *Object Love and Reality*. New York: International Universities Press.

Moore, B. E., & Fine, B. D., ed. (1968), *A Glossary of Psychoanalytic Terms and Concepts*. New York: The American Psychoanalytic Association.

Pumpian-Mindlin, E., reporter (1967), Defense organization of the ego and psychoanalytic technique. *J. Amer. Psychoanal. Assn.*, 15:150-165.

Rangel, L., reporter (1955), The borderline case. *J. Amer. Psychoanal. Assn.*, 3:285-298.

Rinsley, D. B. (1977), An object relations view of borderline personality. In: *Borderline Personality Disorders*, ed. P. Hartocollis. New York: International Universities Press, pp. 47-70.

Robbins, L. (1956), The borderline case. *J. Amer. Psychoanal. Assn.*, 4:550-562.

Schafer, R. (1968), The mechanisms of defense. *Internat. J. Psycho-Anal.*, 49:49-62.

Segal, H. (1964), *Introduction to the Work of Melanie Klein*. New York: Basic Books.

Spiegel, L. A. (1959), The self, the sense of self and perception. *The Psychoanalytic Study of the Child,* 14:81-109. New York: International Universities Press.

Stein, M. H. (1966), Self-observation, reality and the superego. In: *Psychoanalysis—A General Psychology: Essays in Honor of Heinz Hartmann,* ed. R. M. Loewenstein et al. New York: International Universities Press, pp. 275-297.

Stern, A. (1938), Psychoanalytic investigation of and therapy in the border line group of neuroses. *Psychoanal. Quart.,* 7:467-489.

Stone, L. (1954), The widening scope of indications for psychoanalysis. *J. Amer. Psychoanal. Assn.,* 2:567-594.

Wallerstein, R. S., reporter (1967), Development and metapsychology of the defense organization of the ego. *J. Amer. Psychoanal. Assn.,* 15:130-149.

Wender, P. H. (1977), The contribution of the adoption studies to an understanding of the phenomenology and etiology of borderline schizophrenias. In: *Borderline Personality Disorders,* ed. P. Hartocollis. New York: International Universities Press, pp. 255-269.

Winnicott, D. W. (1965), *The Maturational Processes and the Facilitating Environment.* New York: International Universities Press.

Zetzel, E. K., reporter (1954), Panel: Defense mechanisms and psychoanalytic technique. *J. Amer. Psychoanal. Assn.,* 2:318-326.

Zilboorg, G. (1941), Ambulatory schizophrenia. *Psychiatry,* 4:149-155.

Author Index

Subject Index